Warfare, Trade, and the Indies in British Literature, 1652–1771

Warfare, Trade, and the Indies in British Literature, 1652–1771

Peter Craft

FAIRLEIGH DICKINSON UNIVERSITY PRESS
Vancouver • Madison • Teaneck • Wroxton

Published by Fairleigh Dickinson University Press
Copublished by The Rowman & Littlefield Publishing Group, Inc.
4501 Forbes Boulevard, Suite 200, Lanham, Maryland 20706
www.rowman.com

6 Tinworth Street, London SE11 5AL, United Kingdom

Copyright © 2021 by The Rowman & Littlefield Publishing Group, Inc.

All rights reserved. No part of this book may be reproduced in any form or by any electronic or mechanical means, including information storage and retrieval systems, without written permission from the publisher, except by a reviewer who may quote passages in a review.

Fairleigh Dickinson University Press gratefully acknowledges the support received for scholarly publishing from the Friends of FDU Press.

British Library Cataloguing in Publication Information Available

Library of Congress Cataloging-in-Publication Data

Names: Craft, Peter, 1978– author.
Title: Warfare, trade, and the Indies in British literature, 1652–1771 / Peter Craft.
Description: Lanham, Maryland : Fairleigh Dickinson University Press, [2021] | Includes bibliographical references and index. | Summary: "Warfare, Trade, and the Indies in British Literature traces the differences in representations of Mughal and American "Indians" in travel narratives of the long eighteenth century. It contributes to the exposure and eradication of colonial rhetoric and violence by accounting for the origins and (d)evolution of different "Indian" stereotypes"— Provided by publisher.
Identifiers: LCCN 2021020003 (print) | LCCN 2021020004 (ebook) | ISBN 9781683933083 (cloth) | ISBN 9781683933090 (epub)
Subjects: LCSH: Travelers' writings, English—History and criticism. | English prose literature—18th century—History and criticism. | English prose literature—17th century—History and criticism. | Indians in literature. | Imperialism in literature. | Mogul Empire—In literature. | LCGFT: Literary criticism.
Classification: LCC PR756.T72 C68 2021 (print) | LCC PR756.T72 (ebook) |
DDC 820.9/3254—dc23
LC record available at https://lccn.loc.gov/2021020003
LC ebook record available at https://lccn.loc.gov/2021020004

Contents

Abstract	vii
Acknowledgments	ix
Chapter 1: Introduction	1
Chapter 2: Voyage Accounts and Collections from Heylyn to Bernier	31
Chapter 3: Dryden's West "Indian" Emperors	57
Chapter 4: Mughal History and Dryden's *Aureng-Zebe*	95
Chapter 5: British Men of Feeling on "Indians" and Wealth: Addison, Steele, and Mackenzie	115
References	141
Index	151
About the Author	155

Abstract

My monograph builds upon and adapts New Historical and postcolonial interpretations of British perceptions of East and West "Indians" in the long eighteenth century. I argue that extremely popular voyage narratives during this period reflected and shaped British people's tendency to view Mughal Indians as similar and in some ways even superior to Europeans. This special status, which was also accorded to the Chinese, did not extend to American "Indians." I begin my study with the origins of the mistaken term "Indian" as applied to American Indians by European "discoverers" in the late fifteenth century. Although the indigenous peoples of the Americas continued to be called "Indians" by Europeans for centuries after Amerigo Vespucci realized Columbus had "found" a separate continent rather than a new route to India, I argue that British writers were keenly aware of the difference between "Indians" in the Eastern and Western hemispheres by the mid-seventeenth century. In fact, before the death of the Mughal Emperor Aurangzeb in 1707, British men and women greatly admired a country that was far more wealthy, spacious, and militarily powerful than their own. The inhabitants of the Americas, however, were decimated by the European transmission of smallpox and lacked the military technology of India and Europe. Consequently, the European colonization of the Americas, and its accompanying devaluation of the native peoples, began much earlier and lasted much longer there than in India (where the British presence did not become significant until Robert Clive's victory at the Battle of Plassey in 1757). Peter Heylyn's critically neglected 1652 *Cosmographie* (eight editions before 1700), a collection of voyage narratives from sailors, merchants, and Jesuits that represented at least a century of European perceptions of the rest of the world, shows that a sharp distinction was made between, on the one hand, the "Indians" in the Americas and, on the other hand, the inhabitants of the Mughal Empire in

India proper. Drawing also on representations of "Indians" in the works of canonical literary authors in the seventeenth and eighteenth centuries such as John Dryden, Richard Steele, and Henry Mackenzie, my monograph provides a more nuanced account of the origins and (d)evolution of "Indian" stereotypes than scholars have to date. Saidian nineteenth-and twentieth-century models of postcolonial theory must undergo some modifications before they can be applied to seventeenth-and eighteenth-century British literary texts. Yet the ethical commitment to the exposure and eradication of colonial rhetoric and violence that postcolonialism provides is essential to my work.

Acknowledgments

Research for this monograph was conducted with the generous support of the Dolores Zohrab Liebmann Foundation, the University of Illinois' College of Liberal Arts and Sciences, the Illinois Program for Research in the Humanities, Barbara Smalley, and several additional grants and fellowships from the University of Illinois. I also received a summer research stipend from Felician University that expedited the completion of this project. I would like to thank, in no particular order, Jessica Munns, Andrea Stevens, Gordon Hutner, Sandra Lach Arlinghaus, Suvir Kaul, Richard C. Simmons, Geoffrey Parker, Jodi Byrd, Feisal Mohamed, Carol Neely, Melissa Littlefield, Linda DeGrand, Humberto Garcia, Lori Newcomb, Elizabeth Zeman Kolkovich, Curtis Perry, and John Zomchick. The inspiring classes that Paul Battles taught at Hanover College and his helpful office chats were largely responsible for the career path that I chose, and to him I am forever grateful. I would especially like to thank Robert Markley and Anthony Pollock for their time, patience, and guidance over the years. Last but certainly not least I would like to thank my family, whose unwavering encouragement has sustained me through it all.

Chapter 1

Introduction

The very name *Indian*, when applied to the indigenes of the Americas, reveals Columbus' and other fifteenth-century European voyagers' inability to distinguish these peoples from the inhabitants of the Indus river region in South Asia (India proper). As late as 1523, Maximilian of Transylvania wrote that "'the natives of all unknown countries are commonly called Indians,'" and in the Englishman Peter Heylyn's *Cosmographie* (1652), he reported that the "ages foregoing" had produced "monstrous Fables" about the inhabitants of India, including reports of some with "dogs heads" and "others . . . whose ears did reach unto the ground" (Heylyn 1652, 3: 213).[1] Similarly, an illustration from a 1547 Spanish edition of *Mandeville's Travels* represents the indigenous peoples of the East with animal heads, which suggests that the rumors Heylyn reports were widespread in sixteenth-century Europe. While Europeans may have had only a vague notion of the differences between "Indians" of the Eastern and Western hemispheres and plenty of misconceptions before the mid-sixteenth century, they were far from ignorant by the middle of the seventeenth century. This shifting perception occurred largely because of the firsthand voyage narratives of sailors, merchants, and Jesuit missionaries summarized in Heylyn's extremely popular mid-seventeenth-century *Cosmographie* (eight editions before 1700), a book that is surprisingly neglected by scholars of the past few decades. Heylyn's work shows that in the late seventeenth and early eighteenth centuries, the total number of Englishmen in South Asia never exceeded a few hundred and their overseas territories were primarily "factories," or trading posts, rather than large-scale colonial occupations as in the Americas. My monograph will therefore distinguish itself from the work of critics such as Laura Brown and Balachandra Rajan who, as I show later in this introduction, group seventeenth-century English depictions of East and West "Indians" into one subordinate category and, in doing so, retroactively impose nineteenth-century postcolonial models on early modern texts. There have been histories of India and the Americas and analyses of the popular works of literature featured in this monograph, but not an interdisciplinary combination of these subjects, especially with the cumulative Hakluyt-Purchas-Heylyn voyage narrative legacy that largely contributed to the worldview of British[2] men and women as the focal point.

More specifically, I will focus on the eyewitness voyage narratives that helped to move Europeans away from the ignorance about "Indians" in the fifteenth century and toward the complex range of perceptions and understandings of a century and a half later.[3] These accounts were compiled in vast, enormously popular anthologies that were recycled, modified, expanded, condensed, consumed, and cannibalized for at least two centuries. Portions of Richard Hakluyt's *Principal Navigations, Voyages, and Discoveries of the English Nation* (1589) were reused in *Purchas his Pilgrimage* (1613), Heylyn's *Microcosmos* (1621) and *Cosmographie* (1652), and John Harris' *Navigantium Atque Itinerantium Bibliotheca* (1705). This tradition of reusable voyage narratives begins well before the Restoration of Charles II in 1660 and, consequently, has received comparatively little critical attention from scholars of the long eighteenth century in English literature.[4]

My monograph will thus analyze how rhetorical strategies that were widely applied to the peoples of the Americas in the late seventeenth and early eighteenth centuries had to be modified or rejected in portraying the peoples and cultures of the East Indies. This difference in the literature of the period is crucial to understanding how and why the recent emphasis in eighteenth-century studies of the Atlantic world needs to be considered in the contexts of England's very different perceptions of and relations with South Asia. By drawing on this tradition of voyage narratives, I explore the ways in which three canonical English authors (John Dryden, Richard Steele, and Henry Mackenzie) use the term *Indian*, beginning in 1665 with Dryden's *Indian Queen* and ending in 1771 with Mackenzie's *Man of Feeling*. While the word "Indian" encompassed indigenous peoples in both the Eastern and Western hemispheres, my monograph argues that the treatment of these groups in English literature was vastly different, marked by deference to the former and condescension toward or dismissal of the latter. The literature of the late seventeenth and early eighteenth centuries also retained many of the economic concerns of the voyage collection genre and carried on one of the cultural tasks that voyage writing editors undertook in prologues and introductions to the tales they assembled: constructing compensatory fictions about Europeans' status in relation to the Mughal Empire.

In other words, the heightened importance of England in global affairs developed not from the ignorance of late seventeenth-and early eighteenth-century English authors, but because this fiction proved to be a durable marketing technique. English writers composed romanticized fictions in order to combat (often well-deserved) unflattering depictions of themselves on economic and territorial grounds by East Indians, such as the powerful Mughal Emperor

Aurangzeb whose mentor taught him that all of Europe was "no more than some inconsiderable island," and ethical grounds by Amerindians, such as Wahunsenacawh, who asked rhetorically why Europeans destroyed the very Indians who supplied non-natives with food (Bernier 1968, 155; Armstrong 1971, 1).[5] The ideology of these compensatory texts therefore both conserved and helped to change fundamental values of English national identity from Heylyn's *Cosmographie*, the subject of my second chapter, well into the first few decades of the eighteenth century.

WEST "INDIAN" COLONIES AND EAST INDIAN FACTORIES

An important distinction must be made between colonies and factories because these terms reveal the immensely different power relations among England, the Americas, and India in the seventeenth century. Generally speaking, English colonies in the Americas in the 1600s were well-populated, had enough women and children to be self-perpetuating, had relatively sizable portions of land, retained close ties with England itself, and were seized or at least protected by military force from the indigenes. A colony, according to the *OED*, is "a settlement in a new country; a body of people who settle in a new locality, forming a community subject to or connected with their parent state; the community so formed, consisting of the original settlers and their descendants and successors, as long as the connexion with the parent state is kept up" (1989, "Colony").[6]

In the Americas, there were enough English women to satisfy the sexual, marital, and paternal desires of a substantial portion of the male English settlers. There were 37,000 married couples in New England alone by the end of the seventeenth century, which means that the very minimum presence of English women was half of that number: 18,500 (Torrey 1985, xiv). Because they did not have the protection of a powerful emperor such as Jahangir (ruled 1605–1627), Shah Jahan (ruled 1627–1658), or Aurangzeb (ruled 1658–1707) as in India, English men and women in the Americas were forced to rely on their own military strength and reinforcements from England (Keay 2000, *India* 329). Frequent wars with the indigenous peoples of the Americas and linguistic barriers decreased the probability of interracial children. The vulnerability, shared religious beliefs, and language of English women and men in the Americas therefore encouraged the preservation of cultural ties to each other and to the mother country. Children would generally be raised with English values, and in turn pass on those ideologies when they became parents.

Moreover, boatloads of new English settlers arrived frequently and return voyages were also common, largely because the journey was far shorter and safer than the one from England to India. This constant back-and-forth interaction between significant numbers of English colonists in the Americas and England itself ensured that the "connexion with the parent state" was kept up. English navigators had to sail around the Cape of Good Hope in southern Africa in order to reach India or make a combination of shorter sea voyages and at least one long caravan over land through Alexandria or Antioch (*Historical Atlas* 1995, H-10). From London to New England, the largest English territory in the Americas in the seventeenth century, it is approximately 3,250 miles. If one travels by ship from London around Africa to the nearest location in India, by contrast, it is roughly 11,500 miles (H-72). While English voyagers could generally reach North America in three months or less, it took about a year or sometimes longer to sail around the Cape of Good Hope to India. Because of its much shorter duration, the transatlantic England-to-Americas voyage left fewer opportunities for being blown off course by strong winds, ship damage from barnacles and storms, pirate raids, navigation problems, food corruption and depletion by weevils or rats, freshwater shortages, mutinies, and diseases spread from the prolonged exposure of large groups of people in confined quarters. English captains who piloted vessels bound for the Americas were also spared the danger of the notoriously treacherous waters surrounding the Cape of Good Hope. Consequently, English men and women who sailed from England to the Americas, or vice versa, had a much greater likelihood of reaching their destination than those who went to or came back from India.

No English colonies, in the strictest sense of the word, existed in India until after Aurangzeb's death in 1707. Unlike their counterparts in the Americas, Englishmen in India procured firmans[7] from Mughal emperors in order to build factories. A factory, according to Johnson's eighteenth-century *Dictionary of the English Language* (1755), is "1. A house or district inhabited by traders. . . . 2. The traders embodied in one place" ("Factory"). The "trading" component of this definition is crucial because the prospect of large profits was the only incentive that would induce Englishmen to undertake the extremely long and dangerous journey to India. Indeed, East Indian commodities were generally far more lucrative than the raw materials exported from the Americas, but Englishmen could not expect to own large tracts of land in Mughal territory.

Although the Americas had enough land to accommodate 257,000 English settlers by the end of the seventeenth century, Englishmen in India had tiny populations and very little territory of their own. In the Americas, the English occupied a large portion of New England by 1690, which is approximately 66,424 square miles ("New England"; Anderson 1995, lxxix). Madras, by contrast, which was one of the larger English factories in India, consisted of about "one square mile," "300–400" inhabitants, and a fort in 1639. In 1675, the number of Englishmen in Surat had dwindled to thirty and Bombay had only 300 English occupants (Keay 1994, 69; Fawcett 1936, 131). In other words, EIC soldiers, merchants, sailors, and administrators could be counted in the dozens and hundreds in India's factories, whereas the English colonies in the Americas contained a combined population of tens and even hundreds of thousands in the seventeenth century. By the end of Aurangzeb's reign, all but the southernmost tip of India and two Maratha territories were considered part of the Mughal Empire (Keay 2000, 314, 349).

Sir Thomas Roe recognized as early as 1615 that attempts to gain territory in India would prove disastrous: "A warr and trafique are incompatible. . . . Lett this bee receiued as a rule that if you will Profitt, seeke it at Sea, and in quiett trade; for without controuersy it is an error to affect Garrisons and Land warrs in India" (Keay 2000, 34). Roe's advice turned out to be well-founded since the EIC's foolish decision to wage war on the Mughal Empire in the 1680s not only ended in a crushing defeat, but it also led to harsh terms of reconciliation. The EIC's peace envoys from Bombay had their hands bound, were "'obliged to prostrate,'" received a "severe reprimand" from Aurangzeb, forced to beg for the restoration of their "cancelled trading rights," and informed that "all plundered goods and ships" must be returned in addition to a fine of 150,000 rupees (Keay 1994, 146). The vivid image of an Englishman prostrated before an East Indian emperor represents spatially the relative power between the two. Compare this situation to the scene in *Robinson Crusoe* where Friday, a West "Indian," performs a similar gesture in front of the protagonist, an Englishman: "he kneel'd down again, kiss'd the Ground, and laid his Head upon the Ground, and taking me by the Foot, set my Foot upon his Head; this it seems was in token of swearing to be my Slave for ever" (Defoe 1719, 172).[8] I argue that these two very different images reflect England's general view of itself in relation to the inhabitants of Mughal India, on the one hand, and the Americas, on the other. Up through the end of the seventeenth century, then, EIC servants could not hope to gain land through force, but rather had to make do with the small scraps that the Mughal Empire was willing to throw to them. The EIC's military efforts in the seventeenth century were primarily aimed at protecting factories, not from Mughals who could easily reclaim them, but rather from other European nations such as the Portuguese, French, Dutch, and even the Danes and Swedes.

After the death of Aurangzeb in 1707, the distinction between Mughal "Indians" and the natives of the southernmost tip of South Asia and its surrounding islands gradually became less important from England's perspective. However, I argue that there was a period, between roughly 1600 (the foundation of the East India Company) and 1707, when English people were keenly aware of the differences between Mughal Indians and those of southernmost India, its surrounding islands, and the West "Indians" of the Americas. This knowledge directly corresponded to England's desire to become the preeminent European trading country in the East, a position that had long been held by the Portuguese. Awareness of the politics, military strengths, available commodities, cultural values, customs, languages, and distinctions between various "Indians" of the East and West was crucial for success in England's expanding trade network. In 1600, the Indian subcontinent had about 140 million people (100 million of whom were in Mughal territory), whereas England had five million, and all of Western Europe had less than forty million (Keay 2000, 320). With a population of approximately 100 million people, Mughal emperors could and did assemble armies of astounding proportions. Approximately a quarter of the population relied on the military for a living, eighty-two percent of the total annual budget went to Akbar's warlords and their retainers, and there were between 150,000 and 200,000 cavalrymen. Akbar personally commanded 80,000 Infantrymen and gunners, and roughly 4.5 million infantrymen (almost the entire population of England) could be raised by rural leaders on short notice at the Mughal Emperor's command (Keay 2000, 325).

In contrast to the staggering population and army sizes of the Mughal Empire, European colonizers encountered far fewer indigenous peoples in the Americas. The population of Mexico had dwindled from its height during the Aztec Empire at perhaps as many as thirty-seven million people to one or two million in the seventeenth century. Captain John Smith estimated the total population of the Powhatan Confederacy, a loose union of Algonquin-speaking nations that was one of the closest approximations of an "empire" in early seventeenth-century North America, to be 8,500 (modern historians estimates are slightly higher, ranging from 14,000 to 22,000) (Mooney 1907, 130).

Another key difference between English colonies in the Americas and factories in the East Indies was the presence of women and children, or the lack thereof in the latter case. Prior to the 1660s, the EIC had a policy forbidding its servants to bring English wives with them to India's factories. In 1618, William Biddulph, a company servant, insisted on a strict adherence to the letter of this policy in a report he sent from Ahmdābād to the EIC's headquarters in London. This dispatch "Blame(d) Roe for not sending home Steel and his wife, as it is 'an article in your commission that who ever shall have a wife in these parts shall uppon knowledge thereof be forthwith dismissed of his place and service and sent home'" (qtd. in Foster 1906, 20–21).[9] Biddulph's complaint, and perhaps those of other EIC servants who envied Steele for having an English wife in India when they could not, achieved the results he desired. According to Philip Anderson, "There were no English ladies . . .

after the expulsion of poor Mrs. Steele" at the English factory of Surat, a fact that caused the Italian voyager Pietro Della Valle to express his reluctance to take his wife there in 1623 (Anderson 1856, 48; Della Valle 1892, 27).

In the seventeenth century, the tendency of English men to marry Catholic Portuguese women residing in India caused the EIC considerable alarm and led to the importation of Protestant English women. The company feared that the children produced by marriages between English men and Portuguese women would, "thro' their father's neglect, [be] brought up in the Roman Catholic principles to the great dishonour and weakening of the Protestant religion" (Kincaid 1938, 22). When the EIC finally began sending English women to the factories in Bombay in the 1660s, they developed a reputation for having "sickly" children "in consequence of the free and easy way in which the mothers lived, and their inveterate habit of taking strong liquors" (Anderson 1856, 216). These English women not only failed to prevent the "weakening of the Protestant religion," but they were also expensive for the EIC to transport and maintain while they remained unmarried. Consequently, the leaders of Madras "were not going to follow the costly Bombay experiment and import women for their white subjects." Instead they decided to "induce by all means [their] Soldiers to marry with the Native women because it will be impossible to get ordinary young women to pay their own passages" (Kincaid 1938, 51). The women's reluctance to undertake the voyage was understandable considering the dangers involved. Toward the end of the seventeenth century, Alexander Hamilton described Madras as the "most incommodious place [he] ever saw," and its dangerous reefs were notorious for wrecking the EIC's ships (qtd. in Keay 1994, 69–70). These reports would hardly have been reassuring for English women contemplating a voyage to an East Indian factory.

Several conclusions can be drawn from the fact that English factories, unlike their colonies in the Americas, were tiny, completely incapable of taking land by force from the Mughal Empire, sparsely populated, and virtually all-male in India prior to 1675, the year Dryden's *Aureng-Zebe* was first performed. First, there was no evidence that England would eventually take over India. The lack of English women and children meant the factories were not self-perpetuating. Moreover, the few marriages that did occur in English factories were usually to Portuguese and native women, and, as a result, the offspring were of mixed races and ethnicities and therefore not in close "connexion with the parent state" of England, as were the colonies of the Americas. Because the voyage took anywhere from four to eight times as long from England to India as it did to the Americas, the possibility of a colonial "connexion" between England and India was nonexistent before the eighteenth century.

Like most seventeenth-century English writers, Dryden's use of the generic label "Indian" concealed a sophisticated set of distinctions based on race, class, religious affiliation, language, and country. Therefore neither a simple Occident/Orient, nor a European/Other binary opposition comprehensively describes the complex set of perceptions of "Indians" that English men and women held in the seventeenth century. Dryden not only used the term "Indian" to refer to the peoples and countries in the Americas (*The Indian Queen* and *The Indian Emperor*), but he also employed the word to delineate a specific subsection of India's population in *Aureng-Zebe*. The "Indian Lords" listed in the *dramatis personae*, and "The sons of Indostan" who "must reign, or die" according to Aureng-Zebe, were not "Indians" in many senses of the word (1883, II.i.539). The Mughal aristocracy and royal family, those who "must reign or die," were not indigenous to the Indus river area that gave the Indian subcontinent its name,[10] did not speak Hindi, were not Hindus, and did not have dark skin.

Even though the Mughals had ruled most of India for over a century and a half by the time Bernier wrote his *Travels*, they were still considered "foreigners" in the Indian subcontinent. The fact that Mughal rulers spoke Persian rather than Hindi[11] and practiced Islam rather than Hinduism added to their foreignness. Although Dryden and other European authors label the Mughals as Indians, they clearly understood the differences between them and the natives of India. Bernier explains these distinctions as follows:

> To be considered a *Mogol*, it is enough if a foreigner have a white face and profess Mahometanism; in contradistinction to the Christians of Europe, who are called *Franguis*, and to the *Indous*, whose complexion is brown, and who are *Gentiles*. . . . the present acceptation of the term *Mogol* [includes]. . . foreigners whose complexions are white, and who profess Mahometanism; such as *Persians, Turks, Arabs,* and *Usbeks*. (1968, 3, 48)[12]

According to Bernier, "Indous" have "brown" "complexions" whereas "Mogols" were "foreigners" with "white" "complexions." Indeed, some seventeenth-century illustrations of Mughal leaders represent them with pale white skin. Although "Mughal" is the currently accepted spelling of the term,[13] Bernier's typographical variant, "Mogol," gives a clearer sense of the word's origins in "Mongol," a native of Mongolia. Babur, who founded the Mughal dynasty in the sixteenth century, had Mongol blood on his father's side from Tamerlane. In *Aureng-Zebe*, Dryden makes this genealogical link explicit when Melesinda says, "Too truly Tamerlane's successors they [the royal Mughal family]; / Each thinks a world too little for his sway" (1883, III.i.85–6). Because Mongolia was located north of China and bordered Russia to the south, Bernier's claim that the "Mogol[s]" had "white" "complexions" makes sense. Yet for Europeans such as Dryden and Bernier, the monotheistic,[14] white-faced "foreigners" seemed strangely familiar. In fact, Dryden was able to identify with them to such an extent that he made the Mughal Emperor Aurangzeb an idealized projection of his own patron and king, Charles II, as I argue in chapter 4.

These distinctions between Mughals and Indians, factories and colonies, East Indians and West "Indians," and foreigners and natives are especially important in relation to the criticism on Dryden's *Aureng-Zebe*, notably by Balachandra Rajan and Laura Brown. Rajan cites historians who discuss the "deterioration ushered in by Aurangzeb," and Brown includes this play, along with *The Indian Emperor* and *The Indian Queen*, as an example of a narrative about "lost, decaying, or declining empires" (Rajan 1999, 68; Brown 2004, 69). But these critics have the benefit of hindsight, which Dryden did not. In *The British Empire, 1558–1983*, T. O. Lloyd argues that "After the event it looks very much as if his [Aurangzeb's] campaigns overstrained the resources of his empire and made it impossible to hold together, but at the time he was seen as the greatest of conquerors" (1984, 34). Roughly contemporaneous accounts of Aurangzeb's reign, such as the first English translation of Bernier's *Travels in the Mogul Empire* in 1671, support Lloyd's argument by depicting the Mughal ruler as ruthless and powerful. According to Bernier, Aurangzeb's personal "body-guard," who attended him "at all times," consisted of "thirty-five thousand cavalry," "ten thousand" infantry, "seventy pieces" of heavy artillery, "fifty or sixty small field-pieces," "oxen," and "elephants" (1968, 351–52). With a "body-guard" this size, and huge armies in addition, English men and women would have seen Aurangzeb as a powerful emperor in the 1670s. Dryden reveals his awareness of the strength and sophistication of Mughal armies when he describes "guns," "cannon[s]," "horses," "castled elephants," and "forty thousand" dead soldiers after one battle in *Aureng-Zebe* (1883, I.i.120–121, 169, 189). Charles II's bodyguard, which doubled as the complete standing army of England in times of peace, was about 500 men in 1661 and eventually grew to 8,865 troops in 1685, ten years after the first performance of Dryden's *Aureng-Zebe* (Childs 2001, 52). After Aurangzeb's death in 1707, the Mughal Empire began to disintegrate and it had lost all of central India by 1730 to Maratha rebels, but Dryden and his contemporaries could not have known that in 1675 (Keay 2000, 369). When Dryden's play was first performed, Aurangzeb had been in power for seventeen years, had the highest revenues and the most land of any Mughal Emperor, and continued to rule until his death in 1707 (Bernier 1968, 459).[15] Rajan's and Brown's view of Aurangzeb as the leader of an empire inevitably heading toward collapse would therefore not have been shared by Dryden and his English audience in the mid 1670s.

In addition to being unable to foresee the collapse of the Mughal Empire, Dryden and his contemporaries could not have predicted that England would one day make India a colony. This point is crucial in the context of Rajan's claim that

> Indamora (the name is not casually chosen) is described as "a Captive Queen" in anticipation of the captive queen India was later to become. She serves her true master (not his competitors) with loyalty, showing us how fully imperialism looks forward in its metaphors. . . . The East India Company's venture is the acquisition of India (Indamora). . . . Thus the acquiring of India is foreseen even at a time when the British position in India . . . was precarious. (1999, 71, 231)

In fact, neither Dryden, "imperialism," nor the EIC "anticipat[ed]" or "fore[saw]" England becoming the "master" of the "captive queen India was later to become." Put differently, the English factories in India showed no signs of developing into a "colony" in 1675, and Dryden's *Aureng-Zebe* does not even hint at this possibility. It is also significant that the EIC administrators "induce[d] by all means [their] Soldiers to marry with the Native women," but were horrified by the potential moral corruption of children that a union of Protestant English men with Catholic Portuguese women would produce. Equally shocking to the EIC's governors was the "free and easy way" in which the Englishwomen in Bombay lived and their "inveterate habit of taking strong liquors." This moral rather than racial assessment of status and personal worth is consistent with Dryden's *Aureng-Zebe*. Indamora sums up this attitude when she says, "All greatness is in virtue understood: / 'Tis only necessary to be good" (1883, V.i.83–4). Far from "devaluing" India, Dryden follows Heylyn's lead in constructing a moral paradigm that contains the overwhelming power of the Mughal Empire and enables England to appear in contradistinction without looking insignificant.

RELATIVE POPULARITY

All of the major texts featured in this monograph were at least moderately successful commercially in their own day, but the truly jaw-droppingly popular works depicted English men in positions of power over Amerindians. Works that focused on East or Mughal Indians, such as Bernier's English translation of *Travels in the Mogul Empire* (at least three printings between 1671 and 1676) and Dryden's *Aureng-Zebe* (at least twelve reprints between 1676 and 1763) had respectable publication records in their own right. Indeed, Donald Lach and Edwin Van Kley point out that "between 1653 and 1680, at least fourteen European accounts of Asia were translated into English" (1993, 3.1: 574–575). Lach and Van Kley then state that

> The steady publication of all these translated works surely demonstrates a growing interest in Asia among English readers. English observers of the Asian scene, however, contributed almost nothing to satisfy that interest. During the entire two decades from 1660 to 1680 only two pieces that could be called firsthand reports appeared in English. Both of these were pamphlets that revived memories of the Amboina Massacre and subsequent hostilities with the Dutch. (1993, 3.1: 575)

Although the steady supply of translations reveals that the English had a definite interest in Eastern countries such as India during this period, they published almost no original works about them. The few British narratives that took place in Eastern countries were carefully spun along nationalistic lines, and the Amboina Massacre[16] was a Dutch-English conflict rather than an English-Mughal one. In the 1690s, John Fryer and John Ovington, among others, wrote firsthand British accounts of the East, which reveals that the region remained of interest to English readers in the form of voyage narratives.

On the other hand, theatrical and poetic variants of the Spanish conquest of the Americas, Behn's *Oroonoko*, the Pocahontas story, and Defoe's *Robinson Crusoe*, in which European settlers colonize West "Indians," at least for a time, were ubiquitous and developed veritably astounding publication records. Richard Ligon's Inkle and Yarico story (1657, later popularized by Steele in 1711) had forty-five adaptations by 1800 in eight languages, and the George Colman theatrical version was staged 164 times between 1787 and 1800 (Felsenstein 1999 xii, 168). *Robinson Crusoe* (1719) went through eighty-three separate publications (including translations and sequels) between 1719 and 1750.[17] Many of these stories involve West "Indians" mistaking Europeans for gods. No such possibility existed in Mughal India. I argue that the omission of Anglo-Mughal narratives on the part of English literary figures was a deliberate attempt to avoid the embarrassing subject position that the relationship evoked. Publication records show that the English had an obsession with West "Indians" in subjugated positions, roles that inhabitants of the Mughal Empire could not assume if even a semblance of verisimilitude were respected.

Because Heylyn's *Cosmographie* binds itself by the title and genre to treat all areas of the known world, complete omission and denial of India was not a viable option. English authors, playwrights, and poets, however, were under no such generic constraints, and indeed literary depictions of English interactions with Mughal India are almost nonexistent. This apparent discrepancy between England's consumption of accounts of India in translations and voyage narratives and omission of original literature about the country makes more sense when one thinks about the strengths and limitations of various genres. In voyage narrative synopses such as Heylyn's *Cosmographie*, lists of India's trade commodities and elaborate navigation instructions to and within the Indian subcontinent create a disembodied fantasy of profits ripe for the taking, a verbal treasure map. The sailors who wrote the narratives that later found their way into works by Hakluyt, Purchas, Heylyn, and Harris were primarily concerned with the practical business of finding and securing wealth through trade. When India's peoples are discussed in Heylyn's source material, he creates lengthy intrusive religious rhetoric to explain away England's inferiority by contrast. Literature, unlike many voyage collections, generally foregrounds interpersonal exchanges, which unfold in the present tense. The digressive apologetics that Heylyn employs would therefore need to be so elaborate in fictional interactions between English and Mughal characters that the narrative momentum would be constantly disrupted. Such a strategy would be nearly impossible in the main body of plays, where the back-and-forth dialogue between characters leaves little room for an intrusive narrator's commentary. Dryden, one of the few playwrights who does attempt to construct a theatrical version of Mughal India, omits English characters entirely, arguably because they would appear insignificant by comparison with their East Indian counterparts if even a semblance of historical accountability was maintained. Europeans also played no role in the Mughal civil wars that took place in the 1640s and 50s.

THEORETICAL APPROACH: ADAPTED NEW HISTORICISM AND POSTCOLONIAL CRITICISM

In "The Circulation of Social Energy," the first chapter of *Shakespearean Negotiations*, Stephen Greenblatt makes a somewhat unusual comparison between literature professors and "shamans" (1988, 1). This atypical blending of ideas from different discourses represents a practice that persists throughout his opening chapter and in New Historicism in general; Greenblatt mixes terms and ideas from theoretical schools as diverse as Marxism, deconstruction, and psychoanalysis, among others. My monograph follows this flexible, eclectic, interdisciplinary approach to literature, but at the same time my argument fills in some blind spots of New Historicism such as the occasionally paradoxically ahistorical interpretations and the inapplicability of Greenblatt's archival work to social change in the twenty-first century.

Greenblatt demonstrates his range of intellectual influences by adapting psychoanalytic ideas to his conception of what the theater represents and what the critic's role entails. He says, for instance, that theater does not simply mirror reality but rather condenses and distorts it: "And only with the recovery of this strangeness can we glimpse a whole spectrum of representational exchanges where we had once seen simple reflections alone" (1988, 8). In this passage, Greenblatt argues that the theater's apparently simple reflection of the real world is in fact a concentration of multiple meanings. Freud describes the condensation of dream-thoughts in a similar manner: "The first thing that becomes clear to anyone who compares the dream-content with the dream-thoughts is that a work of condensation on a large scale has been carried out. Dreams are brief, meager and laconic in comparison with the range and wealth of dream-thoughts" (1958, 279). According to Freud, then, the pictorial manifest content of dreams does not merely represent its real counterpart. Instead, the dream-content condenses a whole host of dream-thoughts into a symbolic language that is difficult to immediately perceive. Freud goes on to relate this distinction between latent and manifest content in dreams to the role of the analyst: "We have introduced a new class of psychical material between the manifest content of dreams and the conclusions of our enquiry: namely, their *latent* content, or (as we say) the 'dream-thoughts,' arrived at by means of our procedure" (277). Greenblatt envisions a similar role for the literary critic who sifts through the manifest content in order to understand what is beneath or behind it. For instance, he says that metaphorical acquisition "works by teasing out *latent* homologies, similitudes, systems of likeness, but it depends equally on a deliberate distancing or distortion that precedes the disclosure of likeness" (My italics; Greenblatt 1988, 11). Greenblatt's penchant for blurring distinctions resurfaces in this passage which, although ostensibly explaining the process whereby theater represents reality, could apply equally well to the psychoanalyst or literary critic who teases out "latent" meanings and maintains a deliberate distance from the material he or she investigates.

Greenblatt makes this connection to his scholastic approach more explicit when he says, "My vision is necessarily more fragmentary, but I hope to offer a compensatory satisfaction: insight into the half-hidden cultural transactions through which great works of art are empowered" (1988, 4). By offering insight into "half-hidden" cultural transactions, Greenblatt looks beyond the strictly mimetic dimensions of theater so that he can discern how the complex textual traces of life encoded into it are so "uncannily full of the will to be heard" (1988, 1). I adapt this approach, which is most commonly associated with Shakespearean criticism in New Historicism, to the narratives and drama of the long eighteenth century. The collective body of knowledge in voyage narratives gained from direct interaction with "Indians" from the Eastern and Western hemispheres is not only "half-hidden" or "latent" within the literary canon, but it is also directly manipulated by authors and playwrights in order to create a more globally powerful English national image.

Rebekah Mitsein convincingly argues that recent scholarly work on seventeenth-century British literature views these texts as more of a palimpsest that includes input from indigenous cultures rather than simply as completely blank spaces upon which European colonial fantasies were projected (2018, 339, 345). One way that British literary authors received this information, as Mitsein points out, was through voyage collections such as *Purchas His Pilgrimage* (344). Whereas Mitsein focuses on Africa, however, my primary aim is to show the ways in which travel narratives informed British literary representations of the East and West Indies. Even so, there is some overlap between the economic incentives that motivated European travel writers in both Africa and the Indies. Mitsein mentions, for instance, that Richard Jobson, the author of *The Golden Trade* (1623), voyaged up the Gambia River in the early seventeenth century in an attempt to gain direct access to Africa's resources (351).

Like Mitsein's work, Greenblatt's emphasis on the collective rather than the individual production of texts and his persistent use of economic terms such as "trade," "exchange," and "consumption," coupled with his desire to diminish intellectual "private property," leads to a Marxist-sounding idiom (Greenblatt 1988, 5, 7, 20). As with his other borrowings of critical terms, though, Greenblatt manages to take a few ideas from this methodology without wholly immersing himself in it. On the one hand, he repudiates claims that a work of art stands "only for the skill and effort of the individual artist," which sounds like a Marxist attack on the lone Romantic genius who creates in a sphere above and dissociated from the material concerns of everyday life (4). Yet Greenblatt's use of the word "only" in this passage is crucial because he does not privilege the power of the solitary artist to the exclusion of everything else but he also refuses to disregard Romantic individualism completely. He makes this stance more explicit by saying: "The idea is not to strip away and discard the enchanted impression of aesthetic autonomy but to inquire into the objective conditions of this enchantment, to discover how the traces of social circulation are effaced" (5). Through this balanced statement, Greenblatt differentiates his own views from more extreme Marxists such as Bertolt Brecht, who prescribes a method of acting that "purge(s)" the theater of "everything 'magical'" in order to "alienate" the audience so that they can look beyond Romantic illusions and critically view a theatrical production as a social text (136).

Olivera Jokic points out that Marx himself deglamorized the history of the East India Company by claiming that it was run by "'old obstinate clerks, and the like odd fellows'" (2011, 109). She then goes on to say that Marx "anticipates some recent developments in the historiography of colonialism" as follows:

> A variety of postcolonial theorists of historiography have worked to break [uncritical] reading habits among the readers of historical archives. They tampered with the enormous force believed to have reorganized the colonial archive so as to make it "official" and serviceable to the triumphalist narrative of imperial history; they worked to read from it the continuity of native agency and resistance; some read from it the eventual triumph of national self-determination. The recent histories of colonialism that focus on writing attempt to counter the author-effect altogether by giving living space to the microorganisms of colonialism, the "petty clerks, accountants and small claims adjusters" that Ian Baucom has identified as the enablers of modernity as we know it. The new historiography promises little glamour and fame to anyone involved in the exchange, and duly so. This is the history of creatues concerned less with imperial pomp and splendor, or with the theoretical questions of empire building and dismantling; and more with the "minutiae of imperial management, the trivial daily business of global rule, the submemorable chatter of sovereignty by committee." In their unglamorous history nobody ever prevailed: there was no absolute hegemony and no government informants. (Jokic 2011, 110, 126)

Like John Bruce, the East India Company administrator who is the central figure of Jokic's article, Peter Heylyn is a now largely forgotten official historiographer who was obsessed with commerce and minutiae. This monograph therefore participates in Jokic's larger Marx-inspired project of resisting colonialism by shining a spotlight on some of the mundane clerks who perpetuated it.

Moreover, Greenblatt distinguishes his own scholastic approach from the grand historical master narrative that often accompanies Marxism. An example of the latter methodology occurs in Fredric Jameson's work: "One of the essential themes of this book will be the contention that Marxism subsumes other interpretive modes or systems" (Greenblatt 1978, 47). Unlike Jameson, Greenblatt believes that "there can be no single method, no overall picture, no exhaustive and definitive cultural poetics" (19). Although Greenblatt borrows some Marxist terms and concepts, then, he does not wholly subscribe to the tenets of some of its adherents.

By defining his own conception of literature in opposition to a totalizing theory, though, Greenblatt sounds a bit like Derrida, who says that "One cannot determine the center and exhaust totalization because the sign which replaces the center, which supplements it, taking the center's place in its absence—this sign is added, occurs as a surplus, as a *supplement*" (Derrida 1988, 119). Within this passage, Derrida concludes, like Greenblatt, that one cannot contain or "exhaust" meaning within a totalizing structure because there is always an overabundance that escapes its attempts at circumscription. In fact, Greenblatt employs a similar vocabulary of surplus or play when speaking about plays; he says that they cannot "exhaust the negotiation" because they have a "plenitude" and are "made up of multiple exchanges, and the exchanges are multiplied over time, since to the transactions through which the work first acquired social energy are added supplementary transactions through which the work renews its power in changed circumstances" (Greenblatt 1988, 20). Greenblatt not only uses deconstruction-influenced ideas of supplementation, but he also advocates decentering traditional texts by saying, "in the essays that follow I propose something different: to look less at the presumed center of the literary domain than at its borders, to try to track what can only be glimpsed, as it were, at the margins of the text" (4). He therefore argues, in a Derridean fashion, that material previously considered marginal can in fact become the central focus of study. Although Greenblatt does not explicitly mention Marxism, deconstruction, or psychoanalysis in his chapter, then, he implicitly pays homage to them by eclectically borrowing from their ideas and vocabularies. This flexible and interdisciplinary approach is essential to my work since Heylyn's *Cosmographie* contains, among other subjects, anthropology, history, geography, theology, philosophy, biology, politics, and mythology.

Greenblatt's chief interest is the early modern period, which predates Marx, Derrida, and Freud. If he were to situate himself uncritically within one of these post-nineteenth-century camps by claiming that Renaissance theater merely reflects particular instances of general theories that developed much later, he would have to ignore the culturally specific social energies that accompanied each respective time period. Greenblatt articulates this idea directly in "Marlowe, Marx, and Anti-Semitism" when he says that

> Civil society, the rights of man, the political state, the concept of citizenship—Marx's basic terms—would have been quite incomprehensible to an Elizabethan. . . . Marx's discourse is informed by the Enlightenment, the American and French Revolutions, Feuerbach's analysis of religion, and the growth of capitalism. (1978, 40)

By emphasizing the sociopolitical and temporal dissimilarities between the Elizabethan age and Marxism, Greenblatt criticizes the unproblematic superimposition of one set of ideas onto another. He adopts a similar position in "Psychoanalysis and Renaissance Culture":

> But psychoanalytic interpretation is causally belated, even as it is causally linked [to Renaissance texts]: hence the curious effect of a discourse that functions *as if* the psychological categories it invokes were not only simultaneous

with but even prior to and themselves causes of the very phenomena of which in actual fact they were the results. (1986, 142)

The problem with arguing that Renaissance texts merely reflect psychoanalytic theory, then, is that the former, in Greenblatt's estimation, was partially responsible for the latter. In other words, modern theories can implicitly invert causality by making it appear as though historical phenomena prior to themselves are specific instances of their temporally posterior methods. Greenblatt's wariness of identifying himself too strongly with any particular post-Renaissance theory in order to explain early modern texts therefore seems to follow logically from his belief in the cultural specificity of social energies. In fact, I argue, following Lisa Jardine, that Greenblatt's work would benefit from greater attention to historical detail in some instances. In a convincing essay entitled "Strains of Renaissance Reading," Jardine shows that Greenblatt focuses so much attention on the anamorphic skull in Holbein's "The Ambassadors" painting that the historical circumstances surrounding the commission of the work are largely omitted (1995, 296–97). Like Jardine, I impose an even more rigorous attention to the archival and historical specificity of art and literature in this monograph than earlier New Historicist critics.

This historical specificity is especially important in relation to English men and women in the seventeenth century. Although I firmly support and seek to advance in my own work postcolonial theory's moral commitment to revealing and eliminating colonial rhetoric and the violence that it often produces, labels such as "racism" or "imperialism" can actually sometimes impede our understanding of the way English people saw themselves in relation to the rest of the world because these terms are too simplistic, impose modern taxonomies retroactively, and vilify a particular group while implicitly contrasting alleged contemporary progress by extension. This back-patting can in turn limit efforts toward genuine social equality by providing ancestral scapegoats. By revealing that Heylyn and the dozens of European voyagers whose voices he preserved and disseminated across England were far more concerned with wealth than skin color before the mid-seventeenth century, I leave fewer historical screens for twenty-first century Americans to project our own societal ills onto. In fact, the categories of race were not even the same in the latter half of the seventeenth century as they are today. Islamic, Persian-speaking Mughal Indians, for instance, were considered white by contemporary Europeans, as the earlier passage from Bernier reveals. Eugenia Zuroski Jenkins persuasively asserts that British literary texts of the early eighteenth century often take pains to write China into British self-representations, and I argue that the same can be said of India until at least 1707 when the Mughal Emperor Auranzeb died (2013, 5). John Dryden, for example, symbolically identifies England and Charles II with India and Aurangzeb (see chapter 4).

Inequalities of power therefore led to the denigration of Western "Indians" from 1492 until now, and Eastern Indians after the Battle of Plassey in 1757. The negative stereotyping of darker races in white Anglo-American discourses is therefore the product of centuries of economic and martial inequality rather than an instinctive or biological xenophobia. Well-meaning modern critics who project transhistorical notions of ethnic superiority onto seventeenth-century England inadvertently give a power and monolithic character to these stereotypes in the very process of condemning them. I argue that because these attitudes are the product of centuries of collective behavioral conditioning, they can be quarantined within specific historical moments in order to limit their reification in future generations.

Historical specificity also helps to navigate the enormous differences between the peoples of Southeast Asian islands and the Mughal Empire, both of which were grouped under the blanket term "Indian" in the seventeenth century. Critics such as Shankar Raman and Ania Loomba[18] focus on Fletcher's *The Island Princess*, a play about the Portuguese role in Ternate and Tidore. This play, along with Dryden's *Amboyna*, are a more natural fit for Saidian postcolonial models of study. However, the isolated examples of relatively potent Europeans on small Eastern islands in these plays are not necessarily representative of larger seventeenth-century international power relations in the vast mainland of Asia. We must therefore adapt certain parts of Saidian postcolonial theory in order to make them applicable to South Asia in the seventeenth century.

Another potential limitation of New Historicism is that its obsession with the archive and historical specificity can lead it to neglect current social and political problems. Terence Hawkes points out that Greenblatt's desire to "speak with the dead" could productively be adapted to "talk to the living" (qtd. in Robson 2008, 126). Although I wish to avoid grossly anachronistic stretches and parallels, I believe that my work is relevant to twenty-first century discussions of racial equality. In addition to providing fewer historical scapegoats for modern Americans to hide behind, historical explorations of the origins of racial and socioeconomic inequality can help to prevent their modern perpetuation. The international encounters of European sailors, merchants, and missionaries over more than a century, which Peter Heylyn's *Cosmographie* encapsulates and modifies, shows that a sharp distinction was made between the "Indians" decimated by European diseases in the Americas and the inhabitants of the Mughal Empire in India proper who were militarily and financially superior to the English until at least the death of Aurangzeb in 1707. Consequently, the European colonization of the Americas, and its accompanying devaluation of the native peoples, which arguably formed the foundation of stereotypes that persist to this day, began much earlier and lasted much longer there than in India (where the British presence did not become significant until Robert Clive's victory at the Battle of Plassey in 1757). By exposing the denigration of Amerindian peoples as an arbitrary product of historical power relations and chance, I unravel the more persistent essentialist myths of skin color and "inherent" behavioral traits upon which American prejudices continue to be based.

In this monograph, I attempt to forge an anticolonial history of British perceptions of "Indians" in the long eighteenth century that follows Friedrich Nietzsche's imposition of personal values onto the past and avoids Max Weber's attempt at scientific neutrality (even if the latter can never be fully achieved). Nietzsche claims to provide a "history of morality" in *On the Genealogy of Morals* and Weber states his attempt to sketch out a "universal history of culture" in *The Protestant Ethic and the Spirit of Capitalism* (Nietzsche 1967, 21; Weber 1958, 23). However, the way these two thinkers use the term "history" has some important differences. Whereas Nietzsche's "history" rarely mentions specific historical figures or works and even less frequently provides any actual quotations or evidence to embed his claims in concrete real-life details, Weber meticulously cites sources, especially Richard Baxter and John Wesley, and one cannot go more than a few sentences without encountering yet another lengthy footnote that qualifies a point or gives additional examples. Indeed, one might question whether Nietzsche's "history" really deserves that title at all since, from a modern standpoint at least, it tends to pay very little attention to chronology, social movements, and specific details from contemporaneous documents (though it does attempt to question the very moral framework that informed historical scholarship at the end of the nineteenth century); and, in spite of Weber's useful attention to detail in his historical work, his refusal to take an ethical stand on issues led him to the politically quietist position of the "iron cage" (Weber 1958, 181).

In *Genealogy of Morals*, Nietzsche advocates a way of studying history that avoids the evils of both nihilism and teleology. He combats the former as follows:

> I emphasize this major point of historical method all the more because it is in fundamental opposition to the now prevalent instinct and taste which would rather be reconciled even to the absolute fortuitousness, even the mechanistic senselessness of all events than to the theory that in all events a *will to power* is operating. (1967, 78)

In other words, a nihilistic approach to history would find, as its name suggests, "nothing" behind the events of history but "senselessness" and "fortuitousness." In this category are the "objective" scientific accounts of history, which Nietzsche criticizes by saying, "For this 'scientific fairness' immediately ceases and gives way to accents of deadly enmity and prejudice once it is a question of dealing with another group of affects" (1967, 74). Nietzsche, in contrast, claims that "a will to power" always informs both the accounts of history themselves and the events that historians write about. This insight is crucial to later theorists such as Foucault and my own work because it unmasks the ideologically prescriptive nature of supposedly objective descriptions of various phenomena.

At the same time, Nietzsche objects to those historians who would fashion history in such a way that it appears to be marching inevitably toward a goal by saying:

> The "evolution" of a thing, a custom, an organ is thus by no means its *progressus* toward a goal, even less a logical progressus by the shortest route and with the smallest expenditure of force—but a succession of more or less profound, more or less mutually independent processes of subduing, plus the resistances they encounter. . . . the form is fluid, but the "meaning" is even more so. (1967, 78)

In this passage, Nietzsche claims that a "succession" of "more or less mutually independent processes of subduing" is a more accurate way of looking at history. They are linked, not by some cosmic design, but rather through the ideological perspective of the historian and the power struggles in history. Nietzsche makes this idea explicit on the previous page:

> the history of a "thing," an organ, a custom can in this way be a continuous sign-chain of ever new interpretations and adaptations whose causes do not even have to be related to one another but, on the contrary, in some cases succeed and alternate with one another in a purely chance fashion. (1967, 77)

Put differently, the habitual juxtaposition of historical interpretations does not necessarily mean they are causally related. This point is central to Nietzsche's history and he articulates several examples of phenomena that have been linked arbitrarily but are treated as having a natural connection by historians: "good" and "unegoistic," "doer" and "deed," "guilt" and "suffering" (1967, 26, 45, 65). In a similar manner, I argue that "self" and "other," "colonial" and "neo-colonial," "slavery" and "racism," and "England" and "imperialism" have no inevitable natural teleological connection.

What Nietzsche does value as a method of history is philology[19] and close attention to "what is documented, what can actually be confirmed and has actually existed, in short the entire long hieroglyphic of record, so hard to decipher, of the moral past of mankind!" (1967, 21).[20] Later on, of course, Nietzsche complicates even this idea of history by questioning the very nature and desirability (or, to use his word, the "value") of truth itself (153). In doing so, he posits a radical relativism that could potentially unsettle even the longest standing norms, and indeed he did just that by challenging the two-millennia-old institution and ideological products of Christianity. While Christianity is now often associated with conservatism and less prominent in academia than in the nineteenth century, the religion's theoretically egalitarian values have endured as a goal in liberal democratic discourse. While equality for all, or "coexistence without violence" to quote Said, are collective goals worth pursuing, they have led some scholars to oversimplify the past in their zeal for a neat history of "progress" or to indulge in repetitive recountings of Anglo-American human rights' violations to the exclusion of all others (*Edward Said on Orientalism*). The enormous popularity of Said's *Orientalism* (1979) has understandably led many scholars to attempt to apply his general principles in different contexts. Yet Said himself says, "The period of immense advance in the institutions and content of Orientalism coincides exactly with the period of unparalleled European expansion; from 1815 to 1914 European direct colonial dominion expanded from about 35 percent of the earth's surface to about 85 percent of it" (1979, 41).[21] In other words, England had a very different position in the world in the latter half of the seventeenth century, when it claimed far less than "35 percent of the earth's surface," than it did beginning in 1815. Similarly, Srinivas Aravamudan contends that a "transcultural, cosmopolitan, and Enlightenment-inflected Orientalism existed at least as an alternative strain before 'Saidian' Orientalism came about" (2011, 3). Postcolonial theory therefore still has much to offer in the study of seventeenth-and eighteenth-century British literature, but it cannot be applied in quite the same way that Said uses it to analyze the nineteenth-and twentieth-century versions of colonial rhetoric.

Unlike some of Said's followers and Nietzsche, Weber explicitly applauded an emotionally detached scientific method of historical inquiry. For instance, in chapter 5 of *The Protestant Ethic and the Spirit of Capitalism*, Weber says:

> And, I might add, whoever wants a sermon should go to a conventicler. The question of the relative value of the cultures which are compared here will not receive a single word. It is true that the path of human destiny cannot but appall him who surveys a section of it. But he will do well to keep his small personal commentaries to himself. (Weber 1958, 29)[22]

This approach opens up the possibility of turning a blind eye to the genocidal horror that colonial rhetoric often produces, and I therefore oppose it. Suvir Kaul reminds us that our interpretations of the past have a very real impact on the present. He convincingly argues that apologists for the United States and some European countries have attempted to justify wars with Iraq and Afghanistan using timeworn rhetoric that allegedly benefits colonized countries while in fact exploiting them (Kaul 2009, 1).

Although Weber's attempt at scientific detachment should therefore be regarded with suspicion, the quantifying element of his historical method is sometimes useful since numbers were an obsession with voyage writers and their editors, especially Heylyn. The total financial worth of various sovereigns; number of references to specific terms such as "Indian" in a given work; sizes of each country's armies; prices of commodities; number of English colonies; population counts; and the editions, translations, and reprints of selected works give a concrete sense of how contemporaries saw themselves on a global scale and how widespread ideas were at any given moment. Searchable electronic databases I have relied heavily upon in this study such as EEBO, ECCO, ESTC, and others have facilitated the accumulation of these statistics, vastly expanded the corpus of readily available texts, and promise exciting new possibilities for the scholarship of the future.

Nietzsche could not seem to help letting what Weber called "small personal commentaries" overwhelm the histories he told. In one of many examples of this tendency in *The Genealogy of Morals*, Nietzsche fantasizes about "kicking to pieces these rotten armchairs, this cowardly contemplativeness, this lascivious historical eunuchism, this flirting with ascetic ideals, this justice-tartuffery of impotence" (1967, 158). As the words "rotten," "cowardly," and "lascivious" suggest, Nietzsche did not attempt to refrain from adding his own voice to questions of "relative value."

Yet Weber also differentiates his historical approach from Nietzsche's by locating his history of Protestant asceticism's influence on the development of Western capitalism within a larger international narrative. In fact, he foregrounds this approach by saying that he plans to make:

> a survey of the relations of the most important religions to economic life and to the social stratification of their environment, to follow out both causal relationships, so far as it is necessary in order to find points of comparison with the Occidental development. For only in this way is it possible to attempt a causal evaluation of those elements of the economic ethics of the Western religions which differentiate them from others, with a hope of attaining even a tolerable degree of approximation. (Weber 1958, 27)

Here Weber claims that it is "only" possible to understand "the elements of the economic ethics of the Western religions" by figuring out what is particular to them (i.e., what makes them unique in comparison to other economic ethics in non-Western religions). This desire to understand something by its negation or what it is not shares some similarities with both the linguistic theory of Saussure (in which a letter has meaning only in terms of its difference from other culturally constructed signs) and the crucial self/other form of identity politics that informs the work of psychoanalysts such as Freud and Lacan and postcolonial critics such as Said, Bhaba, and Spivak.

Thus both Nietzsche and Weber avoid teleological approaches to history. However, Weber attempts a neutral scientific tone that Nietzsche finds deplorable and false because it is every bit as judgmental and influenced by power relations as the work by religious historians who evaluate the past in relation to their own ethical beliefs. In place of a feigned nonbiased approach to history, Nietzsche makes it quite clear whose side he favors and who he detests based on his conception of what ideas and groups have "hindered or furthered human prosperity" (1967, 17). While his emphasis on the never disinterested nature of all historical writing meshes well with modern critical theorists, some of his particular dislikes, such as femininity and democracy, have not received as warm of a reception. My version of historicism therefore borrows and balances elements from the approaches of Greenblatt, Nietzsche, and Weber, even as I acknowledge the limitations of each. This monograph is also indebted to more recent critics of the history of the long eighteenth century whose work I have built upon and whose anticolonial methodologies I have employed in different geographical and literary contexts such as Robert Markley, Srinivas Aravamudan, Suvir Kaul, Eugenia Zuroski, Rebekah Mitsein, and Olivera Jokic.

CHAPTER DESCRIPTIONS

In the chapter following this introductory one, "Voyage Accounts and Collections," I argue that because Heylyn's *Cosmographie* summarizes the collective observations of dozens of European voyagers over a century and averaged more than one new edition per decade between 1652 and 1700, it reflected literate English people's "common sense" or general knowledge about the world until at least the first publication of Dryden's *Aureng-Zebe* in 1676. Heylyn's work therefore forms a general template of a historically specific worldview which reveals that India's economic prosperity and immense armies made England appear insignificant by comparison. At the same time, Heylyn's work, like other contemporary voyage narratives, downplays the role of diseases in the European conquest of the Americas in the fifteenth and sixteenth centuries. This perspective in turn led to an inflated sense of English power in relation to West "Indians," though indeed by the mid seventeenth century such pronouncements were generally accurate. Heylyn invokes religion and ethics to both excuse England's secular frailty in relation to India and to justify the exploitation of Amerindian peoples, a rhetorical strategy that Dryden and Steele employ later in variant forms. I do not claim that these two authors directly quote, paraphrase, or even necessarily read Heylyn, but rather that his work reflects and reinforces general attitudes toward warfare, trade, and "Indians" that show up, in both transparent and modified form, in the literary texts of these writers.

After this broader conceptual overview in the second chapter, my third chapter, "Dryden's West 'Indian' Emperors," analyzes Dryden's account of Montezuma and Cortez chronicled in *The Indian Queen* (1665) and *The Indian Emperor* (1667), which could have come from any number of sources, including Heylyn. I then examine the specific voyage narratives that explicitly influenced Dryden's *Aureng-Zebe* (chapter 4) and Steele's version of the Inkle and Yarico story (chapter 5). In *Aureng-Zebe* (1676), Dryden relies on Bernier's *Travels in the Mogul Empire* (first English edition 1671), and Steele's Inkle and Yarico tale (1711) is an adaptation of a section of Richard Ligon's *True and Exact History of the Island of Barbados* (1657). The overarching trajectory of my monograph chapters therefore progresses in a roughly chronological order and moves from larger seventeenth-and early eighteenth-century English international perceptions embodied in the Hakluyt-Purchas-Heylyn voyage collection tradition to specific iterations, influences, reflections, and modifications within the theater, prose, and poetry of the period. Chapters also alternate between East and West, but I make distinctions within these larger categories such as mainland/island and metropole/periphery.

In my third chapter, I analyze Dryden's depictions of "Indians" from the Western hemisphere by looking at plays set in this locale, *The Indian Queen* and *The Indian Emperor or The Conquest of Mexico by the Spaniards*. One of the most important ways that Dryden shows the "ignorance" of the Mexican "Indians" is through their disregard for gold, which was a widely accepted medium of exchange and a marker of national wealth in European and Eastern countries by the late seventeenth century. Ironically, Dryden may reveal his own ignorance of Amerindian beliefs if the testimony of Fernando Alvarado Tezozomoc, grandson of Montezuma II, is accurate in the *Cronica Mexicana* (1598), which he composed in both Spanish and Nahuatl (the language of the Aztecs). Tezozomoc claims that upon hearing of the arrival of the Spanish in the New World, his grandfather commissioned craftsmen to make a "throat-band or chain of gold," "a pair of gold bracelets, with chains of gold hanging from them," two great fans with "one side a half-moon of gold, on the other a gold sun," "two gold armlets," and quills filled with golden dust as welcome presents for the Spaniards (qtd. in Leòn-Portilla 2006, 19). Clearly the Aztecs valued gold if they considered it a worthy gift for Spanish conquistadors who some Amerindians believed at the time were returning deities. In addition to allegedly not valuing the proper currency, Dryden implies that the Inca and Aztec "Indians" also worship the wrong gods, which ultimately leads to the destruction of the latter's empire in the sequel to *The Indian Queen*. Zempoalla expresses this view of the relation between worldly power and divine favor by saying, "The Gods themselves their own will best express / To like the vow, by giving the success" (1665, V.i.103–104). Of course, this one-to-one correspondence between divine favor and material prosperity is precisely what Heylyn has to explain away in relation to India. When Europeans actually attained military ascendancy over Central American "Indians," however, Dryden does not hesitate to fall back on this traditional idea. The main problem for Dryden, then, is how to justify conquest and plundering from a moral standpoint (even though Europeans' diseases rather than their military skills and numbers were the real conquerors).

He frames this justification in several ways: by having natives invite the conquerors in during the prologue of *The Indian Queen*, by dissociating the English from the excesses of the Spaniards, by making class distinctions, and by giving the battle between the Old and New World cosmic significance as a contest between gods and systems of belief. In *The Indian Emperor*, the fate of Mexico is based on the strength of its gods, and the Judeo-Christian deity clearly wins. At the same time, though, Pizarro's and the unnamed Catholic priest's torture of Montezuma lends a certain degree of savageness to Spanish Christianity that Dryden would have readers believe English versions of the religion did not share. Dryden further stratifies the lines between morally acceptable and unacceptable forms of conquest by contrasting Pizarro's ruthless methods to Cortez's more benign ones. Pizarro was an illegitimate, uneducated son of a Spanish soldier and by some accounts a former swine farmer, whereas Cortez was born into the minor nobility, trained in law, and a former mayor of Santiago. Social class, education, and legitimacy therefore cut across national differences to some extent in *The Indian Emperor*. The supposed moral superiority of Christianity that Heylyn used to elevate the English over the far more powerful East Indians also enabled Dryden to fashion a rhetoric of ethical dominance over the Spanish, who openly exploited "Indians" in the Western hemisphere and monopolized the South American gold market. In both cases, then, English authors masked jealousy of national material inferiority with an appeal to a biblical code that transcended secular power.

In my fourth chapter, "Mughal History and Dryden's *Aureng-Zebe*," I contend that Dryden deliberately manipulates the information in his primary source material, Bernier's *Travels*, in order to reinforce the connection between the East India Company, Charles II (reigned 1660–85), and the contemporary Mughal Emperor Aurangzeb (reigned 1658–1707). As Poet Laureate and Historiographer Royal, Dryden depended on Charles II for money, who in turn relied on the EIC for gifts and loans that were never repaid. Dryden's flattering and deferential depiction of Aurangzeb therefore reveals a very different attitude than the nostalgic pity reserved for Central American "Indian" rulers who had been dead for centuries. In fact, Dryden's literary representation of Aurangzeb mirrors the way that the Mughal Emperor often portrayed himself in his Persian-language letters (Audrey Truschke estimates that roughly two thousand survive today; 2012, 113). In a letter to his father, Shah Jahan, who Aurangzeb had recently overthrown, he contrasts himself to "uncivilised barbarians" and claims that "the chief business of his life [is] to govern his subjects with equity" (qtd. in Truschke 2017, 37). Although Dryden uses the generic term "Indian" to refer to the indigenous peoples of Mexico, Peru, and India proper, he was, like almost all other literate seventeenth-century Englishmen familiar with voyage narratives, very much aware of the differences between the peoples of the Eastern and Western hemispheres. Dryden's own statements in the dedications to *The Indian Emperor*, on the one hand, and *Aureng-Zebe*, on the other, reveal this awareness. Whereas Dryden says he will portray the "sufferings," "griefs," lack of "Eloquence," and "simplicity," of Mexican "Indians," he compares some of his East Indian characters to historically powerful figures such as Cleopatra and mythical ones such as Cassandra (Indian 1665, 25; *Aureng-Zebe* 1675, 11).

Chapter 5, "British Men of Feeling on 'Indians' and Wealth: Addison, Steele, and Mackenzie," argues that representatives of eighteenth-century British sentimental masculinity and cosmopolitanism in works by Addison, Steele, and Mackenzie simultaneously pity and exploit "Indians." Despite overt expressions of commendation for ideals of global brotherhood, interracial mixing, and the ethical treatment of all human beings, the heroes of *The Spectator* and *The Man of Feeling* nonetheless subtly favor Englishness, whiteness, and financial gain at the direct expense of Others. While these ambivalent ideals were characteristic of British attitudes toward West "Indians," I show that Mackenzie's novel represents a cultural turning point. The English character Edwards' pity toward an East Indian (and simultaneous desire to profit from him) mirrors Dryden's and Steele's attitudes toward West "Indians." Mackenzie's novel therefore reflects the conflation of East and West "Indians" that became possible only after Clive's victory at the Battle of Plassey in 1757 when the British plundered West Bengal and put an end to the last vestiges of the Mughal Empire's power.

The problem with some versions of postcolonial theory's notion of "others" is that they can imply the English lumped all "Indians" into one subordinate category much sooner than the practice actually occurred. While it may be true that the English looked down on the natives of the Americas from a militant and cultural standpoint well before 1757, India, as Heylyn's *Cosmographie* and other voyage narratives reveal, was a different story.

Whereas Dryden and Steele attempted, on some level, to justify ethically the exploitation of "Indians" of the Western hemisphere, Heylyn and other voyage collections writers used religion to explain away the military and commercial inferiority of their own country in relation to India. In the voyage accounts and literature of the late seventeenth and early eighteenth century, Christianity and material prosperity, far more than skin color, served as the dominant gauges by which English men and women assessed "Indian" cultures and their own English reflections by contrast. Appeals to biblical authority were crucial to the rhetorically exaggerated claims to power that English authors employed in order to construct a national image that appeared potent on a global and even a cosmic scale. My monograph therefore analyzes competing representations of reality in order to sketch a more comprehensive picture of the ways in which English playwrights and fiction-writers in the long eighteenth century adapted voyage narratives to forge romanticized, flattering, and therefore marketable depictions of English relations with "Indians" from the Eastern and Western hemispheres.

CODA

The terminology for the indigenous inhabitants of the areas I treat in my monograph poses some challenges as I try to retain the early modern sense of "Indians" while respecting more recent preferences.[23] In the seventeenth and eighteenth centuries, "Indians," as applied to the peoples of the Western hemisphere, included the inhabitants of North, South, and Central America, the Caribbean, and Canada. Today, this term is used in a much narrower sense. North American descendants of these peoples are still designated by this word, though the phrase "First Nation" is generally preferred for groups such as the Inuit in Canada (Pritzker 2000, xv).[24] The term "Indian" for inhabitants of the Caribbean and Central and South America has been largely replaced by specific national affiliations such as "Barbadians," "Mexicans," or "Peruvians."

Although Native Americans today refer to themselves as "Indians" without the quotation marks, I include them when I discuss indigenous inhabitants of the Western hemisphere in order to avoid confusion with the peoples who originally were known under that rubric, namely the occupants of the Indus River valley in South Asia and its surrounding areas. The specific native peoples I discuss in this monograph were inhabitants of present-day Peru, Mexico (Dryden's *Indian Queen* and *Indian Emperor*), India (Dryden's *Aureng-Zebe* and Mackenzie's *Man of Feeling*), Barbados, and an unspecified "Main[land] of *America*" that could refer to the coastal regions of either the North or South American continents (Steele's Inkle and Yarico story)

(Addison and Steele 1711, 44). Wherever possible, I provide the group and individual names of these peoples in a manner that is the least Anglicized and the most acceptable to indigenous descendants, but of course problems arise with variant spellings, lack of consensus, and shifting meanings.[25]

NOTES

1. Heylyn is careful to distance his own work from these "monstrous Fables." He vows to "not let them pass without some censure" and assumes his audience is capable of separating fact from fiction: "But these relations, and the rest of this strain, I doubt not but the understanding Reader knoweth how to judge of, and what to believe" (1652 3: 213). For a discussion of the problematic terminology that a work of this scope entails and my selective use of quotation marks around the word "Indian," see the coda at the end of this introduction. All italics within this monograph are the authors' own unless I specifically state that I have added them for emphasis.

2. I specifically use this term rather than "English" here so that my claim encompasses Richard Steele, who was Irish, and Henry Mackenzie, who was Scottish. At the same time, I wish to point out that "British" is not wholly satisfactory either in relation to some of the earlier texts I include since the Parliaments of England and Scotland were not joined until 1707 (though English monarchs had ruled both since James I's coronation in 1603), and the United Kingdom of Great Britain that included Ireland did not officially come into being until the Act of Union in 1800.

3. Of course, the eyewitness accounts of merchants, sailors, and Jesuit missionaries were biased, subjective, and often written for personal advancement or popular consumption in Europe. Yet, even so, these accounts had the advantage of firsthand contact with "Indians" and were therefore at least grounded in empirical observations.

4. For an analysis of Hakluyt's work by a scholar who specializes in the early modern period, see Mancall.

5. From an economic standpoint, the English were indeed "inconsiderable" compared to Mughal emperors, as the following sample of annual revenues suggests: Elizabeth I 392,000 (1588); Akbar 32,000,000 (1593); Jahangir 50,000,000 (1611); Charles II 1,200,000 (1661); James II 2,000,000 (c. 1685); Aurangzeb 77,438,800 (1697) (Thomas 445, "History").

6. Samuel Johnson's roughly contemporaneous definitions in 1755 are similar to the *OED*'s: "1. A body of people drawn from the mother-country to inhabit some distant place. . . . 2. The country planted; a plantation" ("Colony").

7. The *OED* defines a firman as "An edict or order issued by an Oriental sovereign . . . a grant, licence, passport, permit" ("Firman").

8. Other Eastern countries forced Europeans to perform humbling gestures as well. In *Gulliver's Travels*, for instance, Swift describes the real practice of *fumi-e*, a "Ceremony" that involves Dutchmen "*trampling upon the Crucifix*" before a Japanese emperor. Englishmen were not even allowed in Japan after 1638 (Swift 2001, 291).

9. Richard Steel (also spelled "Still" and "Steele") was an Englishman who wrote an account of his voyages in the East in 1614 that was included in *Purchas his Pilgrimes*.

10. See "India," *OED*.

11. See Della Valle, *Travels of Pietro*, 97.

12. Like Bernier, Heylyn asserts that in northern India the "The natural Inhabitants for the most part, are of white complexion, like the Europaeans" (*Cosmographie* 1652, 3: 235). Skin color was not genetically predetermined in seventeenth century English minds, as Heylyn's description of the Chinese reveals: "The people are for the most part of swart complexion, but more or less, according to their neerness to the heats of the Sun" (3: 207). Derek Hughes points out that the term "race" included a "range of possible intellectual combinations that is not easily reproduced today" and "primarily meant family, genealogy, or nation" (Hughes 2007, xv). Yet skin color already had some of the connotations that it would acquire in later centuries. Ania Loomba argues convincingly that seventeenth-century English men and women held "a Bible-centered conception of the world in which humanity was graded according to its geographical distance from the Holy Land. . . . Blacks became identified with the descendants of Ham, and their color a direct consequence of sexual excess" (42). For a study of race in the eighteenth century, see Wheeler.

13. See "Mogul," *OED*.

14. As I show in chapter 2, Heylyn, like Dryden, does not find fault with the Muslim religious practices of the South Asian subcontinent. Yet Heylyn abhors the polytheistic Hindu rituals of India such as virginal deflowerings by pagods, sati, and self-mutilation. This perspective, a sympathetic identification with Muslim religious practices at least to the extent that they were the lesser of two evils, contributes to the growing body of research about the complex range of early modern British perceptions of Islam. As Gerald MacLean points out, "English attitudes towards the Ottoman Empire in the early modern period were not as uniformly hostile or as fearful as we have often been led to believe by followers of the school of Richard Knolles" (MacLean 2004, xiii). For additional studies of England and Islam in the early modern period, see Vitkus, Burton, Andrea, and Matar.

15. For a chart that compares the average annual incomes of the Mughal emperors, see Thomas, 445. Although Dryden could not have predicted that Aurangzeb would continue to rule for many years after the publication of the play, all indicators pointed to that outcome, as the playwright would have known from Bernier's descriptions of the Mughal Emperor's wealth and land in relation to his predecessors.

16. Dryden himself resurrected this theme in theatrical form in his 1672 tragedy *Amboyna*.

17. It is important to note, however, that much of the second volume of the Crusoe trilogy takes place in the East Indies.

18. See Raman, *Framing*; Loomba, "Break."

19. See *On the Genealogy of Morals* pages 17, 31, and 37.

20. In spite of this claim, Nietzsche rarely cites sources and therefore fails to produce the "documented" evidence that "can actually be confirmed" that he applauds in theory.

21. Elsewhere in *Orientalism*, Said locates the beginning of "modern Orientalism" in "the last third of the eighteenth century," but regardless of whether one starts in the late 1760s or 1815, my point about England's lack of a colonial presence in India prior to Clive's victory at the Battle of Plassey in 1757 and its accompanying reevaluation of the English global position remains the same (Said 1979, 22).

22. Another example of Weber's attempts to provide an objective history occurs in the following passage: "But this brings us to the world of judgments of value and of faith, with which this purely historical discussion need not be burdened" (182).

23. Bruce Trigger and Wilcomb Washburn make a compelling argument about the perils of using the word "Indian" as a blanket term: "In response to complaints from historians, most notably James Axtell, that referring to collective members of indigenous groups in the singular is an ethnocentric and 'nonsensical convention left over from the nineteenth century,' . . . in this volume such groups are called Hopis, Hurons, and Utes, just as people normally speak of Germans, Italians, and Russians" (1996, xviii). While I agree with Trigger and Wilcomb's point and I attempt whenever possible to provide specific group names, there are times when the use of "Indian" in a broader sense is necessary to convey an understanding of English people's perspectives in the long eighteenth century, especially when particular group names are not specified, as in the case of Ligon's and Steele's respective versions of "Inkle and Yarico."

24. At one time in the second half of the twentieth century, the term "Indian" was considered derogatory in the United States when applied to Native Americans, possibly because of the "cowboys and Indians" stereotypes it evoked. However, just as with the word "queer" in reference to gay men, "Indian" is no longer intended to offend the group it designates by most people who use it, and many Native Americans use this term to describe themselves.

25. On the problems of naming groups in South America, see Salomon and Schwartz, especially pages 11–17.

Chapter 2

Voyage Accounts and Collections from Heylyn to Bernier

Even though Peter Heylyn's *Cosmographie* is far better organized, larger in scope, and sold more copies than similar works of its kind, both before and after its publication in 1652, it has received little attention from literary scholars of the long eighteenth century. While the names of other voyage[1] collection writers and editors such as Hakluyt and Purchas are still well-known, Heylyn has somehow managed to slip through the cracks of history, despite his being one of the bestselling authors of the seventeenth century. In one of the few recent articles on *Cosmographie*, Robert Mayhew portrays this enormous geographical work as an "intellectual priest hole" in which Heylyn's "persecuted elements" (Caroline polemics) could be both "expressed and concealed by the bulk of other material" (Mayhew 2000, 32). Yet the scope of Mayhew's essay, along with most other scholarship on Heylyn, never moves beyond Europe. Consequently, all countries outside the West in *Cosmographie* become, to some extent, "the bulk of other material" that conceals what Mayhew considers the author's important theological concerns. Robert Markley is an exception to this trend.[2] Whereas Markley analyzes Heylyn primarily in relation to China and Japan, I concentrate on Heylyn's work as it relates to the Americas and India.

This chapter argues that what appears marginal or superfluous to Mayhew (Heylyn's depiction of non-European cultures) is in fact crucial to understanding his conception not only of England's place in the world during the 1640s and early 50s, but also his own relationship to the tradition of Hakluyt and Purchas. Moreover, the large gap between the desperate circumstances that Heylyn as an English royalist found himself in during this period and the consolatory, self-aggrandizing rhetoric that he employed in reaction to these conditions makes him a paradigm that can, with minor modifications, be used to understand marketable ideas about warfare, trade, and "Indians" in British fiction in the century and a half that followed the initial 1652 publication of *Cosmographie*. Whereas Purchas edited the voyage accounts he inherited from Hakluyt, Heylyn rewrote them to provide a comprehensive historical geography of the "entire" world. In other words, Heylyn offered general, "authoritative" principles based on specific voyage accounts and observations. By sifting through, categorizing, and summarizing these massive tomes, Heylyn actively prioritized those elements of each country's descriptions that warranted attention from his English readers. Consequently, his work, to a far greater extent than some of his predecessors', contextualizes voyage narratives in relation to contemporary concerns about military might, wealth, and trade. Heylyn's work also helps to contextualize the exaggerated claims made by Bernier, Dryden's main source for *Aureng-Zebe*, which I analyze later in the chapter.

SEVENTEENTH-CENTURY AUDIENCES FOR VOYAGE COLLECTIONS

While publication records show clearly that English men and women bought voyage collections, it is more difficult to gauge who exactly purchased these works. Sailors and merchants would certainly have been primary targets since the commodities and geographic descriptions of various countries in voyage collections were directly relevant to their success at international trading. Common sailors and especially officers had both the money and the reading skills to buy and consume these volumes. Money was one of the few perks of a grim life at sea. A sailor or merchant could save by taking long voyages where room and board (hard, sometimes weevil-filled biscuits) were included, and the outlets for spending wages were few on the ship itself. If the seaman finally did reach land, he generally had sufficient funds to purchase books for the next long maritime journey that awaited him. The length of these voyages, which could span months or even years, also provided men at sea with time for reading, and an impressive number of them were literate. Between 1700 and 1750, approximately eighty to one hundred percent of the highest ranking officers (captains, first, second, and third mates, surgeons) could read. Even among unskilled workers (common seamen, apprentices, quartermasters) the literacy rate ranged between 62.5 to 100 percent, with a total merchant shipping industry average of 75.4 percent (Rediker 1987, 307). These numbers are especially important because merchants appear to have been the primary targets for the consumption of secondhand voyage collections such as Heylyn's *Cosmographie*. Even though voyage collections were primarily by, for, and about sailors and merchants, a much larger portion of England's population had to have purchased these collections for a work such as Heylyn's *Cosmographie* to have gone through eight editions in a half of a century.[3]

Because some voyage collections such as *Cosmographie* stretched to thousands of pages in length, it is more likely that they were read sporadically rather than cover to cover. Heylyn's *Microcosmus* and *Cosmographie*, unlike Hakluyt's *Principal Voyages of the English Nation* or Purchas' *Hakluytus Posthumus*, facilitated this approach by providing concise summaries of countries that authors of fiction and others could refer to with relative ease. Of course, Heylyn's cosmographies were not the first to provide manageable synopses of the cultures, resources, history, inhabitants, wildlife, wealth, religious practices, and armies of various countries. Yet other roughly contemporaneous books similarly organized through the use of country names for their category headings, such as Botero's *Travellers Breviat* and d'Avity's *Estates, Empires, and Principallities of the World*, only have one extant English translation each, which suggests that they were less popular and less widely consulted in England than Heylyn's work. Heylyn's *Microcosmus* went through at least eight editions in twenty-five years and his *Cosmographie* had the same number within a fifty-year period (Bennett 1970, 170; Markley 2003, 494). With a combined total of sixteen editions between 1621 and 1700, Heylyn's two major works were ubiquitous.

When writers such as Richard Head or Dryden needed information on India or the Americas for their prose fiction and plays, the most logical place to look would therefore have been Heylyn's bestsellers: *Microcosmus* or *Cosmographie*. However, even if some of these authors[4] did not directly consult Heylyn's work, the ideas about "Indians," warfare, and trade in the Americas and India helped to form the popular conceptions that inspired fictional representations. Heylyn therefore not only reflected, but also shaped and refined, seventeenth-century English literary tastes. In the pages that follow, I argue that the commercial success of Heylyn's *Cosmographie* was partially the result of specific historical circumstances and his corresponding interpretation of them. He contained potentially unsettling contemporary information within his book, such as the inferiority of England's military in relation to India's, within not only a cyclical view of history, but also spiritual and nationalistic rhetoric that his successors in English literature would later reiterate and adapt.

THE BIOGRAPHICAL AND HISTORICAL CONTEXT OF *COSMOGRAPHIE'S* PUBLICATION

In order to comprehend Heylyn's purpose(s) in expanding his *Microcosmos* (1621) into a *Cosmographie* (1652) and a contemporary audience's reactions to this revised work, one must first explore the historical context in which it was written. Although no source appears to exist that records the exact dates when Heylyn began and finished *Cosmographie*, a seventeenth-century biographer, John Barnard, claims that the book was begun around 1648 and finished, or at least published, in 1652 (1683, 214–15).[5] Barnard was in a position to make such a claim with some accuracy since he was married to Heylyn's daughter. One knows that Heylyn was working on the "General Introduction" in 1648 since he includes that date in a discussion of the age of the earth (1652, 1: 3). While he wrote *Cosmographie*, the House of Commons tried and executed Charles I, Heylyn's patron and sovereign, to whom he dedicated *Microcosmus*. For Heylyn, this was yet another tragic incident in a long string of misfortunes. A few years earlier, according to the *Dictionary of National Biography*, Heylyn joined Charles at Oxford and acted as his "historian of the war," which led to Parliament's decision to strip Heylyn's house at Alresford of its contents and plunge him into destitution ("Heylyn").

Indeed, Heylyn explicitly refers to this bleak situation in the preface to *Cosmographie*:

> For being, by the unhappiness of my Destiny, or the infelicity of the Times, deprived of my Preferments, and divested of my Ministerial Function, (as to the ordinary and public exercise thereof) I cannot chuse but say, I have leisure enough; the opportunity of spending more idle hours (if I were so minded) than I ever expected or desired. (1652, A3)

Moreover, no immediate relief appeared to be within view; the New Model Army, led by Cromwell, was the biggest and most expensive in English history up to that point. If viewed from an Old Testament perspective in which God rewarded His "chosen people" with military victories and economic prosperity, Heylyn seemed to be on the losing, punished, forsaken, or "sinful" side. One way around this conclusion, as Heylyn shrewdly realized, was to cast the apparent wrath of God at the English royalist party in terms of a Job-like test. In the Old Testament, Job's divinely approved behavior in the midst of afflictions eventually restore him to even greater wealth and prosperity than he had before, which in turn signifies an even higher degree of favor with God:

> The Lord gaue Iob twice as much as he had before. . . . euery man also gaue him a piece of money, and euery one an eare-ring of gold. So the Lord blessed the latter end of Iob, more than his beginning: for he had fourteene thousand sheepe, and six thousand camels, and a thousand yoke of oxen, and a thousand shee asses. (*King James Bible* 1611, Job 42.10–12)

According to this passage, the Lord rewards Job's successful endurance of his trials of faith by giving him more material wealth (gold and animals) "than his beginning."[6]

In the "To The Reader" section that prefaces *Cosmographie*, Heylyn casts himself in this Job-like role fairly explicitly by explaining the "wants and difficulties" that he "struggle[d]" with while composing this work.[7] More specifically, he advertises his own learning by posing the following indirect question: "Books I had few to help my self with of mine own" and "it rather may be wondred at by an equall Reader, how I could write so much, with so little help"? Of course, the reason Heylyn lacked books was that Parliament confiscated his possessions at his Alresford home. While he does not come right out and denounce Parliament, which would have been dangerous, he implicitly casts its members in the role of Satan. After all, Satan, like the Puritans in Heylyn's life, was the actual agent of deprivation in Job's trials (1611, Job 2.6–7). Moreover, just as Job's suffering forged a closer bond between himself and God, Heylyn claims the same process took place during the writing of *Cosmographie*: "And to say truth, the work so prospered in my hand, and swelled so much above my thought and expectation, that I hope I may with modesty enough use those words of Jacob . . . The Lord God brought it to me." Far from being forsaken, then, Heylyn claims to be the medium through which God speaks. By making this claim, Heylyn identifies himself, his work, and the destiny of the English nation in terms of Old Testament typology.

With a need to reaffirm his place in the cosmos and with time on his hands because he had lost his "Ministerial Function," then, Heylyn decided to revise and expand one of his earlier works. Aside from the immediate purpose of publishing to make some much-needed money, his decision to expand the scope of *Microcosmus* into a *Cosmographie* appears to have been motivated by a desire to contain the events in England within a larger biblical narrative of providential history in order to position Heylyn and his fellow royalists as God's chosen people in the midst of a temporarily painful test that would eventually lead them to unprecedented prosperity. India proved especially conducive to this endeavor since its vast military forces, which effectively dwarfed the Commonwealth government's seemingly unlimited power, revealed the New Model Army's relative vulnerability. In fact, India's armies serve as a kind of metaphor for nearly absolute power that Heylyn believed he and his loyal English followers would attain once they passed their divine test and the cycle of history put them in a position that more accurately reflected their supposed importance in the eyes of the Judeo-Christian God. In terms of purely secular prosperity, Shah Jahan (ruled 1628–1658) and the Indian emperors who preceded him served as models for the type of power and wealth that Heylyn and other Englishmen desired for themselves and their countrymen.

HEYLYN'S FOCUS ON INDIA'S ARMIES IN *COSMOGRAPHIE*

Given the bellicose climate of England in the seventeenth and eighteenth centuries, it makes sense that Heylyn should devote a significant portion of his *Cosmographie* to an assessment of the relative military strengths of countries around the world. Yet this assessment is far more thorough and respectful in Heylyn's section on Mughal India than it is in his discussion of the Americas. If a relatively well-informed Englishperson were to peruse this work in the middle of the seventeenth century, he or she would be struck by Heylyn's repeated emphasis on the enormous size of India's armies. By repeatedly listing these figures in an incantatory way, Heylyn whets his readers' appetites for a revival of the East India trade, a project that both Charles I and Cromwell endorsed. Each of these rulers used the EIC as a creditor, or more accurately as a benefactor since neither of the two men repaid their loans (Markley 2006, 64). Consequently, Heylyn's promotion of trade to the East Indies was a further testament of his loyalty to Charles I that could be safely made in print without causing Heylyn further trouble with the Commonwealth government. With this universal support in place, Heylyn was free to dwell on the trade benefits that India could offer England. For instance, he says, "Only we may conjecture by the great wealth of those several Princes, and the vast Armies by them raised in their several Territories; that his *Annual Revenues, Casualties*, and united Forces must be almost infinite" (1652, 3: 246).[8] The phrase "almost infinite" that Heylyn uses in this passage sums up one of the main points that he urges his readers to grasp about the Mughal Empire. By constantly emphasizing the enormous numbers of Mughal troops, and the accompanying wealth that the maintenance of those soldiers suggested, Heylyn clearly conveys his envy of India's power. A strong army also provided rulers with the ability to seize and defend strategic ports. Thus wealth led to the equipment and provision of armies, who in turn captured and protected wealth. These large forces could guarantee, at least in theory, safe trade with the English. India's vast military would also require a steady supply of gunpowder so England's saltpetre merchants could find a ready market for their exports. Interestingly enough, the sentence about the infinite nature of Mughal military might and wealth is the last line that Heylyn writes about India before closing with his stock phrase: "And so much for" India (1652, 3: 246).

Although Heylyn concerned himself with this aspect of Indian culture in his *Microcosmus* as well, it became an obsession in *Cosmographie*. Whereas *Microcosmus* contains about six numerical references to the size of armies, *Cosmographie* has twenty-seven (*Microcosmus* 1621, 348–56; *Cosmographie* 1658, 213–46). One might argue that he simply followed Purchas' lead. After all, five of the six references to the size of Indian armies in *Microcosmus* come from *Purchas his Pilgrimage*, and many of the military statistics in *Cosmographie* are also taken directly from Purchas. Of Purchas' geographical books, *his Pilgrimage* (1613) would have been the most conducive to a relatively facile transcription of India's army counts because it is organized by country and contains digested summaries of voyagers' letters rather than the actual epistles themselves. Yet *Purchas his Pilgrimage* only has twelve numerical references to India's troops, which leaves fifteen unaccounted for in Heylyn's *Cosmographie*. Heylyn therefore must have searched out actively and taken the rest of his figures from other sources.

Heylyn's use of *Purchas his Pilgrimes* (1625), which is over four thousand pages and fills twenty volumes in the 1905 edition, reveals a significant degree of selectiveness and prioritizing. While this tome, much longer than *Purchas his Pilgrimage* in 1613, had not yet been published when Heylyn wrote the first edition of *Microcosmus* (1621), it had been in print for decades by the time he composed *Cosmographie* (1652). Moreover, none of Purchas' indices and prefaces contain easy reference points such as "Indian Armies" or "Military Statistics" that might have facilitated the intensive labor that Heylyn undertook.

Yet the figures Heylyn lists are almost certainly not completely accurate since the sheer task of counting troops in that quantity would be difficult, especially under the duress of an impending battle. Moreover, the rounded sums, usually to the hundred or even thousand, that Heylyn consistently gives suggest estimation rather than exact counts. The few times Heylyn gives precise numbers tend to be smaller than one thousand and easily countable; for instance, at one point Heylyn mentions that an army had 537 elephants, animals whose size would make them distinguishable from the rest of the troops with little difficulty (*Cosmographie* 1652, 3: 227, 233).[9] By uncharacteristically using a nonrounded number for elephants, Heylyn also draws his English readers' attention to this part of the military description and, in doing so, enhances its rhetorical power.

Heylyn's source for this unusually precise number appears to be Giovanni Botero. Although Heylyn does not cite sources frequently in *Cosmographie*, the 1621 edition of *Microcosmus* features extensive marginal citations. In one of them, Heylyn cites Boterus, the Latinized name of Giovanni Botero, as the source for the number of elephants that an army brought to battle against Prince Idalcan in the Narsinga province of India. Interestingly enough, this number changes between Botero's *Traveller's Breviat*, Heylyn's *Microcosmus*, and again in *Cosmographie*: 557, 558, and 537, respectively (1652). Botero lists the numbers of foot soldiers, cavalrymen, and elephants in nine separate battalions of troops, but he does not provide a total for the entire army. One can only assume, therefore, that Heylyn manually added up these figures. The one-elephant discrepancy between Botero's *Breviat* and Heylyn's *Microcosmus* was most likely a typographical or mathematical error on the latter's part. Because Heylyn does not list his sources in *Cosmographie*, however, it is possible that he found the 537 figure from someone other than Botero. Yet Botero lists two battalions that contain twenty elephants so another possibility is that Heylyn forgot to add in the second regiment. Thus the figures Heylyn listed were not perfectly consistent with either his sources or his own later work,[10] but they nonetheless gave readers a general idea about the huge forces India was capable of producing.

The fact that he took the trouble to count Botero's nine separate battalions (with three different troop subdivisions and hundreds of thousands of foot soldiers) reveals the importance that Heylyn placed on sum totals for Indian armies. In other words, Heylyn tallied these numbers and, in doing so, presented an overwhelming homogenous force rather than individual regiments. The awe and rhetorical effect that the idea of over 500 elephants in one place engendered in readers' minds would be far greater than listing twenty or so at a time, as Botero does. Cromwell's entire army, by contrast, enlisted roughly 34,000 soldiers in England alone in 1652 and 70,000 troops in England, Ireland, and Scotland combined that same year (Schwoerer 1974, 52; Childs 2001, 88).

Even if numbers had been painstakingly counted, the temptation to exaggerate would have been overwhelming. From a victorious army's standpoint, a greater number of enemy troops meant more glory and renown for those who won and, from a voyage writer's perspective, larger armies created a more wondrous, unusual, and therefore marketable tale. Defoe emphasizes this idea in his *A New Voyage Round the World* by saying that an account of a routine voyage "in it self" has "no Value," but that the story of an unusual journey "may be worth publishing" (1725, 2). Even with exaggerations taken into consideration, though, numeric trends are fairly consistent by country in Heylyn's work. Of his twenty-seven numerical references to India's army sizes, only eight have fewer than 100,000 troops. The largest of these armies exceeds 3,000,000 troops. In all of the Americas, however, the biggest army had 300,000 troops, and that was *before* the Spanish invaded and diseases decimated the population. Moreover, this army of 300,000 is the only one of the five references in all of the sections on the Americas to exceed 100,000 troops, and that army had been disbanded well before the arrival of the Spanish conquistadors. The oral nature of much pre-European American history and the inherent possibility of miscommunication that translation presents further cast doubt on the accuracy of this number. However, in spite of these potential inaccuracies, Heylyn's *Cosmographie* provided seventeenth-century English readers with a clear sense of the overwhelming differences in the sizes of Amerindian armies versus South Asian ones.

In the section on the Americas in *Cosmographie*, Heylyn scarcely mentions armies composed of native peoples. This omission is especially interesting considering the section on the Americas is about three times as long as the one on India.[11] In the 1652 edition of *Cosmographie*, Heylyn devotes thirty-three pages to India and ninety-five to the Americas. For the relatively short section on India, Heylyn crams in twenty-seven numerical references to the size of India's armies, nearly one per page. The sections on the Americas, in contrast, only list five numerical allusions to indigenous armies, which is about one reference for every twenty pages of text. Heylyn's omission of references to armies in the Americas is especially pronounced when one considers the vast amount of territory and peoples that he envisions. As the map from *Cosmographie* shows, when Heylyn describes the Americas he means South, Central, and North America, the Caribbean, and what is now Canada.

GUNPOWDER AND CLOTHING

By the time Heylyn put together his *Cosmographie*, then, it seems clear that he thought these numbers were important for India. In one of these references, he claims that King Badurius of Cambaia had an army that consisted of "150000 Horses, 500000 foot, 2000 Elephants armed, 200 Pieces of brass Ordnance, of which were 4 *Basilisks*, each of them drawn with 100 yoke of Oxen: and 500 Carts loaded with Powder and Shot" (Heylyn 1652, 3: 237). The references in this passage to "Ordnance," "Basilisks," and "Carts loaded with Powder and Shot" are especially important because India's armies had more than just numbers; they were also equipped with gunpowder and cannons. In fact, the first recorded reference to the use of gunpowder in India dates back at least to 1290 and the earliest known records of artillery use in battle were in 1368. England's first known recorded use and description of cannons in battle, in contrast, occurred in 1327 (Chatterji 2001, 20–21). In other words, India's armies had been using gunpowder-based projectiles for more years than Europeans. The latter therefore had no technological advantage over South Asians. Many of the armies Heylyn described also had "Horse," or cavalry, and war elephants. The depiction of Indian armies that Heylyn presents, complete with cavalry, war elephants, hundreds of thousands of troops, gunpowder, and cannons, would have been highly impressive to his contemporary English readers, especially since their own military had no war elephants and only a small fraction of India's soldiers.

For Heylyn, cavalry and "ordnance," both of which Amerindians lacked in the fifteenth century, were the hallmarks of a civilized army and could compensate for overwhelming odds. When Heylyn describes a combined European and South American army, he differentiates the "Savages" or Aztecs from the Spanish cavalry (*Cosmographie* 1652, 4: 134). Heylyn repeats this word "savages" when referring to an indigenous army of New Spain. In the year 1518 at the town of Potonchon, Heylyn says that 550 Spaniards led by Cortez were able, "by the help of . . . Horse and Ordinance . . . [to] discomfit . . . 40000 of the naked savages" (4: 134). Heylyn's emphasis on the "naked" nature of the Amerindians reveals his dismissal of armies who lacked armor and ordinance, and his consistent use of the word "savages" to describe Amerindian troops forms a distinct contrast to his respectful descriptions of India's armies.

The frontispiece of *Cosmographie* reinforces the distinction between clothed Asians, on the one hand, and naked Amerindians (and Africans), on the other. In fact, the woman representing Asia is indistinguishable from a European in dress, physical features, and skin color. This identification between Europeans and Asians based on these characteristics is also present on the title page of Gerhard Mercator's 1635 edition of *Historia Mundi: or Mercator's Atlas* (1635). Mercator's cover illustration further emphasizes these poles (European and Asian vs. African and Amerindian) by creating a hierarchical image with two women representing Europe and Asia on the top corners. These fully clothed women have civilized buildings in the background, whereas the backgrounds of their nude African and American counterparts in the two lower corners consist solely of wildlife and flora.

In addition to clothing, firearms also seem to have marked a crucial difference between ethnic groups. Like Heylyn, Defoe's Robinson Crusoe believes guns compensate for overwhelming odds in battle against Amerindian peoples. After telling the reader that "perhaps two or three hundred Canoes" full of "Savages" could show up on his island, Crusoe says: "I dream'd often of killing the Savages, and of the Reasons why I might justify the doing of it" (1719, 156). Machine guns did not exist in Crusoe's time, and the heavy muskets often took a half of a minute to reload in order to fire a single shot, as Bernier's quotation reveals later in this chapter. Consequently, Heylyn's and Defoe's ideas of the role of guns in battle against Amerindians were not realistic. In the eighteenth-century illustrations included in various editions of *Robinson Crusoe*, the protagonist is never without his gun, and in several he is in the process of firing it. The possession of guns therefore formed a crucial component of Englishmen's feelings of superiority over Amerindians, and since Mughal Indians were as well armed as the English, if not better, the same condescending attitude could not be adopted toward South Asians.

DIVINE CYCLICAL HISTORY

While the "Indian" armies of the Americas were largely overlooked or trivialized by Heylyn, the forces of India proper were a different story. He states that King Badurius of Cambaia's army, which was approximately nine times the size of the Commonwealth government's combined forces in all of England, Ireland, and Scotland, was still insufficient to defeat the soldiers of another Indian king named Merhamed (*Cosmographie* 1652, 3: 237). Heylyn then tells his readers that even this victorious empire, which for a time possessed a huge chunk of India, began to stagnate within a relatively brief period and then started to be overrun by "puissant Rebels" (3: 237). From this cycle of victory and defeat on a massive scale, Heylyn draws the following conclusion: "Nature or Divine providence have given to Empires, as to men, a determinate growth, beyond which there is no exceeding" (3: 237). For English royalists such as Heylyn who opposed the reigning Puritan government, the idea of a natural or divinely ordained "determinate growth, beyond which there is no exceeding," which pertained to even the largest armies and strongest empires, would have been particularly attractive and comforting precisely because it could be applied to Cromwell's regime, whose fall or at least decline would appear inevitable. This view also offers an explanation for the defeat of the royalists that, to some extent, clears them from charges of mismanagement and tyranny. After all, if the decline of all nations is unavoidable, Charles I's specific policy decisions do not seem to be directly responsible for the collapse of his government.

Heylyn's decision to expand the scope of *Microcosmus* into a *Cosmographie*[12] and to add a religio-historical "General Introduction" therefore assumes added significance when one views it in light of his personal situation in the middle of the seventeenth century. On the local level in England, Cromwell's army must have seemed large and powerful, much to the royalist Heylyn's chagrin. From the more universal perspective that Heylyn creates, however, the situation was not nearly so bleak. After all, if Indian empires with hundreds of thousands of troops and seemingly infinite wealth could be subsumed into a biblical master narrative of "determinate growth," then the Cromwellian government's comparatively puny forces and finances, which had not even lasted a decade at that point, appeared far less threatening. From Heylyn's royalist perspective, the cycle of history would eventually restore the Stuarts to their rightful throne.

As one of the most influential works of its kind in England in the seventeenth century, then, *Cosmographie* demonstrates at least one Englishman's recognition (and probably others') of the real-life limitations of his own country, and his simultaneous attempts to transcend those limitations by reproducing selected portions of extant non-European histories to serve as a fantasy with at least two components. First, Heylyn finds consolation as he recounts the wealth and might of Indian rulers whose thriving monarchical governments seem to validate royalist ideology. When he then reached the parts of Indian history in which the empire began to decline, he received pleasure of a different sort. The ultimate failure of these pagan rulers served as a confirmation that the Judeo-Christian biblical histories and prophecies, in which non-Christian groups of people could not survive indefinitely, still governed the fates of countries with other religions or "idolatries." In the "To the Reader" section of the 1652 edition of *Cosmographie*, Heylyn makes this link between morality and long-term national prosperity explicit: "If now we look into the causes of that desolation which hath hapned in the Civill State of those mighty Empires; to what can we impute it but their crying sins"?[13] The "crying sins" of "mighty Empires" therefore eventually led to their inevitable ruin from Heylyn's perspective.

Moreover, Heylyn was not above graphically recounting these "crying sins" for his readers, which leant a sensational aspect to his writing, and doubtless accounted for some of its popularity. In one of the more gruesome descriptions, Heylyn tells of an Indian village where "Fathers devoured their Children, the stronger preyed on the weaker; not only devouring their more fleshly parts, but their entrails also: nay, they broke up the skuls of such as they had slain, and sucked out their brains" (1652, 3: 245). The idea of fathers eating their own children is horrifying in itself, but Heylyn prolongs the shock value by including vivid visual images that likely both repulsed and fascinated readers in equal measure. In another passage, Heylyn describes a regional Indian king who "cutteth off his nose, ears, lips, and other parts" (3: 232). It is significant that this local ruler is from Travancor, which is located in Kerala, the southernmost tip of India, because this region was not under Islamic Mughal rule and therefore retained its Hindi customs. The map of India in Heylyn's *Cosmographie* shows that his conception of the country's basic shape agrees with modern cartographers, and the same map reveals the approximate location of Aurengzeb's court at Agra in the north. As a monotheistic religion that venerates Christ and other biblical figures alongside the prophet Muhammad, Islam was generally more respectable to Heylyn and other Englishmen than Hinduism's more alien polytheistic beliefs.

In addition to self-mutilation and cannibalism, there are sections in *Cosmographie* that graphically narrate self-immolations, live burials, euthanasia, torture, polygamy, public nudity, bloody rituals, and virginal defilements.[14] Sensational descriptions such as these fit naturally into the exotic adventure fiction of the next few decades, and may have even inspired them. The line between voyage narratives and exotic adventure fiction was so thin that an authentic version of the former, *Madagascar, or Robert Drury's Journal* (1729), was attributed to Defoe by some critics until 1945 (Edwards 1994, 169–70).

There is no question, for instance, that Richard Head plagiarized *Cosmographie* for the section of *The English Rogue* (1665) where Meriton Latroon travels to India. Compare, for instance, the following two passages from these respective works:

> The people are of coal-black colour (differing therein from the rest of the *Indians,* swarth and complexioned like the *Olive*) well limbed, and wearing their hair long and curled: about their heads an hankerchief wrought with gold and silver, and about their middle a cloth, which hangeth down to conceal their nakedness. (Heylyn 1652, 3: 227)

> These Malabars are coal-black, well limb'd, their hair long and curled; about their heads they only tye a small piece of linen, but about their bodies nothing but a little cloth which covers their secrets. (Head 1996, 267)[15]

Phrases and terms from these excerpts by Heylyn and Head such as "coal-black," "well-limb[e]d," and "hair long and curled" are identical. These passages not only reveal *Cosmographie*'s direct influence on popular seventeenth-century fiction, but they also show Heylyn's distinction between the "coal-black" skin color of Malabar natives on the southern coast of India and "the rest of the *Indians*" under Mughal rule, who are "complexioned like the *Olive*." The inhabitants of central and northern India therefore generally looked more like Europeans, and more importantly from Heylyn's perspective, shared more of their religious beliefs, than the Hindi natives of southern India and its surrounding islands.

Heylyn's moralistic approach to his subject matter provided hope and pleasure for English readers who shared his views because it enabled him to refer to biblical origins in order to reason away any apparent historical[16] contradictions (such as the seemingly infinite number of inhabitants of India and the relatively short time since Noah's flood) that he encountered. By addressing these potential historical problems, Heylyn followed in the tradition of other seventeenth-century writers such as James Ussher, Isaac Newton, and John Wilkes. Moreover, because Heylyn provided a lengthy biblical explanation of history in his "General Introduction," a section that did not even appear in

Microcosmus, the shift between the historical claims of his sources and the ways in which they could be reconciled with Judeo-Christian historiography often led him to reiterate or expand upon points he had made in the earlier work. For instance, Heylyn used this rhetorical strategy to explain away a potentially unsettling disparity between the reported size of one Indian army and the biblical explanation of history: how could King Staurobates of India have a "greater force made up of natural *Indians* only" than Queen Semiramis, whose own army was "three Millions of men and upwards,"[17] within "four hundred years" of the great flood's destruction of all human beings except Noah and his family (1652, 1: 6)? The presence of this enormous population in a single area of the world posed a direct challenge to the Mosaic narrative of history.

Heylyn further complicated this question by noting that the descendants of Noah were said to be scattered to the far corners of the earth after the Tower of Babel or "*Confusion of Tongues*," described in the eleventh book of Genesis (1652, 1: 7). In order to resolve these apparent incongruities between the statistics in his sources and the biblical account of time, Heylyn used about three double-columned pages with microscopic print in his "General Introduction" and then another column in his section on India (1: 6–8; 3: 218). The argument that Heylyn begins in the "General Introduction" and then continues in the India section is too lengthy to deal with here, but the gist of it is that people lived longer in those days and therefore had more opportunities to have children; also, Heylyn believed that Noah's Ark landed in the area "on the top of Mount *Caucasus* in the Countries of *Tartary*, *Persia*, and *India*" and that the people in these countries started reproducing rapidly before the Tower of Babel scattering took place (1: 7). Per usual, Heylyn summarizes popular European values since this argument derives from Sir Walter Raleigh's *History of the World*. Heylyn's constant shuffling back and forth between a specific country's description and the way that it fit into the biblical view of history and time enabled him to impose a rigorous master narrative on individual events that might have seemed chaotic or threatening if viewed in isolation.

However, Heylyn's pleasure in returning to what he believed was the "Real" or "True" version of interpreting world affairs, a macrocosmic divine perspective, is counterbalanced by a different sort of enjoyment that is almost proprietary or self-identifying in nature. The endless lists of army sizes sound like a monarch basking in his power or a miser repeatedly counting his coins. Indeed, the association between wealth and military size would have been natural to the English in the seventeenth century for several reasons. On a practical level, India would have to be incredibly spacious and endowed with an abundance of natural resources to support a population capable of producing armies of that magnitude.

TAXES AND TRADE

More specifically, the way that the English government was structured in the seventeenth century made the link between money and armies self-evident since the taxes that the government collected went almost entirely to military expenditures. Between 1689 and 1697, for instance, seventy-four percent of England's overall government expenditure was devoted to the military (Brewer 1989, 40). No large-scale welfare programs existed and specific tolls rather than general income taxes paid for necessary public amenities such as roads and bridges. Heylyn makes this association between wealth and armies quite explicit:

> if *Badurius*, which was King of *Cambaia* only, could bring into the field at once 500 Tun of Gold and Silver to pay his Army; and after the loss of all that treasure, advanced upon the sudden the sum of 600000 Crowns, which he sent to *Solyman* . . . What infinite *Treasures* must we think this Prince to be Master of, who hath more than four times the estate of the King of *Cambaia*? (1652, 3: 237)

As this passage suggests, the size of India's armies reveals a complex network of associations that connect the physical numbers of the army to the cost of maintaining those troops to the wealth of the ruler who can afford such sums.

What they could not take by force, then, Englishmen attempted to gain through trade. Yet trade was not favorably balanced in the seventeenth century because England's main export, wool, was not especially valuable and the English were running out of natural resources such as timber, which was crucial for the production of ships, buildings, and heat during England's cold winters. Heylyn follows in Purchas' footsteps by attempting to provide an ideological justification for this trade imbalance through theological rhetoric:

> But nothing more sets forth the Power and Wisdom of Almighty God, as it relates to these particulars, than that most admirable intermixture of Want with Plenty, whereby he hath united all the parts of the World in a continual Traffique and Commerce with one another: some Countries being destitute of those Commodities, with which others abound; and being plentiful in those, which the others want. (*Cosmographie* 1652, 1: 5)[18]

In this passage, which idealistically posits that nations will "Traffique and Commerce with one another" rather than forcibly taking the things they need by warfare, Heylyn argues that the Judeo-Christian God created a world in which the intermingling and interdependence of all His people was not just encouraged, but actually required. In practice, Englishmen were forced to trade with "Indians" in India if they wanted to gain access to valuable spices and commodities since a military takeover of the Mughal Empire was out of the question.[19] Yet, by framing this weakness as obedience to divine mandates, Heylyn enables his fellow countrymen to maintain a sense of dignity and importance in global affairs. Seventeenth-century readers of Heylyn's work could view a visual representation of his advocacy of trade in his monetary conversion chart from English pounds to twenty-four international currencies on the last page of *Cosmographie*.

HOBBESIAN ANXIETIES ABOUT A STATE OF WAR

Heylyn's focus on the military strength of India reflects his experience of the nine-year British Civil Wars, but his preoccupation with, and Hobbesian anxiety about, warfare in *Cosmographie* persisted for at least a half-century after its initial publication in the worldviews of English men and women. Heylyn was obsessed with the military and rightly imagined his readers would be as well, and his martial concerns during the Civil Wars produced an authorial intrusiveness not apparent in the 1621 publication of *Microcosmus* that both reflected and influenced popular taste in the mid-seventeenth century and beyond. Hobbes' *Leviathan*, published in 1651, a year before the first edition of Heylyn's *Cosmographie*, gives a sense of the effect that nearly a decade of civil wars engendered in British people's minds. In *Leviathan*, Hobbes describes a "time of Warre" as follows:

> Whatsoever therefore is consequent to a time of Warre, where every man is Enemy to every man; the same is consequent to the time, wherein men live without other security, than what their own strength, and their own invention shall furnish them withall. In such condition, there is no place for Industry; because the fruit thereof is uncertain: and consequently no Culture of the Earth; no Navigation, nor use of the commodities that may be imported by Sea; no commodious Building; no Instruments of moving, and removing such things as require much force; no Knowledge of the face of the Earth; no account of Time; no Arts; no Letters; no Society; and which is worst of all, continuall feare, and danger of violent death; And the life of man, solitary, poore, nasty, brutish, and short. (1651, 62)

This passage is important for several reasons. First and foremost, of all the dire consequences that war engenders, Hobbes ranks "continuall feare" and "danger of violent death" as the "worst of all." Second, Hobbes traces a direct line from war to the disruption of industry and trade, which in turn leads to the collapse of "Knowledge," "Arts," "Letters," and "Society." The sum total of all the problems warfare causes is Hobbes' famous line that life becomes "poore, nasty, brutish, and short."

When Hobbes discusses war and its ramifications, however, he does not simply mean the duration of time when two countries or groups of people are actively fighting or even necessarily when there has been an official declaration of war. Instead, he frames his notion of a "time" or "condition" of war in terms of the lack of a collective peace of mind, as the following passage suggests:

> Hereby it is manifest, that during the time men live without a common Power to keep them all in awe, they are in that condition which is called Warre; and such a warre, as is of every man, against every man consisteth not in Battell onely, or the act of fighting; but in a tract of time, wherein the Will to contend by Battell is sufficiently known: and therefore the notion of *Time,* is to be considered in the nature of Warre; as it is in the nature of Weather. For as the nature of Foule weather, lyeth not in a showre or two of rain; but in an inclination thereto of many dayes together: So the nature of War, consisteth not in actuall fighting; but in the known disposition thereto, during all the time there is no assurance to the contrary. (1651, 62)

In this passage, Hobbes describes war as a psychological state of fear induced by the constant threat of battle. At the end of the British Civil Wars in 1651, there was indeed "no assurance" that England would enjoy a prolonged period of peace and stability. The British Civil Wars produced the violent overthrow of a longstanding monarchical system of government, much of the fighting was within England's own borders, and the fear of being involuntarily recruited by either the king's or Parliament's armies was pervasive. The obsessive attention Heylyn lavished on India's military forces in *Cosmographie* and the receptiveness of his readers toward these descriptions therefore makes sense given the omnipresence of martial concerns in mid-seventeenth century England. Heylyn and Hobbes wrote during one of the most acute phases of this "condition which is called Warre" in British history, and their respective works reflect the uncertainty and trepidation of that era.

This fear associated with an unsettled civil state remained in effect long after the British Civil Wars were over through the system of impressment and the continual threat of war in the seventeenth and eighteenth centuries. Parliament began using impressment, or forced recruitment, almost immediately in 1642, whereas King Charles I did not resort to the practice on a large scale until the spring of 1644 (Gentles 1998, 103). Nor was the practice of impressment over after the British Civil Wars. In 1666, Pepys recorded in his diary that a British fleet spent an entire fortnight in the harbor solely to press men, a practice that he called "a shame to think of" (qtd. in Hutchinson 1914, 9). The *OED* cites another instance of the press gang at work in 1693, and, very early in her reign, Queen Anne authorized the forcible recruitment of musically inclined boys for drummer and fife players in the English army ("Press-gang"; Hutchinson 1914, 241). While the authorization was only temporary, it set the precedent for later abuses. In 1705, for instance, a fiddler named Richard Buller was handed over to the press gang because of his musical ability (Hutchinson 1914, 241–42). Although men were the direct targets of the press gang, women suffered under the system as well through the constant fear of losing husbands, fathers, sons, and friends, not to mention the danger of rape that the roving bands of press-gangs presented.

The recruiting tactics of press-gangs were especially aggressive during wartime, and there was certainly no shortage of English wars in the seventeenth and eighteenth centuries. Between 1625 and 1719, England not only fought three civil wars (1642–51), but the country also battled Spain (1625–29, 1655–60, 1702–13); France (1627–29, 1689–97, 1702–13); the Netherlands (1652–54, 1665–67, 1672–74); Scotland (1639–40, 1644, 1650–51, 1666, 1679, 1715); and Ireland (1641, 1649).[20] Skirmishes between English soldiers and Amerindians also took place during this period: the First (1609–13) and Second (1644–6) Anglo-Powhatan Wars; the Pequot War (1637); King Philip's War (1675–76); the Tuscarora War (1711–15), and the Yamasee War (1715–16). In the ninety-five year period between the ascension of Charles I (1625) and the publication of Defoe's *Farther of Adventure of Robinson Crusoe* (1719), England was at war for sixty-two of those years. *Cosmographie*'s eight editions between 1652 and 1700 therefore continued to reflect anxieties about warfare in the minds of the literate public.

In addition to England's martial conflicts, there were frequent changes of power. From 1558 to 1625, Elizabeth I and James I had been the only rulers of England. In the next sixty-seven year period, though, from 1625 to 1692, England went through eight different regimes: those of the executed Charles I (1625–49), the English Council of State (1649–53), the Roundheads Oliver and Richard Cromwell (1653–58 and 1658–59, respectively), Parliament (1659–60), the libertine Charles II (1660–85), Catholic James II (1685–89), and foreign William III (1689–1702). In fact, the beheading of Charles I in 1649 ushered in a new era of uncertainty for the English people. Even in theory, the divine right of kings no longer ensured a relatively peaceful succession to the throne. James II's religious affiliations, for example, caused him to be temporarily excluded from ruling overwhelmingly Protestant England even though his Stuart bloodline entitled him to the throne. The psychological uncertainty and fear produced by the Civil Wars on the imaginations of

British people, including fiction writers, then, lasted far beyond Heylyn's 1652 publication of *Cosmographie*.

Frequent conflicts of the next half-century and the ever-present fear of press-gangs were not the only agents that caused this collective psychological fear to persist; there was also a strong economic component. The increasing numbers of able-bodied men who were pressed into naval service during times of war were one demographic factor that contributed to domestic labor shortages, which in turn decreased commodity production. Rival navies also interfered with English trade vessels, a practice that made the already risky endeavors of seafaring merchants even more hazardous and limited the amount of materials that England could safely import. These economic problems were partially responsible for England's first national debt. At the beginning of the Nine Years War, England was debt-free. By the end, however, the government was £16,700,000 in debt (Brewer 1989, 30).

Thus the continued popularity of Heylyn's *Cosmographie* (eight editions before 1700) suggests that this product of Civil War culture offered a "standard" view of the world for decades after its initial publication. Although the most tumultuous years were over by 1651, Hobbes' work, like Heylyn's, continued to reflect general apprehension about warfare in English culture for over half a century. Between 1669 and 1686, for instance, not a single year passed without at least one reprint of Hobbes' work or a treatise that specifically mentioned his name in its title. In fact, the psychological mindset (or state of war) that Hobbes described persisted in England for the next few decades, and colored every aspect of the citizens' perspectives, including their tastes in literature.

Even several decades after Heylyn's *Cosmographie* and Hobbes' *Leviathan*, English readers maintained a generally fearful and hostile view of both their fellow countrymen and outsiders. The Earl of Rochester reveals this perspective in his poem "A Satyr Against Mankind":

> Whilst wretched man is still in arms for fear.
> For fear he arms, and is of arms afraid:
> From fear, to fear, successively betray'd.
> Base fear, the source, whence his best passions came,
> His boasted Honor, and his dear bought Fame. (Wilmot 1675, 140–44)

During the 1670s, English men and women read reports of the Americas that often contributed to these fears since voyage narratives about their colonists' conflicts with "Indians" in North America were ubiquitous. Between 1675 and 1677, there were at least fourteen books about King Philip's War published in London. Not surprisingly, these accounts tended to vilify

Amerindians and revel in the death of their leader, Metacomet. A few of the more descriptive titles of these works will serve to illustrate this point. One such treatise, published by Benjamin Tompson in 1676, had the following title: *Sad and Deplorable Newes from New England. . . . A True Narrative of New-Englands Lamentable Estate at Present, Occasioned by Many Un-heard of Cruelties, Practised upon the Persons and Estates of its United Colonies, Without Respect of Sex, Age or Quality of Persons by the Barbarous Heathen*. This title polarizes the indigenes of the Americas and the English by claiming the "Indians" practiced "Un-heard of Cruelties" indiscriminately against colonists. Moreover, the terms "Barbarous" and "Heathen" form a stark contrast to the supposedly civilized and Christian colonists.

Other titles from this two-year period stress the English victory over the indigenous peoples of the Americas, such as *The Warr in New-England Visibly Ended* by Richard Hutchinson (1677) and Increase Mather's *Brief History of the War with the Indians in New-England . . . when Philip, Alias Metacomet, the Principal Author and Beginner of the War, was Slain* (1676). The latter title places the blame for the war solely on Metacomet's shoulders, as if English encroachment on North American territory had nothing to do with it. Moreover, Mather's "Brief History" reports Metacomet's death as a victory for the colonists and by extension their mother country. These titles suggest that publishers, authors, and readers insatiably produced and consumed narratives about supposedly heroic English conquests of West "Indians." The glorification of English settlers at the expense of Amerindians therefore represented a major trend in popular histories of the late seventeenth century. By reading accounts of their countrymen's military triumphs over indigenous peoples in the Americas, English men and women were able to find a temporary reprieve from, and vicarious mastery of, their economic, political, and national fears.

While the English could revel in their martial victories over Amerindians in the seventeenth century, the same could not be said for their interactions with Mughal India. England's first significant armed conflict with India did not occur until Clive's victory at the Battle of Plassey in 1757. In other words, England had been fighting with Amerindians at least 148 years (the first Anglo-Powhatan War in 1609) before the earliest important engagement with India. When Heylyn published *Cosmographie* in 1652, England was still over a century away from controlling West Bengal, and EIC soldiers were vastly outnumbered and outgunned by Shah Jahan's troops. When war did break out briefly in the late 1680s between the EIC and Aurangzeb, the former were easily defeated.[21]

European countries before Clive's victory at the Battle of Plassey in 1757 had to send ambassadors to ask permission from the Mughal Emperor to set up trading posts in India through elaborate ceremonies that depended on the exchange of gifts. In Bernier's time at the Mughal court, for instance, he observed and recorded a Dutch ambassador's successful appeal to Aurangzeb in 1662.[22] Dirk van Adrichem, or "Monsieur Adrican" as Bernier calls him, performed the *"Indian ceremony of the Salaam,"* passed his letters "through the medium of an *Omrah*," or Indian lord, presented expensive gifts to Aurangzeb, and was detained until several members of his party were gravely ill and his secretary died (Bernier 1968, 127–28). In a gesture that Bernier describes as especially "courteous and condescending," Aurangzeb allowed van Adrichem to "salute him *à la Frank*" (127).[23] While Europeans could revel in victories over supposedly barbarous "Indians" in the Americas, then, a different approach was necessary when dealing with the regal, civilized, and militarily superior Mughal Empire in the 1660s.

BERNIER'S ACCOUNT OF AURANGZEB

The few reports of Europeans' hypothetical ability to defeat India's armies in this period should therefore be regarded with considerable skepticism, especially Bernier's since he dedicated his work to Louis XIV. Bernier makes a claim in his 1670 book *Travels in the Mogul Empire*[24] about French military prowess in an imagined war against Indian armies that contradicts his own account of Dara's (Aurangzeb's brother and rival for the Mughal throne) armies and India's warfare more generally:

> These immense armies frequently perform great feats; but when thrown into confusion it is impossible to restore them to discipline. I could never see these soldiers, destitute of order, and marching with the irregularity of a herd of animals, without reflecting upon the ease with which five-and-twenty thousand of our veterans from the army in *Flanders*, commanded by *Prince Condé*, or *Marshal Turenne*, would overcome these armies, however numerous. . . . By receiving the onset with their usual steadiness, the French troops would throw any Indian army into consternation. (1968, 55)

The idea that 25,000 Frenchman could defeat "any Indian army," "however numerous," seems out of place with some of Bernier's own descriptions. According to him, just one of Dara's three divisions of troops contained 30,000 soldiers, and the picture of Indian armies that Bernier paints in other parts of his narrative of India's armies is impressive: "bannes" (explosives) throwers, saber-wielding horse archers who could shoot six arrows before a musketeer could fire twice, war elephants, cannons chained together to impede the enemy cavalry's advance, camel-riders with small pieces of ordnance mounted on swivels, and musketeers (Bernier 1968, 47–48).

Against this impressive force, Bernier claims that the French could prevail with "ease" through "steadiness" and good commanders alone. Yet elsewhere in his *Travels*, Bernier claims that India's armies also possess these two traits: the cavalry "preserve excellent order, and keep in a compact body"; Dara was an "intrepid commander"; and Aurangzeb showed "bravery and resolution" (1968, 48–50). In fact, Bernier's entire set of assumptions about India's disorganized armies rests on a single incident: Dara temporarily dismounted from his visible position atop his elephant, which fueled rumors of his death and disheartened his troops. Aurangzeb, meanwhile, "remained during a quarter of an hour *steadily* on his elephant, and was rewarded with the crown of *Hindoustan*" (Emphasis added; 54). Bernier reduces all military success to strong leadership and "steadiness," two non-quantifiable, and therefore difficult to disprove, traits.

The apparent contradiction between Bernier's description of India's impressive armies and the supposed "ease" with which 25,000 French troops could defeat them makes more sense when one looks at the dedication to *Travels in the Mogul Empire*. Bernier dedicates his work to the reigning French king Louis XIV as follows: *"for I have always remembered, no matter how far away I may have been, that I had a Master to whom I was accountable, being,* HIS MAJESTY'S *Most humble and most obedient Subject and Servant, F. Bernier"* (1968, xlvi). Because Bernier "always remembered" that he was a "Subject and Servant" who was "accountable" to Louis XIV, the flattery of French troops and their strong leadership in imaginary battles against India's armies seems sycophantic. Rather than taking Bernier's boast that 25,000 French troops could defeat any Indian army, however large, as an honest assessment of the relative military strengths of these two countries, then, his unrealistic nationalist bravado should be viewed as a transparent attempt to secure royal patronage. Louis personally participated in the War of Devolution in 1667, and the quality of the French army was something in which he took special pride and interest, which makes Bernier's flattery particularly apt.

The connection between writers such as Bernier and Heylyn and the popular fiction of the ensuing decades is of vital importance. Heylyn is especially significant since he was not just a lone bestselling author; he summarized firsthand accounts by European travelers such as William Hawkins, Ralph Fitch, and dozens of others. Heylyn's religiously saturated *Cosmographie* and Bernier's *Travels in the Mogul Empire* provide insight into the ways in which Europeans saw themselves in relation to the rest of the world and perform the cultural work of national identity formation that the more secular and fictionalized media increasingly would come to share.[25]

NOTES

1. I prefer the word "voyage" rather than "travel," the more common label for this genre, because the latter connotes leisurely trips for pleasure, which was not an early modern concept. Although aristocrats wandered throughout Europe during Grand Tours in the long eighteenth century, trips to the Americas and Asia were considered far too long and dangerous for mere entertainment by most English men and women. By "voyages" I mean extended journeys at least partially by sea with financial gain or religious conversion as the primary goals.

2. See *Far East* (2006) 9, 60–64, 136, 180.

3. This statement takes into account the relatively small percentage of England's overall population that men at sea constituted. If one combines all of the nautical professions in Gregory King's 1688 tables (merchants and traders by sea, naval officers, and common seamen), the number of men was 234,000 (2: 184). Because England's total population was, according to King's chart on the same page, about 5,500,520 at this time, men at sea only comprised approximately four percent of the country's whole populace.

4. Head unquestionably read Heylyn since there are descriptions of Indians directly lifted from *Cosmographie* in *The English Rogue*, as I show later in the chapter.

5. For a different contemporary biography of Heylyn, see Vernon.

6. All biblical quotations in this chapter are from the 1611 edition. The explicitly materialist wealth of post-tribulation Job also justifies Heylyn's and other Englishmen's fascination with the riches of India. Yet India's wealth, in Heylyn's view, was acquired over time independently of God's favor.

7. All references to *Cosmographie* in this paragraph will refer to this section, which is not paginated.

8. Heylyn is similarly impressed by China's population, size, military, and wealth:
> Of both Sexes it is thought that this Countrey containeth no fewer than 70 Millions. Which though it seem to be a number beyond all belief; yet it is knowingly averred, and may be thought probable enough, if we consider the spaciousness of the Countrey. . . . The forces which this King is able to draw into the Field must needs be infinite, considering that incredible number of subjects under his command. . . . This Countrey one-is [sic] computed at 70 millions; which is more by 15 millions than all [European countries] together. Proportionably his Levies must be so much greater than can be ordinarily raised out of those Countries. (3: 208, 211–12).

9. Heylyn provides the numerical size of this army twice in the 1652 edition of *Cosmographie*, and he lists the quantity of Badurius' Indian forces three times (3: 221, 225, 237). The repetition of these figures further illustrates the importance Heylyn placed upon them. In the 1621 edition of *Microcosmus*, in contrast, Heylyn repeats none of these numbers. These differences between *Microcosmus* (1621) and *Cosmographie* (1652) support the idea that the British Civil Wars (1642–1651) and Heylyn's troubles during them contributed to his increase in emphasis on the numerical sizes of India's armies in the later work.

10. Even within the 1652 edition of *Cosmographie*, Heylyn lists the same army with different numbers of troops, as the following figures show: "606000 Foot, 29650 Horse, and 537 Elephants" (3: 227); "606000 foot, 30000 Horse, 537 Elephants" (3:

233). Botero's records of cavalrymen in this army add up to 29,650 so Heylyn likely rounded the sum.

11. I compare India to all of the countries in the Americas, rather than just one, in this paragraph in order to show Heylyn's larger trends in referring to East and West "Indian" armies. If one were to take a single country in the Americas such as Mexico there would be even fewer military references, which reinforces the same statistical pattern.

12. This expansion from the respective first editions of *Microcosmus* (1621) and *Cosmographie* (1652) was enormous. The difference between these two works in sheer page numbers is 488, but because *Cosmographie* averages three times as many words per page as its predecessor, an adjusted and more accurate difference in length between them would be approximately 1,464 pages.

13. This section is not paginated.

14. Examples of these phenomena appear on 3: 214, 223, 227, 232, 234–5, 241, 245.

15. I cite only Richard Head since Francis Kirkman, who cowrote portions of later volumes of *The English Rogue*, was not yet a contributor in the first book.

16. On seventeenth-century historiography, see Guibbory, *Map*.

17. In the India section, Heylyn claims that the same army was "four Millions and upwards" (3: 218). Heylyn's main source, Purchas, lists the army at 3,500,000 (*Pilgrimes* 1.1: 72).

18. Richard Steele's *Spectator* coauthor, Joseph Addison, voices a nearly identical sentiment six decades later: "NATURE seems to have taken a particular Care to disseminate her Blessings among the different Regions of the World, with an Eye to mutual Intercourse and Traffick among Mankind, that the Natives of the several Parts of the Globe might have a kind of Dependance upon one another, and be united together in their common Interest. Almost every *Degree* produces something Peculiar to it" (213). The passage predates Heylyn in Purchas' work and thus reveals that the same rhetoric extends over a century.

19. The EIC's army in 1668, for instance, only contained about 267 troops (St. John 77–78). When the EIC interfered with pilgrims from Surat to Mecca, they were temporarily banished from western India, and only allowed to return in 1690 by Aurangzeb after paying a £15,000 fine (Kadian 15).

20. The march of Monck's Army in 1659 was an internal English conflict, but not technically part of the three British Civil Wars between 1642 and 1651, and when the Duke of Monmouth rebelled in 1685, supporters from The Hague, Scotland, and southern England rallied to his cause (including a young Daniel Defoe). For an analysis of the role that these incessant wars played in England's economy, see Brewer.

21. John Keay points out the absurdity of the Company's Mughal War in the following passage: "two ships carrying exactly 308 Company soldiers sailed up to Hughli to press the Company's suit and challenge an empire which had at the time at least 100,000 men in the field" (*India* 371).

22. Although both the first (1652–54) and second (1665–67) Anglo-Dutch Wars were essentially stalemates, the Dutch were more powerful than the English in the East Indies. Moreover, the Verenigde Oostindische Compagnie was better funded

than the British East India Company and more successful at trading. See Markley, *Far East* (2006)146.

23. The word "condescending," as Bernier uses it here, carries negative connotations for the person who receives this action rather than, as many twenty-first century Americans indoctrinated in the ideals of democracy would assume, the person who performs it. As Bernier uses the word, the most accurate definition is "to sink willingly to equal terms with inferiors" ("Condescend").

24. This book was first translated into English in 1671, and it records Bernier's travels in India from 1656–68. Like Heylyn's *Cosmographie*, Bernier's *Travels* was a bestseller. In various forms, it went through a total of thirteen reprints in forty-one years, and was translated into German, English, Italian, and Dutch.

25. This statement does not mean that secular novels and plays were suddenly published more frequently than religious works or that the categories of "secular" and "religious" could not overlap. As Ian Watt points out in *The Rise of the Novel*, religious works were still "by far the greatest single category of books published in the eighteenth century, as in previous centuries" (49). However, the theaters were closed in England from 1642 until 1660 and scholars such as McKeon argue that "the novel" had not yet been born as a recognizable generic entity; consequently, readers at the time that Heylyn's *Cosmographie* was published (1652) would have had fewer choices of secular fiction than, say, readers of Defoe's *Robinson Crusoe* (1719).

Chapter 3

Dryden's West "Indian" Emperors

With all of their grandiose language, Heylyn and Bernier sound like people who possessed much more power and control of their situations than the historical facts seem to warrant. Rather than viewing English authors of this period through a nineteenth-and twentieth-century Saidian postcolonial lens, as arrogant and powerful oppressors of unfortunate "others," then, scholars should envision seventeenth-century writers and readers as insecure citizens of a globally marginal country producing and consuming unrealistic self-aggrandizing stories to console and distract themselves from the fear and economic scarcity that the constant threat of war engendered. With a few exceptions, the men and women who wrote fiction in the seventeenth and eighteenth centuries were not even particularly wealthy or "well-bred" by the standards of their own society, let alone those of certain parts of India. Let us turn, then, to some of the more influential, popular, and canonical works of English fiction from this period to see more specifically how voyage collection writers in the mid-seventeenth century influenced and set the stage for the bestselling literature of the next seventy years.

Dryden's three "Indian" plays, *The Indian Queen* (1665), *The Indian Emperor* (1667), and *Aureng-Zebe* (1676)[1] are rarely studied directly in relation to one another, though the assumptions about England's growing colonial power in relation to "Indians" are often transferred, incorrectly, from the plays set in the Western hemisphere to the one set in the East. The few analyses that do overtly explore the relationship between the works, such as Laura Brown's article "Dryden and the Imperial Imagination," focus on the heroic[2] and exotic nature of the plays rather than their "Indian" subjects. Brown groups these plays together into a thematic whole, noting that they "often treated lost, decaying, or declining empires" (2004, 69). While generic and thematic analyses of these plays are useful, I argue that Dryden's rhetorical strategies are very different in his plays set in the Americas (*The Indian Queen* and *The Indian Emperor*) in the sixteenth century, on the one hand, and his contemporary play that takes place in Mughal India (*Aureng-Zebe*), on the other.

In the first two plays, Dryden justifies English territorial expansion into the Americas, whereas *Aureng-Zebe*, which I analyze in the next chapter, offers an idealized, flattering version of Charles II based on a reigning Mughal ruler who, as Heylyn's *Cosmographie* and other seventeenth-century voyage collections reveal, was far wealthier and more powerful than England's sovereign.

In this chapter, I argue that Dryden reproduces and elaborates an ideological, providentialist view of European superiority to the indigenes of the Americas and of English moral superiority to the Spanish. The first section contends that Dryden attempts to justify English territorial expansion in the West Indies by constructing a consensual invitation to rule by the indigenous inhabitants in *The Indian Queen*. Part two explores Dryden's invocation of the Black Legend in *The Indian Emperor* as a way to differentiate England's supposedly benign form of colonialism in North America from Spain's allegedly crueler version in Peru and Mexico. This fantasy allows Englishmen to appear comparatively blameless since the Spaniards provide a convenient scapegoat for the worst aspects of colonialism. In this triangulated relationship between England, Spain, and the Americas, English colonial violence could be displaced onto the Black Legend of the Spanish. The third section complicates East/West and English/Spanish binary oppositions by showing that Dryden's use of Cortez as a surrogate Englishman reveals a solidarity, albeit limited, among members of the upper classes against inhumane forms of conquest by Europeans. At the same time, I argue that a limited sympathetic identification develops between the Anglicized character and the Mexican ones on the basis of a shared victimization by Spain. I conclude the chapter with an analysis of the parallels between Dryden's Cortez and Charles II in order to show that much of the anti-Catholic rhetoric that often accompanied English constructions of the Black Legend is absent in Dryden's *Indian Emperor*, most likely because the playwright was already a crypto-Catholic at this time.

INDIGENOUS INVITATIONS TO RULE

Brown's decision, and most other critics', to group two of Dryden's three "Indian" plays together, *The Indian Queen* and *The Indian Emperor*, makes sense beyond the fact that they both belong to the heroic genre. Written, or at least performed, approximately one year apart, these two plays set in Mexico form a natural pairing. Unlike *Aureng-Zebe*, which does not even mention foreign invasions since all battles occur between the armies of rivals within the royal Mughal family, *The Indian Queen* and *The Indian Emperor* are preoccupied with the conquest of one group of peoples by another. In fact, *The Indian Queen*, the first play in the two-part series, begins Dryden's rhetorical justification for European invasion of the Americas in the very prologue[3] itself.

An unnamed "Indian" boy and his female companion, Quevira, awaken from their slumber and begin a conversation about an impending battle. Ostensibly, this martial conflict occurs between the Peruvian Ynca's armies, commanded by the general Montezuma, and the indigenous "Mexicans," who defend the usurping Queen Zempoalla (Dryden, 1665, I.i.1–3). In reality, this battle never took place. Even at the height of their respective empires, the Aztecs and Incas were too geographically distant from one another for conflicts between them to occur (*Historical Atlas* 1995, H-3; Moseley 1992, 9). Montezuma (also called Motecuhzoma Xocoyotl or Motecuhzoma the Younger) was indeed a general before becoming a ruler, as Dryden's *The Indian Queen* reveals, but the Aztec warrior was the son of Axayacatl and the great grandson of the first Motecuhzoma, both of whom were previous monarchs in the Tenochtitlan (the capital city of the Aztec empire) dynasty (Tsouras 2005, 18–19; Gillespie 1989, 7–9). In other words, Montezuma was not a "man of unknown Race" with "Base blood" who was unworthy of marrying Orazia, as Dryden's Yncan emperor alleges, but rather a legitimate royal heir (1665, I.i.38, 50). He was elected to rule by a council of Mexica lords and priests, not by the eventual grudging capitulation of an Incan emperor, presumably Huayna Capac, who ruled Peru from 1498–1525.[4] Dryden's distortion of Meso-American history therefore demands an alternative explanation for the looming battle that is the central topic of the prologue.

The language that the "Indian" boy and Quevira use when speaking about the ensuing invasion not only reveals the substitution of an Inca-Mexica battle for a Spanish-Mexica one, but it also serves as a generic invitation for European conquest. The Indian boy says:

> By ancient Prophesies we have been told
> Our World shall be subdu'd by one more old; . . .
> Why should we fear these are Enemies,
> That rather seem to us like Deities? (Dryden 1665, 11–12, 17–18)

When the Indian boy employs the word "Deities," he suggests that Europeans will not only be welcomed in the Americas, but they will also be worshipped by the indigenous peoples. Another instance where Dryden refers to and clarifies the "ancient Prophesies" in the prologue of *The Indian Queen* occurs in *The Indian Emperor* when Montezuma consults an "Earthy Spirit" who warns that:

> A God more strong, who all the gods commands,

> Drives us to exile from our native lands;
> The Air swarms thick with wandring Deities, . . .
> A Nation loving Gold must rule this place,
> Our Temples Ruine, and our Rites Deface:
> To them, O King, is thy lost scepter given. (Dryden 1665, II.i.25–27, 35–37)

In this passage, Dryden converts the Mexican prophecy of Quetzalcoatl into Judeo-Christian terminology, affirms the Europeans' right to rule the indigenous Central Americans based on the omnipotence of the biblical God, and simultaneously condemns Spain as a greedy and destructive "Nation loving Gold." Like Heylyn, Dryden assimilates non-European cultures into a Judeo-Christian master narrative. Yet Dryden could claim a one-to-one correspondence between European military victories in the Americas and divine favor that Heylyn was unable to assert for the English in Mughal India or his own royalist party in England in 1652.

By using the word "Deities" in *The Indian Emperor*, Dryden alludes to the ubiquitous early modern stories of Europeans' initial receptions by "Indians" in the Americas. More specifically, the dialogue between the "Indian" boy and girl in the prologue recalls European accounts about the Aztecs' initially believing Cortez was either the god Quetzalcoatl himself, or one of his divine messengers. By the second half of the seventeenth century, several different versions of Cortez's invasion of Mexico were available for Dryden to choose from. There were at least three Spanish firsthand narratives of Cortez's conquest of Mexico, besides his own dispatches to King Charles V: those of Andrés de Tápia, Bernal Diaz del Castillo, and a Spaniard whose identity has never been ascertained. Numerous writers compiled further accounts in the next few decades based on conversations with the Spanish eyewitnesses and the Aztecs themselves (Diaz del Castillo 1928, 21–22). Richard Eden translated Pietro Martyre d'Anghiera's account of Cortez's invasion of Mexico into English in 1555, and in 1600 Edward Haies mentions "a right honest and discreete Gentleman" who claimed that stories of "the conquest of *Hernando Cortes* about *Mexico,* and those of *Francisco Pizaro* in *Peru* about *Casamalcha* and *Cusco*" were "extant to be had in the English tongue" (qtd. in Maltby 1971, 23; Hakluyt 1600, 3: 167). Dryden therefore had multiple English translations of Spanish renditions of Cortez's adventures in the Americas to use as sources by the time he wrote *The Indian Queen* and *The Indian Emperor* in the 1660s.[5]

Out of all these available English translations, the account in *Purchas his Pilgrimes* is the most likely inspiration for Dryden's prologue because of its simplicity and idealization. In 1518, according to Purchas' Spanish sources, Meso-Americans:

discouered a Fleete at Sea, in the which was the Marquise of *Valle Don Fernande Cortes*, with his companions, newes which much troubled *Moteçuma*, and conferring with his Counsell, they all said, that without doubt, their great and auncient Lord *Quetzakoalt* was come, who had said, that he would returne from the East, whither he was gone. (1625, 3: 1,021–22)

A Mexican god, "Quetzakoalt," promising one day to return "from the East" is especially important because it coincides with the "ancient Prophesies" the "Indian" boy alludes to in Dryden's prologue to *The Indian Queen*.

In Purchas' version of this story, the "Indian" ambassadors then proceeded to "worship" Cortez "as their god" and delivered the message that his "seruant *Moteçuma* sent to visit him, and that he held the Country in his name as his Lieutenant, that he knew well it was the *Topilein* which had beene promised them many yeares since, who should returne againe vnto them" (1625, 3: 1,022).[6] The idea of Meso-American kings being "Lieutenant(s)" waiting for the rightful European god-like rulers to come perhaps inspired Dryden's prologue in which the invading "Enemies . . . rather seem . . . like Deities" to two symbolic figures of the Amerindian population. The lack of a name for the male "Indian" character who speaks all four of the lines discussed so far suggests a general consensus among the indigenous peoples about the ideas he expresses. In other words, this figure becomes a representative, composite, or mouthpiece of Mexican "Indian" attitudes toward foreign conquest in general.

Dryden transforms the legend of Quetzalcoatl and the "Indians'" invitation and supposed desire to be conquered from one European country to another: Spain to England. Because the English were relatively late arrivers in the European conquest of the Americas, there were fewer accounts of English voyagers to the Americas being mistaken for "Deities" by Amerindians. However, this idea was nonetheless a shopworn literary convention by the seventeenth century. Heylyn, for example, recounted a tale about *"English"* explorers in the Americas who the indigenous peoples "took for Gods," and in Behn's *Oroonoko* one of the narrator's kinsman "set some paper a-fire, with a burning-glass," an action that caused the Surinamese natives to "adore . . . him for a god" (Heylyn 1652, 4: 123; Behn 1688,122).[7] Tales of divine comparisons to Dryden's fellow Englishmen by West "Indians" would certainly have been flattering to his readers and Charles II, his patron and sovereign. As I will discuss later in this chapter, Cortez serves as a surrogate Englishman in *The Indian Emperor* since no actual voyagers from that country accompanied the conquistadors in the 1519–21 invasion of Mexico. Dryden therefore combines the legend of Quetzalcoatl, in which an Anglicized version of Cortez is received as a god by Amerindians, with actual and desired seventeenth-century accounts of the same phenomenon occurring specifically in relation to English voyagers in order to create a symbolic welcoming invitation for further conquest[8] by his countrymen from the indigenous peoples of the Americas.

Dryden reinforces the "Indian" boy's permission and even eagerness for new rulers by naming his female companion "Quevira." According to Heylyn's 1625 edition of *Mikrokosmos*, "Quivira" was a place on the "most Westerne part of *America*" where "it is supposed that the inhabitants first came into this new world" (788). Thus Dryden's "Quevira" both acts as the female half of the "Indian" invitation to Europeans to invade the Americas and represents the land itself as a perceived geographical entry point into the Americas for foreigners to impregnate and populate. Dryden followed in the footsteps of prior Englishmen by equating unsullied, ripe, newly discovered lands with a virginal female body, a practice that dated back at least as early as the naming of Virginia after Elizabeth I, the "Virgin Queen."[9]

By drawing attention to that fact that Amerindians were not actually native to the Americas, but rather migrated eastward from Asia through Quevira into the Americas centuries before the Spanish "found" the continents by traveling westward, Dryden suggests that "Indians" too were immigrants, albeit from a much earlier time.[10] Consequently, the "Indians" did not have a divine birthright to the land from Dryden's perspective, but rather a chance prior discovery by their ancestors. European colonization therefore became justifiable as one set of foreigners competing against others rather than a usurping nation laying claim to a land that belonged to another people by heavenly birthright. Quevira, as the spokeswoman for the land itself, asks, "Why should men quarrel here, where all possess / As much as they can hope for by success?" (Dryden 1665, 7–8). As Quevira suggests, "quarrel[s]" had occurred and would continue to do so in the Americas between indigenous peoples themselves, and between Amerindians and Europeans, not only in the *The Indian Queen* and *The Indian Emperor*, but also in historical accounts of the seventeenth century.[11] Moreover, military "success" was indeed the key to which countries would "possess" various regions of the Americas.

Yet Quevira questions the necessity for such "quarrel[s]" because in the Americas, in her words, "Nature is so kind / As to exceed Man's Use" (Dryden 1665, 9–10).[12] Indeed, some English settlers adopted less violent means of obtaining the goods they desired from the indigenous inhabitants of the Americas. Christopher Newport, an English captain in Virginia, for instance, traded swords for turkeys with Powhatan in 1608 (Price 2005, 79). Behn's semiautobiographical account of her stay in the English colony in Surinam from 1663–64 includes the following description:

> With these people [Amerindians] . . . we live in perfect tranquillity, and good understanding, as it behoves us to do; they knowing all the places where to

seek the best food of the country, and the means of getting it; and for very small and invaluable trifles, supply us with what 'tis impossible for us to get. (1688, 77–78)

However, tension underlies each of these examples. Newport was about to leave the region indefinitely when he agreed to Powhatan's trading conditions, and John Smith was displeased with the English captain for selling European weapons that could be used by Amerindians against English settlers (Price 2005, 78–79). Behn's narrator makes it clear that her fellow English colonists trade with the Surinamese rather than enslaving them only because "their numbers so far surpass" her own "in that continent" (1688, 78). Convenience and insufficient troops therefore made bartering "trifles" a more attractive option for obtaining the resources of the indigenous inhabitants of the Americas than outright conquest for some English colonists. Quevira's statement that "Nature" in the Americas so far "exceed[s] Man's Use" that "quarrels" are unnecessary therefore idealistically overlooks the question of who will harvest resources.

Dryden gives a more detailed description of the land where "Nature is so kind" that it "exceed[s] Man's Use" in the sequel to *The Indian Queen* when Vasquez rapturously exclaims:

> Methinks we walk in dreams on a fairy Land,
> Where golden Ore lies mixt with common sand;
> Each downfall of a flood the Mountains pour,
> From their rich bowels rolls a silver shower. (Dryden 1665, I.i.27–30)

Similarly, Behn recounts Amerindian tales of "mountains of gold" where "gold dust" comes "streaming in little small channels down the high mountains ... when the rains f[a]ll," an image that makes such labor questions irrelevant since precious metals would not even require mining (1688, 124–25).[13] In Defoe's *A New Voyage Round the World*, he describes "Mountains, where Gold is to be had in such Quantities, and with so much Ease, that every poor *Chilian* gathers it up with his Hands, and may have as much as he pleases" (1725, 2: 111). Because England possessed no territories in the Americas that even came close to containing the booty depicted in these variants of the El Dorado legend, however, warfare and trade with Amerindians for limited resources and land was commonplace.

However, at least one Amerindian in *The Indian Emperor* does not welcome the European invasion. Almeria, Montezuma's Machiavellian love interest, bitterly chides the aging emperor for considering peace:

> Go, go, with homage your proud Victors meet,

>Go lie like Dogs, beneath your Masters Feet.
>Go and beget them Slaves to dig their Mines,
>And groan for Gold which now in Temples shines. (Dryden 1667, III.i.65–68)

This passage is important for several reasons. Vasquez's description of the Americas as a "fairy Land" "Where golden Ore lies mixt with common sand" makes it sound as though Spaniards can easily collect as much of the precious metal as they desire with little or no labor. Almeria, in contrast, represents Spain's longing for gold as obtrusive and destructive for the indigenous peoples. Unlike "common sand," which is so plentiful that even large quantities could be removed without affecting Amerindians, the looting of gold that "in Temples shines" dramatically disrupts their religious practices. Three of the sentences in this passage begin with the word "go," which represents the power of the "Victors" or "Masters" to issue this command to their "Dogs" or "Slaves." The reiteration of "go" mirrors the repetitiveness of the labor Amerindians will be forced to undertake by the Spaniards, and this cycle will continue in future generations, as Almeria's statement "beget them Slaves to dig their Mines" suggests. Because the English did not find large quantities of bullion in their West "Indian" colonies, Dryden could safely chide the Spaniards for looting temples and creating indigenous gold miners.

Although Dryden endorses the specific critique of the Spanish version of colonization that Almeria articulates, the playwright nonetheless discredits this character's resistance to European ideals. She asserts, for instance, that "Repentance is the Vertue of weak minds" and "'Tis foolish pity spares a Rivals Blood" (Dryden 1667, III.i.100, 104). Immediately after delivering the speech to Montezuma about the consequences of surrender, Almeria says, "Your shameful story shall record of me, / The Men all crouch'd, and left a Woman free" (III.i.69–70). Almeria's image of "Men all crouch'd" and a defiant "Woman free" who stands alone inverts traditional gender roles and shames Montezuma into fighting. Shortly after this speech, Montezuma says, "I am for War" (III.i.87). Guyomar appeals to the same notions of chivalry that Almeria invokes in an antiwar stand when he asserts that his warriors "cannot harm" armored Europeans and will only "exasperate" them, which will in turn lead to "The rape of Matrons" (III.i.79). Yet Guyomar's desire to protect the women of the Aztec Empire falls on deaf ears; Montezuma sides with his would-be lover over one of his own sons.

Montezuma's intense desire for Almeria in *The Indian Emperor* forms a natural counterpoint to his previous relationship with Orazia in *The Indian Queen*. Odmar makes this connection explicit very early in the play when Montezuma expresses an interest in Almeria: "If, sir, Almeria does your bed partake, / I mourn for my forgotten mothers sake" (Dryden 1667, I.ii.61–62).

In the preface to *The Indian Emperor*, Dryden tells us that Orazia is "lately dead," which suggests that Montezuma, like Hamlet's mother, has not allowed sufficient mourning time to pass before rushing into the arms of another (13). Dryden's preface also informs his audience that "about Twenty years [have] elapsed" since the coronation of Montezuma in *The Indian Queen* (14). Consequently, Montezuma attempts to seduce a woman who is much younger than he is. His desire seems to be even less socially acceptable when we learn that both of his sons court Almeria's sister Alibech.

Montezuma killed Almeria's father Traxalla, and her mother Zempoalla committed suicide because of Montezuma's cruel rejection. For these reasons, Almeria understandably refuses to requite Montezuma's love:

> I take this Garland, not as given by you,
> But as my merit, and my beauties due.
> As for the Crown that you, my slave, possess,
> To share it with you would but make me less. (Dryden 1667,
> I.ii.85–88)

Indeed, Almeria's assertion that Montezuma is her "slave" has some merit since his decision to be "for War" with the Spaniards directly results from a wish to please her. Later in the play, Montezuma admits that his obsession with Almeria makes him indifferent about his empire. In a fortune-telling, spirit-conjuring scene reminiscent of Zempoalla, Montezuma says, "Love rules my heart, and is your Monarchs King; / I more desire to know *Almeria*'s mind, / Then all that Heaven has for my state design'd" (II.i.6–8). Almeria's bitterness, rage, arrogance, and subversion of European ideals make her a voice of indigenous dissent that Dryden does not wholeheartedly condone. She openly tells her brother Odmar that she plans to exact "pleasing vengeance" on Montezuma and "force [him] to obey" her every whim (I.ii.75, 84). The spelling of Almeria's name closely resembles "America," and as Montezuma obsessively pursues her, he simultaneously follows the spirit of war and self-destruction. Almeria therefore represents the nonpliant Amerindian spirit more generally, and because Dryden supports the English variant of colonialism in the Americas, he casts this character in a primarily villainous role.

Dryden adds further discord to the tranquil and welcoming image of the sleeping "Indian" boy and girl in the prologue of *The Indian Queen* when the Ynca of Peru promises Montezuma a reward for defeating the Mexican armies:

> Thrice have the *Mexicans* before us fled,
> Their armies broke, their Prince in Triumph led;

> Both to thy valour, brave young man, we owe;
> Ask thy Reward. . . .
> I am impatient till this debt be paid,
> Which still encreases on me whil delay'd;
> A Bounteous Monarch to himself is kind;
> Ask such a Guift as may for ever bind
> Thy service to my Empire, and to me. (Dryden 1665, I.i.1–4, 11–15)

At the very start of the play, the recognizable seventeenth-century European values of civil order, reciprocity, gift-giving, and fealty prevail. A misunderstanding quickly ensues, however, that shatters a properly working monarchical system that would have been comfortable for Restoration theatergoers, particularly after the chaos and uncertainty of the British Civil Wars. In an aside, Montezuma contemplates the Ynca's offer:

> What can this Guift he bids me ask him be!
> Perhaps he has perceiv'd our [Orazia and Montezuma's] mutual fires,
> And now with ours wou'd crown his own Desires;
> 'Tis so, he sees my Service is above
> All other payments but his Daughters Love. (I.i.16–20)

The Ynca's command, "Ask such a Guift as may for ever bind / Thy service to my Empire, and to me," might understandably lead a seventeenth-century character in an English play to come to the same conclusion that Montezuma does since women were often held in an almost hostage-like role to "bind" powerful men to "service." Men would be far less likely to betray and attack an ally if their daughter, mother, or sister lived under the roof of that ally and was at his mercy. When they arrived in their new homes, women were expected to further the interests of the families they had left. This common marital arrangement therefore doubly cemented alliances between powerful nobles and members of royal families.

Like many members of the English court who watched the play in the 1660s, Dryden's Montezuma cloaks this pragmatic and somewhat ruthless convention of exchanging women within the idiom of romantic love. Montezuma says, "I beg not Empires, those my Sword can gain; . . . / I only ask from fair *Orazia*'s eyes / To reap the Fruits of all my Victories" (Dryden 1665, I.i.30, 35–36). Montezuma's words in these two passages invoke a conventional seventeenth-century language of romance: "fires," "Desires," "Love," and "fair *Orazia*'s eyes." He makes a distinction between Orazia as a romantic object to be won and "Empires," but because the Ynca has no other children, she is his sole heir. By marrying Orazia, then, Montezuma would take control of the empire after the Ynca's death. The distinction Montezuma attempts to make between his love for Orazia, on the one hand, and empires, on the other, therefore mystifies the political and economic arrangements that characteristically determine marriages among the upper classes. Of all the women in the kingdom, Montezuma coincidentally "falls in love" with the one whose dowry will include an empire when her father dies.

Yet Dryden gives Montezuma credit for at least maintaining the façade of gallantry. In fact, Dryden employs the language of courtliness in his dedication of *The Indian Emperor* to the Duchess of Monmouth:

> Under your Patronage *Montezuma* hopes he is more safe than in his Native *Indies*: and therefore comes to throw himself at your Graces feet; paying that homage to your Beauty, which he refus'd to the violence of his Conquerors. He begs only that when he shall relate his sufferings, you will consider he is an *Indian* Prince, and not expect any other Eloquence from his simplicity, than that, with which his griefs have furnished him. (Dryden 1667, 12–18)

Like his character, Dryden uses the speech of courtly love when he says that Montezuma pays "homage to" the Duchess' "Beauty." The compliment plays out much like a ventriloquist speaking through a puppet. These sentences are especially important because they highlight Dryden's general rhetorical strategy in the West "Indian" plays. Unlike the "violence" that the Spanish "Conquerors" inflict upon the native peoples of the Americas, the English approach colonization passively. By the end of *The Indian Emperor*, Montezuma becomes the sovereign of the conflated Inca-Aztec Empire, which represented two of the three major civilizations in the Americas. He therefore embodies the peoples of the Americas more generally. In Dryden's idealized dedication, rulers of the West Indies, who seek safety and consolation, throw themselves at the feet of the aristocratic English.

The alleged consent of the indigenous peoples partially exonerates English encroachments in North America, but Dryden also addresses the question of hereditary succession. After all, if the divine right of kings applies to the aristocracy, English disruptions of that natural order of rule and succession in the Americas could potentially be seen as an affront to the Judeo-Christian God. Dryden shrewdly circumvents this problem by applying a different set of standards to the West "Indian" nobility. When Montezuma threatens to kill the Ynca in *The Indian Queen*, Acacis reprovingly says, "Subjects to Kings shou'd more obedience pay" (Dryden 1665, I.i.76). Dryden, through Montezuma, cleverly replies, "Subjects are bound, not strangers, to obey" (I.i.77). As "strangers" to the Americas, the English are therefore free to commit regicide in those lands in order to confiscate the wealth and lands of West "Indian" royalty. The same rule does not apply when the English are in their native country since they would be "Subjects" there. Because Dryden dedicates the sequel of *The Indian Queen* to Charles II's illegitimate son's wife, this qualified endorsement of regicide was necessary in order to avoid offending the very patron that the playwright attempts to please.

Dryden further undermines the indigenous peoples' sovereignty in the Americas by portraying the ruling characters as unstable and ineffective. Years before the events of the play take place, Zempoalla usurps the Mexican throne from her brother. A rapid series of power changes then occur: the Ynca overthrows Zempoalla, Montezuma defeats the Ynca, Zempoalla captures Montezuma, Amexia dethrones Zempoalla, and Montezuma finally inherits the empire from his mother. This instability manifests itself formally in the dialogue between characters. When Montezuma confesses his love for Orazia, the structure of the couplets changes. Before this statement, the Ynca and Montezuma average four to six lines per utterance. After Montezuma's declaration, however, the Ynca is temporarily speechless. Dryden fills in this momentary aphasia with minor characters who each speak a single line in asides. One Peruvian onlooker says, "Our *Ynca*'s Colour mounts into his face," and the second observes that the emperor's "Looks speak Death" (Dryden 1665, I.i.36–37). The second Peruvian reveals the sudden tension of the scene through a mixed synaesthetic metaphor in which a visual sign ("Looks") becomes an audible representation ("speak") of an abstract phenomenon ("Death").

These asides disrupt the flowing symmetrical couplets that the Ynca and Montezuma exchange, and the Peruvian spectators foreshadow a dramatic shift in the tone of the play. The Ynca attempts to regain his composure by delivering another flowing speech:

> Young man of unknown Race,
> Ask once again, so well thy merits plead;
> Thou shalt not die for that which thou hast said:
> The price of what thou ask'st thou dost not know;
> That Guift's too high. (Dryden 1665, I.i.38–42)

Before the Ynca can finish his speech, however, Montezuma interrupts by saying, "And all beside too low" (43). A flood of interruptions and broken couplets follow in the next eight lines:

> *Ynca.* Once more I bid thee ask.
> *Mont.*   Once more I make
> The same demand.
> *Ynca.* The *Ynca* bids thee take
> Thy choice, what Towns, what Kingdoms thou wouldst have.
> *Mont.*   Thou giv'st me only what before I gave.
> Give me thy Daughter.

Ynca. Thou deserv'st to die. (Dryden 1665, I.i.44–48)

The Ynca and Montezuma become an amalgam of Amerindian rulers as they finish each others' sentences and mimic one another. In the first four lines, each character repeats the first word of the sentence freshly spoken by his rival ("Once" and "The"). Equally stubborn and unwilling to compromise, the two characters possess interchangeable personalities despite their disagreement about the specific question of Orazia's fate. Montezuma's final utterance in this exchange, "Daughter," is a one-word summary of the cause of the tension. The word ends a sentence that does not, like the first thirty-six lines of the play, have an accompanying rhyming couplet. This jarring sonic dissonance mirrors the upheaval of previously stable power relations: the supposedly low-born general Montezuma now delivers a command to his emperor ("Give me"). The unity and harmony reflected by rhyming couplets therefore breaks down just like the alliance between Montezuma and the Ynca.

With the possible exception of Amexia, who only rules long enough to transfer power to her son, all of the emperors in *The Indian Queen* have glaring character deficiencies. The first emperor that readers encounter in Dryden's West "Indian" plays is the Ynca. When Montezuma hesitates to name his reward for defeating the Mexicans, the Ynca says, "I am impatient till this debt be paid" (Dryden 1665, I.i.11). This impatience quickly turns into homicidal rage when Montezuma asks for the Ynca's daughter's hand in marriage as a reward; the reigning emperor responds to the request by saying: "Thou deserv'st to die" (I.i.47). The Ynca also demonstrates rapid changes of mind. In his opening speech, he praises Montezuma's role in the battle that has just taken place: "Thrice have the *Mexicans* before us fled, / Their Armies broke, their Prince in Triumph led; / Both to thy valour, brave young man, we owe" (I.i.1–3). These lines make it sound as though Montezuma's "valour" was the main cause of victory. After Montezuma voices his desire for marriage as a "Reward," however, the Ynca dramatically revises his previous statement: "My Fortunes gave thee thy success in Fight; / Convey thy boasted Valour from my sight; / I can o'recome without thy feeble aid" (I.i.53–55). Within the first fifty-five lines of the play, Montezuma has gone from a "brave young man" who was essential to victory to an inconsequential braggart who only prevailed because his armies were so well-funded by the Ynca. The Ynca's rapid revisionary history of Montezuma's part in the battle makes the reigning emperor seem insincere and incapable of governing even his own emotions. These negative character traits seriously compromise any claim he might have to being an effective ruler.

Like European royalty, indigenous claims to sovereignty are based on divine approval in Dryden's "Indian" plays. When Montezuma, who the Ynca initially believes is a "man of unknown Race," asks to marry into the imperial family, the emperor says: "O thou great Author of our Progeny, / Thou glorious Sun, dost thou not blush to shine, / While such base Blood attempts to mix with thine!" (Dryden 1665, I.i.38, 48–50). Unlike Judeo-Christian ideology, in which a divine being encompasses and supersedes heavenly bodies such as the sun, Dryden creates a pagan deity as the foundation of Peruvian royal legitimacy. As Montezuma's reaction to these lines shows, this deity either has limited power or approves of mixing base and divine blood: "That Sun thou speakst of did not hide his face, / When he beheld me Conquering for his Race" (I.i.51–52). This statement undermines the idea that the Peruvian solar deity is capable of intervening in human affairs in order to express its displeasure since Montezuma's desire to have sex with Orazia should have been met with a symbolic defeat rather than a victory. At the end of the play, Dryden reveals that Montezuma is the son of Amexia, who is "the lawful Queen of Mexico" and an embodiment of the country itself, as the partial anagram "mexi" within her name suggests. Although the revelation of Montezuma's royal blood perhaps vindicates the sun's failure to intervene in the battle, Dryden lets the deity appear to be powerless for the entire play. The undermining of indigenous gods allows Dryden to justify England's American colonies, which became increasingly important.

For the English in the seventeenth century, the Americas offered a solution to a growing population problem and diminishing resources. As Robert Markley points out, England's population more than doubled between 1500 and 1650, and it peaked at 5,650,000 in 1657, only seven years prior to *The Indian Queen*'s first performance, before beginning to decline to more manageable numbers. Moreover, grain prices rose 600 percent whereas wages only went up 200 percent in this century and a half (Markley 1999, 819, 824). Partially because of population pressures on resources, and in some cases for greater religious freedom, a substantial number of English men and women immigrated to colonies in the Americas, especially during the Great Migration of the 1630s, where 21,000 people boarded ships bound for New England (Canny 1998, 1: 29–30).

> Prior to *The Indian Queen*'s first performance in 1664, the English established colonies in the Americas, with varying degrees of success, at Roanoke (1585–86, 1588–90), Guiana (1604), the Lesser Antilles (1605), Jamestown (1607), Sagadahoc (1607), Newfoundland (1610), Bermuda (1612), Plymouth (1620), St. Christopher (1624), Barbados (1625), Carolina (first Charter, 1629), Massachusetts Bay (1630), Maryland (1632), Connecticut (1634), St. Mary's (1634), Providence (1636), New Haven (1637), Albemarle Sound (1653), Jamaica (1655), and New York (1664). By 1635, there were eight English towns settled in the Boston area and twenty-four in New England alone. In 1690, New

England had at least sixty-three towns (R. Anderson 1995, 1: lxxvii-lxxviii, lxxix). At the end of the seventeenth century, the English population in the Americas was at least 257,000, and the presence of 37,000 married couples in New England alone before 1700 ensured a self-sustaining and multiplying population (Cressy 1987, 70; Torrey 1985, xiv).

With such a substantial colonial population in place and more English immigrants arriving all the time, disputes over territories and natural resources with the indigenous peoples were inevitable in the Americas. In response to Quevira's question about why "quarrel[s]" occur in such a superabundant location, the "Indian Boy" delivers his line about the "ancient Prophesies" foretelling the inevitable subjugation of their people by one "more old." Dryden therefore answers his own rhetorical question in this dialogue between the two characters by appealing to a divine, preordained destiny. While there was allegedly sufficient land for all in Dryden's view, indigenous peoples could be subjugated by Europeans based on heavenly mandates. As compensation for losing their land and natural resources, Amerindians would gain the opportunity to live among "Deities," and, as Dryden writes later in *The Indian Emperor*, the benefit of worshipping the Judeo-Christian God "who all the gods commands." Quevira says that if "these be they," the "Deities" destined to "subdu[e]" her world, then she "welcom[es]" them. All that she and the "Indian" boy desire in return for their surrender is "protection" and "Mercy" from the returning gods. From a moral standpoint, this dialogue that exonerates and welcomes European conquerors, provided they show "Mercy," was necessary since England had already made significant territorial encroachments into the Americas.

ENGLISH "MERCY," EUROPEAN WEAPONS, AND THE BLACK LEGEND OF THE SPANISH

By constructing a fantasy invitation to conquer from indigenous peoples to the English, Dryden positions his own people as heirs to the Americas. Yet while the English colonies in the Americas helped to ease some of the population burdens of England, the desires of seventeenth-century English men and women were not fully satisfied by their colonies in the Americas. Glyndwr Williams argues convincingly that

> The hope that the precious metals which existed in such profusion in Peru and Mexico might also be found farther north lured many English across the Atlantic to the eastern coastline of North America; but they found no Potosí in New England, no Zacatecas in Virginia. (1973, 27)

Dryden's fictional amalgamation and distortion of historical elements of the separate Spanish conquests of Peru and Mexico that occurred eleven years apart (such as Montezuma being a general in the Ynca's army, Pizarro taking part in the Mexican conquest, etc.) in *The Indian Queen* and *The Indian Emperor* was not coincidental since those were two of the largest bullion-producing countries of Spain's empire in the Americas and represented two of the three major pre-Columbian civilizations (the Incas, Aztecs, and Mayans). Michael Moseley claims that "Despite tantalizing finds of gold work from Mexico south, truly large quantities of the coveted metal eluded the European explorers until the conquistadors reached Cajamarca, a mountain town in northern Peru" (Moseley 1978, 5). Dryden's forced incorporation of the Incan Empire, the wealthiest Spanish colonial possession because it included Peru and Bolivia, into *The Indian Emperor or The Conquest of Mexico by the Spaniards*, reveals his preoccupation with bullion, a longstanding European cultural obsession.

Moreover, the torture scene of Montezuma in order to discover the whereabouts of his gold has no historical validity. Accounts of Montezuma's death vary, but no extant ones coincide precisely with Dryden's theatrical rendition. Heylyn says that the Mexican ruler "was by one of his own Subjects killed"; Cortez claims that Montezuma "received a blow on his head from a stone; and the injury was so serious that he died three days later"; and Durán's Mexica sources protest that their king was "stabbed to death by the Spaniards" (Heylyn 1652 4: 134; Tsouras 2005, 82–83). In Dryden's *Indian Emperor*, the stage directions indicate that Montezuma "stabs himself" with "His sword" after being tortured by Spanish soldiers and then "Dyes" as a result of the wound (Dryden 1667, V.ii.234, 237, 250). Yet Pizarro was present during the capture and ransom of the Peruvian ruler Atahaulpa, and, after the gold was delivered, the Spanish garroted the Incan Emperor. Consequently, N. D. Shergold and Peter Ure contend persuasively that this historical event partially inspired Dryden's fifth act in *The Indian Emperor* (369).

The frustrated dreams of "precious metals" that English men and women encountered upon arriving in England's American colonies led them to look with envious eyes southward at Spain's Mexican, Peruvian, and Bolivian territories. Williams argues that "From the mid-seventeenth century onwards an infinite variety of schemes was put forward to tap the silver lifeline of the Spanish empire" (1973, 27). These "schemes" by Englishmen to "tap the silver lifeline of the Spanish empire" had been in place since Sir Francis Drake's voyages and Sir Walter Raleigh's seizure of Spanish ships in the sixteenth century. While concern for the well-being of "heathen" souls may have partially inspired some Englishmen to end Spain's monopoly in Central and South America, the gold and silver bullion from those countries, both real and imaginary, was probably the most salient incentive for most.

A seventeenth-century reprint of Sir Francis Drake's voyages urges Englishmen to emulate his bullion-seeking adventures right in the title of the work itself: "*Sir Francis Drake Reuiued: Calling vpon this Dull or Effeminate Age, to folowe his Noble Steps for Golde & Siluer, by this Memorable Relation, of... a Third Voyage, made by him into the West-Indies, in the Yeares 72. & 73*" (Nichols 1626). In the Dedicatory Epistle of this work to Queen Elizabeth, Drake refers to Spain as England's "great enemy," and indeed the two countries continued to fight until after the monarch's death in 1603 (A4). In 1596, Sir Walter Raleigh expresses concern over, and resentment of, Spain's monopoly on the South American bullion market. Raleigh claims that "many millions" of "pesoes" of "golde" and "siluer" were "daily brought out of *Peru* into spaine" (1596, 11). Because of this "abundant treasure," Raleigh concludes that

> the Spanish King vexeth all the Princes of Europe, and is become in a fewe yeares from a poore king of *Castile* the greatest monarke of this parte of the worlde, and likelie euery day to increase, if other Princes forsloe the good occasions offered, and suffer him to adde this Empire to the rest, which by farre exceedeth all the rest: if his golde now indanger vs, hee will then be vnresistable. (11–13)

This passage served as a call to arms to England and other European nations. Because this plea was written, or at least published, only eight years after the Spanish armada invaded England in 1588, Raleigh's fears of Spain's hegemonic inclinations must have seemed well-founded to his English contemporaries. Raleigh makes it clear that an English takeover of Peru would not only limit Spanish power, but it would also provide "many millions" of "pesoes" of "golde" and "siluer" on a "daily" basis. Although such figures may have been exaggerated, they would nonetheless serve as a tantalizing temptation for English voyagers for two centuries (Williams 1973, 27).

While the imaginary value of gold and silver in Mexico, Peru, and Bolivia in the minds of Englishmen such as Sir Walter Raleigh was essentially infinite and therefore exaggerated (in El Dorado for instance), the Aztec and Incan Empires genuinely did yield high amounts of bullion. Pizarro's capture and ransom of the Inca ruler Atahualpa for "one room full of gold" and "two of silver" represented "only a very small percentage of the precious metals in the land" in 1532 (Moseley, 1978 5; Pan American 1954, 12). Henry Kamen argues that the actual amount of bullion entering Spain from the Americas peaked in between 1591–95 at thirty-five million pesos and then began to decline steadily to three million pesos by the 1656–60 period. Even through the reign of the Spanish king Carlos II, 1665–1700, however, "the five-year totals [of bullion exported from the Americas] regularly exceeded 40 million" pesos. But by that time, "most of this" bullion "did not enter Spain but went to foreign traders" (Kamen 1991, 271). By "the mid-seventeenth century," according to Glyndwr Willaims, "Spain's bullion imports and her trans-Atlantic trade in general were in serious decline," but the English continued to attempt to "tap the silver lifeline of the Spanish empire" until at least 1762 (Williams 1973, 27, 52). When Dryden wrote *The Indian Emperor* in 1665, Spain had already depleted a significant quantity of the precious metals from the Americas, which was a source of irritation to the English that had been festering for over a century. By dwelling on the idea that the Spanish were morally unfit rulers of the indigenous peoples of Central and South America in the torture scene in act five of *The Indian Emperor*, Dryden displaces and vents England's frustration at having been excluded from the most lucrative bullion-producing regions of the Americas.[14]

Spain's monopoly on West "Indian" bullion was especially psychologically torturous to the English since precious metals were one of the few commodities that the EIC could export in exchange for the spices, cottons, and luxury goods that were exponentially valuable. The practice of exporting large quantities of bullion from England was so widespread and controversial that by 1620 Thomas Mun, a director of the Company, felt compelled to defend it in his *Discourse of Trade unto the East Indies* (Keay 1994, 119). The English therefore viewed the Spanish gold and silver monopoly as a failed opportunity to create a highly profitable international trading network by exploiting West "Indians'" natural resources and labor and using the bullion yields to help finance a lucrative trade with East Indians of the Mughal Empire and its surrounding islands. In *The Indian Queen* and *The Indian Emperor*, Dryden contributes to Raleigh's legacy, the interests of the EIC, upon whom Charles II, like Cromwell before him, depended for money,[15] and Englishmen's futile desires "to tap the silver lifeline of the Spanish empire" by perpetuating the Black Legend about Spain's conquistadors.

The concept of mercy was crucial in the discourse of Dryden's and other seventeenth-century English writers' justifications for their own attempts at colonial expansion in North America, the Caribbean, and Surinam because this ethical characteristic supposedly differentiated them from other countries such as the Netherlands[16] and Spain. The latter country was especially maligned by the English for Spain's alleged use of excessively sadistic Inquisition-related torture. Tales of the cruelty and greed of the Spanish Inquisitors appeared in English in the works of such authors as John Foxe (whose *Acts and Monuments*, also known as *The Book of Martyrs*, went through ten editions between 1554 and 1641), Bartolomé de las Casas, Reginaldus Gonsalvius Montanus, and Hakluyt (Maltby 1971, 12, 35).

The two separate English translations of Las Casas' *Brevissima Relaçion de la Destrucción de las Indias* (one by M. M. S. in 1583 and the other by John

Phillips in 1656) are especially important for an analysis of Dryden's *The Indian Emperor* because they focus specifically on the Spanish Inquisition in South and Central America (Maltby 1971, 13).[17] Las Casas was a Spanish priest who accompanied Diego Velászquez and Cortez on their expedition from Hispaniola to Cuba in 1511. What Las Casas saw there shocked him: massacres of natives who refused to submit, enslavement of those who surrendered, and the execution by fire of the native leader Hatuey (Koch 2006, 27–28). English men and women searching for material to bolster their anti-Spanish stereotypes were able conveniently to overlook the fact that Las Casas was himself a Spaniard seeking reform within his own country and focused instead on the carnage depicted in his work.

The full title of the 1656 English translation of Las Casas' *Brevissima Relaçion* by John Phillips, which Dryden may have consulted when writing *The Indian Emperor*, summarizes the contents and attitude of the work:

The Tears of the Indians being an Historical and True Account of the Cruel Massacres and Slaughters of above Twenty Millions of Innocent People, Committed by the Spaniards in the Islands of Hispaniola, Cuba, Jamaica, &c.: as also in the Continent of Mexico, Peru, & other Places of the West-Indies, to the Total Destruction of those Countries.

Interestingly enough, this title attributes the deaths of "Twenty Million . . . Innocent" Amerindians to "Cruel Massacres and Slaughters" by the Spanish with no mention of European diseases, which actually accounted for far more casualties than any Spanish weapons made of steel. The sheer quantity of murders is staggering and implies that the Spanish possessed an insatiable and unnatural bloodlust if the indigenous peoples were indeed all killed in "Massacres." Las Casas' *Brevissima Relaçion* therefore shows no real understanding of etiology and an eagerness to explain enormous casualties from a moral perspective.

In addition to staggering body counts, another component of the Black Legend that was firmly rooted in the minds of Dryden's English audience was the notion that corrupt priests of the Spanish Inquisition used horrible torture methods and were far more interested in confiscating wealth than in saving souls. This stereotype was partially perpetuated by the well-known story of a wealthy English merchant named Nicholas Burton living in Spain in 1560 that was printed in the works of Hakluyt, Montanus, and Foxe (Maltby 1971, 35). In Foxe's version of the tale, the example of Burton's treatment by the Inquisitors illustrates the "extreme dealing and cruell reuenging of those Catholicke Inquisitours of Spayne, who vnder the pretensed visour of Religion, do nothyng but seeke theyr owne priuate gaine and commoditie, with crafty defending and spoyling of other mens goodes" (Foxe 1583, 2:

2,036). According to Foxe's *Actes and Monuments*, whose ten editions before *The Indian Emperor*'s first performance made it likely that Dryden's audience was familiar with the story, a "Iudas (or as they terme them) a Familiar of the Fathers of the Inquisition" visited Burton under false pretenses and wanted to "know where he laded hys goods" (2: 2,036). Other Inquisitors soon arrived to arrest Burton and when he asked what crime they were charging him with, they refused to answer and threw him in jail for two weeks. Burton then had "His tongue . . . forced out of hys mouthe" and was "most cruelly burned" to death. "Immediately" after Burton's arrest, "all the goodes and Marchaundise whiche he brought with him into Spayne" were "seised, and taken into the Sequester" (2: 2,036–37). Foxe's widely read account of Burton's suffering, death by fire, and the "Immediate" confiscation of his goods while he sat rotting in jail for weeks reveals early modern English perceptions of the Spanish Inquisitors as ruthlessly greedy torturers.

Diseases, however, rather than Spanish cruelty, are the only plausible explanation for the majority of the casualties suffered by Amerindians after the arrival of Europeans. Recent estimates of indigenous populations in the Western hemisphere prior to European contact in 1492 vary widely, anywhere from forty million to eighty million. However, in a highly persuasive and meticulously researched revised study conducted in 1992, William Denevan estimates the entire Amerindian population of the Caribbean and Central and South America to have been 50.1 million inhabitants in 1492 and 5.6 million in 1650 (xxviii, xxix). In other words, there were approximately 44.5 million fewer "Indians" in the Americas 158 years after the Spanish "discovered" it, a population decline of roughly eighty-eight percent.

Conventional sixteenth-century Spanish weapons were incapable of accounting for all, or even most, of these deaths, even in the hands of the most depraved sadists. Cortez invaded Mexico from 1519–21 with approximately 1,600 Spanish soldiers, a dozen light cannons, and a few dozen horses and muskets, and Pizarro had about 300 Spaniards who were lightly armed when he conquered Peru (León 28–29). Crossbows and portable guns ranging in size from small cannons to muskets known as "arquebuses" or "harquebuses" were in short supply, and they took time to load, thereby leaving Spanish soldiers vulnerable to native spears, clubs, knives, and arrows ("Arquebus"). This loading delay, partially caused by the need for two types of gunpowder kept in separate flasks for each shot, also allowed Amerindians inclined to fight or flee plenty of time to do so. Moreover, the matchlock arquebuses that the Spaniards used in the sixteenth century required a lit match, which made them difficult if not impossible to use in damp environments or rainstorms (Ricketts 1962, 13, 15). In weighty[18] full or even partial armor in scorching equatorial countries during long marches, Spanish swordsmen and pikemen would eventually be incapable of prolonged slaughter from sheer exhaustion and heat stroke. Tropical diseases, including syphilis, that Europeans were not immunized against, further weakened and killed off their soldiers, and cavalrymen lost the advantage of speed in dense jungles. Moreover, much of the killing was done by "Indian" allies such as the Tlascalans of Mexico since the Spanish did not have sufficient troops on their own to battle the indigenous peoples, and the Peruvians had just finished a brutal civil war when Pizarro and his troops arrived that further decimated the population (Moseley 1992, 5). The notion that Spanish conquistadors killed *"Twenty Millions of Innocent People,"* as Las Casas alleges, or 44.5 million simply through conventional warfare or "Slaughter" is therefore unrealistic.

European diseases such as smallpox, and not the "Cruel Massacres" of the Spanish conquistadors, were the most lethal force in the Americas during the sixteenth century, against which the indigenous peoples had no immunity. By 1574, there were at least 200 Spanish settlements in the Americas, and the Spaniards explored the Americas in every direction (Stearn and Wagner 1945, 19). Moreover, many West "Indians" sought new places to live after their villages were decimated by smallpox. This widespread movement of contagious Spaniards and Amerindians led to a rapid spread of smallpox and other diseases throughout the Americas. Smallpox destabilized the entire social structure of indigenous societies: famines were widespread because so many harvesters succumbed to the epidemic; "Indian" royalty, including Montezuma's younger brother Cuitlahuatzin, died as well leaving their peoples leaderless; and the loss of loved ones and the terror of an unknown scourge demoralized the indigenous peoples of the Americas. Even well into the nineteenth century, when Amerindians had some immunity to the disease, it had a fatality rate ranging from 55% to over 90% in some tribes (Stearn and Wagner 1945, 14–15, 18–19). The physical, social, and psychological havoc wreaked by European diseases on indigenous peoples was therefore by far the most devastating factor in the Spanish conquest of the Americas, but the sheer quantity of Amerindian deaths was attributed to the conquistadors' bloodlust by Las Casas and many English men and women. At the same time, Europeans' military technology and prowess in relation to indigenes was highly exaggerated in the minds of many English subjects because contemporaneous narratives of Spanish conquistadors focused on very small numbers of European soldiers defeating vast hordes of West "Indians." Diseases, intertribal warfare, famines, migrations, civil wars, uprooted social structures, and the devastated morale of Amerindians did not directly reinforce the Black Legend of the Spanish and, as a result, these factors were minimized or omitted altogether. The superiority many Europeans felt toward indigenes was therefore based on limited or inaccurate knowledge of the circumstances that led to the conquest of the Americas. England's distorted view of the military weakness of West "Indians" made Mughal India, which had not suffered an unprecedented epidemic, appear to be even more powerful by contrast.

Dryden provides an explicit link between the two West "Indian" plays in a preface to *The Indian Emperor* entitled "Connexion to *The Indian Queen*," and the preface is especially important because it shows Dryden's own preoccupations with warfare and trade in relation to "Indians." Dryden explains his play's connection to the historical voyage narrative source that he uses as follows:

> I have neither wholly followed the story nor varied from it; and, as near as I could, have traced the Native simplicity and ignorance of the Indians, in relation to *European* Customes: The Shipping, Armour, Horses, Swords, and Guns of the Spaniards, being as new to them as their Habits and their Language were to the Christians. (1667, 22–27)

In this passage, Dryden conceives of "*European* Customes" almost entirely in military terms, with "Shipping" having both trade and naval applications. Of the eight characteristics that Dryden employs to differentiate Europeans from Amerindians, five of them relate to the military.

Many "*European* Customes" appear in *Aureng-Zebe*, a play that features no European characters. Mughal Indians, unlike Dryden's Mexican characters, use "guns" and "horses" for cavalry (Dryden 1667, I.120, II.1). An EEBO search for the word "sword" in *Aureng-Zebe* reveals sixteen results, and at one point Dryden specifies that Mughal weapons are made of "polished steel" (I.119). The latter point is especially important because steel, which was often forged in Damascus, was more durable than the comparatively brittle weapons of Amerindians. Dryden shows his awareness of this fact in *The Indian Emperor* when the Mexican warrior Guyomar describes his fight with a Spaniard:

> I fell'd along a Man of Bearded face,
> His Limbs all cover'd with a Shining case:
> So wondrous hard, and so secure of wound,
> It made my Sword, though edg'd with Flint, rebound. (1667, II. iii.25–28)

For Dryden, being "*European*" was to a large extent dependent upon having an advanced military. Because the Mughal Indians possessed technologically advanced armies, then, they were similar to Europeans in an essential way from Dryden's perspective. Military sophistication correlates strongly with national character traits in Dryden's three "Indian" plays. The word "simplicity" never occurs in *Aureng-Zebe*, and Dryden's few uses of the term "ignorance" in the play are either feigned or theoretical reflections on humanity in general.[19]

When Dryden retells the story of the Spanish conquest of the Americas in *The Indian Emperor*, he invokes a time when the disparity between European and West "Indian" military technology was especially pronounced. By the time Dryden wrote his West "Indian" plays in the 1660s, that technological gap had partially closed. In 1631, Governor Thomas Dudley complained that English merchants, "dishonestly for their gaine," sold "guns, swords, powder and shott" to Amerindians in Massachusetts (qtd. in Russell 1957, 7). A New England law in 1641 expressly forbid this practice because English colonists feared the weapons would be used against them, and the Apaches and Pueblos had horses by the 1660s (Russell 1957, 41–42; Trigger and Wasburn 1996, 8). Dryden, however, like Heylyn and numerous other Englishmen, focuses on a time when guns were completely new to Amerindians; Montezuma says:

> All's lost –
> Our Foes with Lightning and with Thunder Fight,
> My men in vain shun death by shameful Flight;
> For deaths Invisible come wing'd with Fire,
> They hear a dreadful noise and straight expire. (1667, II.iii.31–35)

In the 1660s, when Europeans had been in the Americas for over a century, the indigenous peoples would not have reacted to guns with the same terror of the unknown that their ancestors did. The sight of "Lightning" and the sound of "Thunder" that Montezuma associates with guns would have had less mystical shock value for Amerindians since at least some of them had used firearms themselves.

Dryden's return to a time when European weapons had a greater psychological impact on Amerindians makes the Spaniards look especially vicious since the combat resembles slaughter more than seventeenth-century conceptions of honorable warfare. Guyomar says, "We but exasperate those we cannot harm, / And Fighting gains us but to dye more warm" (Dryden 1667, III.i.75–76). Guyomar claims that he and his fellow Mexicans "cannot harm" the Spaniards, presumably because the Europeans' "Shining case[s]" (armor) make Amerindian weapons "edg'd with Flint . . . rebound." No mention is made of atlals or bludgeoning instruments such as clubs that were more effective against European armor, which gives the Spaniards the appearance of near invincibility. Consequently, the battle seems to be unfair, especially when the Spaniards mercilessly take advantage of the power inequalities. In Cortez's most villainous moment in the play, he issues the following order to his soldiers:

Their eager Chase disorder'd does appear,
Command our Horse to charge them in the rear.
You to our old *Castillian* Foot retire,
Who yet stand firm, and at their backs give Fire. (Dryden 1667, II.iii.13–16)

By using his cavalry to chase down fleeing Mexicans and "Fire" "at their backs," Cortez exploits the technological advantage that his soldiers possess and violates the wartime etiquette of giving quarter to enemies who refuse to fight.

European weapons seem to be especially powerful since Dryden minimizes the role of Spain's Amerindian allies in the conquest of Mexico. In *The Indian Emperor*, Spain's tiny army of "four hundred foot and forty horse" completely dominates its indigenous allies when they threaten to disobey Cortez's orders and kill Montezuma (Dryden 1667, I.i.33). A representative of the Taxallans, who Dryden gives the symbolic name "Indian," fearfully exclaims:

O mercy, mercy, at thy feet we fall,
Before thy roaring gods destroy us all;
See we retreat without the least reply,
Keep thy gods silent, if they speak we dye. (I.ii.224–227)

Historically, Spain's Amerindian allies greatly outnumbered the meager European force and played an essential role in the overthrow of the Aztecs. Yet Dryden gives the impression that these allies were of minimal importance since they, like all Amerindians in the play, exhibit a supernatural fear of Europeans' guns or "roaring gods."

CONFLICTING SYMPATHETIC IDENTIFICATIONS

In *The Indian Emperor*, Dryden's fictional versions of Pizarro and an unnamed "Christian Priest" embody the alleged torturous inclinations of Spaniards perfectly and, in doing so, they become stock villains that English Restoration theatergoers could easily recognize and love to hate. These two characters, accompanied by "Spaniards with Swords drawn," interrogate Montezuma and an "Indian High Priest," both of whom are tied up, in a prison. Pizarro begins the scene by reprimanding Montezuma as follows: "Thou hast not yet discover'd all thy store" (Dryden 1667, V.ii.1). When Montezuma refuses to divulge the location of his hidden treasure, the Christian Priest says, "How wickedly he has refus'd his wealth, / And hid his Gold, from Christian hands, by stealth" (V.ii.7–8). As with the example of Nicholas Burton's torturers in

Foxe's *Actes and Monuments*, Dryden's corrupt representatives of the Spanish Inquisition are interested in "Gold" rather than religious conversions, confessions, or the detection of heresy. Yet the Christian Priest uses the vocabulary of religion as a thin veil for the ruthless pursuit of ill-begotten material goods.

Because the Christian Priest and Pizarro are unable to obtain the information they desire through verbal interrogation, they decide to take a more aggressive approach toward Montezuma and the Indian High Priest. Pizarro begins by addressing the two uncooperative Mexican captives and then issues orders to the Spanish soldiers:

> Since neither threats nor kindness will prevail,
> We must by other means your minds assail;
> Fasten the Engines; stretch 'um at their length,
> And pull the streightned Cords with all your strength. (Dryden 1667, V.ii.11–14)

The stage directions then state that the Spaniards "fasten" Montezuma and the High Indian Priest "to the racks, and pull them" (V.ii.14). This violent scene allowed Dryden and his English contemporaries to feel morally superior to the Spanish since, at least in theory, England's Common Law forbid the use of torture. In *Torture and English Law: An Administrative and Legal History from the Plantagenets to the Stuarts*, James Heath argues that, although Charles II threatened the reinstatement of torture in a few instances after 1666, actual records of it taking place are dubious, and "Common Law . . . condemn[ed] torture in any context" in England (Heath 1982, 172–78). Moreover, in a 1680 trial, Baron Weston claimed that torture had not occurred in a sanctioned English administrative context "since Queen Elizabeth's time," and "God in heaven knows" that "no such thing" happened during Charles II's reign (qtd. in Heath 1982, 179). Dryden implies that England's more humane laws differentiate its colonial expansion in North America, Surinam, and the Caribbean from the Spanish[20] version in Central and South America.

In addition to using the word "wicked" to describe Montezuma's refusal to surrender his gold to "Christian hands," the Christian Priest calls the Mexican king an "impious heathen" who "our true God denies" because of Montezuma's refusal to tell the Spaniards where the cache of gold is hidden (Dryden 1667, V.ii.5–6). The notion that an Amerindian's desire to prevent his captors from stealing his treasure is a denial of "our true God" is a non sequitur that clearly reveals the nameless priest's greed and hypocritical use of religious rhetoric. Like the generic "Indian Boy" in the prologue of *The Indian Queen*, the Christian Priest's lack of a name makes him a composite representative and spokesperson of a group in general, in this case the Spanish

Inquisitors rather than the "Indian" people. The greed and torture employed by Dryden's fictional Pizarro and the Christian Priest, both of whom symbolized seventeenth-century English perceptions of Spain, forfeited any ethical or proselytizing right the country might have claimed as a justification to rule in the Americas.

As an illiterate, illegitimate, cruel Spanish swineherd, Francisco Pizarro was a logical choice for a villainous role in Dryden's *The Indian Emperor* (Chapman 1967, 30). Pizarro's illegitimate birth was probably not grounds, in and of itself, for Dryden's unflattering fictional depiction since he dedicatated the play to Anne, the wife of Charles II's bastard son, in October of 1667 (Dryden 1667, 23). Dryden says the Duke of Monmouth, James Scott (or Cross), is a "Noble Lord" who has no parallel in "masculine Beauty, and goodliness of shape," and that he and Anne are "Angels sent below to make Virtue amiable in [their] persons" (23). Other members of Dryden's audience, however, may not have viewed Pizarro's birth out of wedlock so lightly. After all, the English social structure of primogeniture depended on legitimate children for the transfer of leadership and property rights from one generation to the next, and the Duke of Monmouth's own status as Charles II's bastard son rather than rightful heir would later be one of the causes of the rebellion of 1685.

More importantly, Pizarro, unlike Dryden's Cortez, was not a nobleman. In fact, Heylyn's 1652 edition of *Cosmographie* claims that Pizarro was abandoned on a "Church-porch" by "the poor whore his mother" and, because no nursemaid could be found for several days, he was forced to get milk by "sucking a Sow" (4: 156). At least as early as the fourteenth century, the word "swine" had the figurative meaning of a "sensual, degraded, or coarse person" ("Swine"). Thus Pizarro's onetime vocation as a swine*herd*, a leader of swine, might also be applied figuratively by Dryden and his audience, primarily aristocrats and some of the more successful merchants, to the Spanish soldiers under Pizarro's command.

Dryden's intended and actual audience, English Restoration aristocrats such as the Duchess of Monmouth, and Charles II himself, who saw the play performed at court in January of 1668, valued wit, learning, and humane behavior (Van Lennep 1965, 127).[21] In various proclamations between 1660 and 1661, Charles II presented himself to the public as a merciful sovereign by issuing a "General Pardon" to all his "Subjects," except for a few scapegoats chosen by Parliament, for any "Crime whatsoever, committed against [him], or [his] Royal Father" provided the offenders confess in "publick" and reaffirm their "Loyalty and Obedience" to the new regime (Stuart 1661, *A Proclamation Concerning His Majesties Gracious*). Other proclamations by Charles II during this period state that "clemency" is "most agreeable to [his] Nature," and that his decrees are "more ample in the things pardoned, and [have] fewer Exceptions than have been usual in Pardons granted upon like occasion at the Coronation of his Majesties Predecessors" (*His Majesties; A Proclamation, Concerning His Majesties Coronation*). Because Charles II's father was executed eleven years earlier and he himself was forced into exile with the consent or active involvement of men still living in England during the Restoration, he could indeed have been far more vengeful than he was. Thus while Dryden and other Englishmen's rigid dichotomies between English mercy and Spanish cruelty were often exaggerated, there was at least some historical validity to the former claim during Charles II's reign. Charles II's *public* displays of clemency, however, may have been motivated more by a need for political stability in his realm, proactive riot prevention, and the cultivation of his people's loyalty through the creation of a performative persona rather than being simply "agreeable to [his] Nature," as he argued in his *Gracious Speech to Both Houses of Parliament* (1660). The official persona that Charles II cultivated, which in turn set the standard for his courtiers, equated gentility with mercy.

The few small theaters in London at the time of the first performance of Dryden's *Indian Emperor* in 1665 attracted this exclusive audience due to their limited seating capacity and high production costs that were in turn passed on to ticket buyers. In the early 1660s, theaters were former tennis courts that could only seat about 400 people, whereas the Globe in Elizabethan England accommodated 3,000 and was one of eight playhouses.[22] Because greater London's population in the early 1660s was about 500,000 and Charles II granted exclusive control of the theatrical industry to Thomas Killigrew and Sir William Davenant, the demand for dramatic entertainment vastly exceeded the supply. In James Wright's 1699 work *Historia Histrionica*, the author sets up a dialogue about theatrical conditions before and after "the Wars" (1642–51) between two fictional characters named "Lovewit" and "Trueman." The latter lists eight pre-Cromwellian playhouses and five acting companies. In response, Lovewit asks why "two can hardly subsist" in the 1660s. Trueman answers this question by saying that the town was far less "populous" before the British Civil Wars and "the Prices were small" (Wright 1699, 5). In other words, because of limited seating capacity in fewer theaters, higher admission prices, and a much larger population than Elizabethan or Jacobean England, wealthy Londoners made up a substantial portion of the audience at the time of the first performance of Dryden's *Indian Emperor* in 1665.

Edward A. Langhans argues that the cultivation of a select clientele was deliberate on the parts of Killigrew and Davenant as they renovated their theaters: "[they] selected small buildings in reputable neighborhoods because they anticipated a limited, aristocratic audience that would prefer intimacy and would not fill larger houses" (Langhans 2003, 2). Because this "aristocratic audience" was to some extent dependent upon Charles II for the continuance and improvement of their titles, estates, and wealth, they were likely to share his values, or at least appear to do so, in order to stay in royal favor. Dryden's vilification of a fictionalized Pizarro based on an actual man who was the antithesis of Stuart values therefore likely received a favorable response from London theatergoers.[23]

Because no Englishmen accompanied the conquistadors on their invasion of Mexico, Dryden Anglicizes a Spanish character to voice the opinions of an English audience. Cortez was a natural choice because he was a member of the nobility, educated in Latin, law, and grammar, and a wealthy Chief Magistrate of Santiago, Cuba by the time he was thirty-two years old (Madariaga 1942, 20; Wood 2000, 24, 26). In addition to these positive traits, at least one sixteenth-century historian portrayed Cortez as a humane individual. Bernal Díaz de Castillo wrote that the news of Montezuma's death made Cortez weep, which probably inspired the tears in Dryden's fictional version of the historical figure (although Dryden's Cortez cries during the Mexican ruler's impending demise, rather than afterward) (Tsouras 2005, 85). More importantly, the legend of Cortez being a god-like figure returning to his native country from self-imposed exile to resume his place as the rightful and legitimate ruler established an implicit parallel with Dryden's chief patron, Charles II. The historical Cortez was also, like Charles II, a notorious womanizer and gambler, though of course Dryden does not mention this well-known fact in the play (Wood 2000, 26). Dryden's Anglicized, heroic, merciful Cortez therefore serves as a fictional version of Charles II who expresses popular English anti-Spanish sentiments. From a financial standpoint, this strategy enabled Dryden to flatter his chief patron while simultaneously incorporating a crowd-pleasing theme into his play to help ensure its longevity on the Restoration stage.[24]

Dryden further humanizes Cortez through his love interest, Cydaria. Critics such as Eugene Waith argue that Cortez is "dangerously swayed by passion," but his romantic relationship with Cydaria makes him a more sympathetic embodiment of Spanish colonization (Waith 1971, 209–10). Whereas Almeria represents indigenous hostility toward European colonialism, Cydaria, much like Quevira in *The Indian Queen*, symbolizes a passive and welcoming Amerindian attitude. In fact, Cydaria literally stands "*Betwixt the two Armies*" (Dryden 1667, II.ii.1). Under her influence, Cortez reevaluates his priorities. This change begins as soon as he meets her. While Vasquez and Pizarro make demands and enter into a lengthy debate with Montezuma about religious conversion, Cortez, according to the stage directions, "*spies the Ladies and goes to them, entertaining* Cydaria *with Courtship in dumb show*" (I.ii.265). Consequently, Cortez, like the English, is conveniently absent during many of the unpleasant scenes of early colonialism. Another instance of

Cydaria's pacifying effect on Cortez occurs before a battle. In response to protestations of love and devotion from Cydaria, Cortez exclaims:

> No more, your kindness wounds me to the death,
> Honour be gone, what art thou but a breath?
> I'le live, proud of my infamy and shame,
> Men can but say Love did his reason blind,
> And Love's the noblest frailty of the mind.
> Draw off my Men, the War's already done. (II.ii.66–72)

Cydaria's appeal to the peaceful side of Cortez "wounds [him] to the death," a martial metaphor that indicates "kindness" or love conquers where weapons cannot. Cortez's willingness to "Draw off [his] Men," lose his "Honour," and live in "infamy and shame" for the woman he loves makes him sympathetic from the perspective of the gallant ideals that Dryden himself employs in the dedication to the Duchess of Monmouth.

This gesture of romantic devotion, however, is ultimately in vain. Pizarro, significantly the bearer of bad tidings and possibly the instigator of a premature engagement, says, "Your orders come too late, the Fight's begun" (Dryden 1667, II.ii.73). Despite Cortez's attempts at aristocratic English "good" colonialism based on ideals of gallantry and indigenous cooperation, then, lower-class Pizarro initiates a more brutal, Spanish, "bad" variant of the subjugation of Amerindians. Colonialism works best, from Dryden's perspective, when Europeans with chivalrous English values encounter indigenous peoples with Cydaria's and Quevira's welcoming attitudes. The process becomes less pleasant, however, when Amerindians display the obstinacy and rebelliousness that Almeria embodies.

Cortez's adherence to the principles of chivalry extends beyond romantic love to warfare. As a surrogate Englishman in spirit, Cortez rebukes his fellow Spaniards and a "Christian Priest" for their excessive violence. A morally outraged Cortez says:

> On pain of death kill none but those who fight;
> I much repent me of this bloody night:
> Slaughter grows murder when it goes too far,
> And makes a Massacre what was a War:
> Sheath all your weapons. (Dryden 1667, V.ii.106–110)

Cortez's allegations that his countrymen are committing a "bloody . . . Massacre" or "murder" that "goes too far," beyond the equal or consensual valorous fighting among men that constituted seventeenth-century notions of "War," echoes and reinforces the stereotypes of unnatural Spanish bloodlust found in the works of Las Casas, Montanus, Hakluyt, Purchas, and Foxe.

Along with the popular story of Nicholas Burton, at least three other Englishmen who met cruel and unusual deaths at the hands of Spanish Inquisitors were recorded in Samuel Clarke's 1640 *Generall Martyrologie*, some of whose phrases and incidents are lifted verbatim from Foxe (Clarke 1640, 261). Accounts of Englishmen victimized by Spanish Inquisitors found their way from the books of history onto the Restoration stage before Dryden's *The Indian Emperor* was first performed in 1665. In one scene of William Davenant's *The Play-House to be Let, Containing the History of Sir Francis Drake, and the Cruelty of the Spaniards in Peru* (first performed in 1663), the curtain opens to reveal a "dark Prison" with "Racks" and "other Engines of torment," where "Spaniards are tormenting the Natives and English Mariners." One of these "Natives" is an "Indian Prince" (Davenant 1673, 111). Even though this incident takes place in Peru rather than Mexico, N. D. Shergold and Peter Ure argue that it was a source for the torture of Montezuma in Dryden's *The Indian Emperor* (1966, 369).

Such a claim makes sense because Dryden amalgamates many of the events in *The Indian Queen* and *The Indian Emperor* from two separate Spanish campaigns that occurred eleven years apart. One was the invasion of Mexico by Cortez in 1519–21, which Pizarro did not join since he was a landowner in Panama City during those years (Pan American 1954, 3–4; Prescott 1892, 1: 201). The other was the Spanish conquest of Peru led by Pizarro in 1532. For the purposes of this chapter, the most interesting aspect of Davenant's scene is that "English Mariners" and an "Indian Prince" from the Americas are tortured simultaneously by Spanish Inquisitors. A sympathetic identification therefore forms between the English and Amerindians on the basis of being victims of the Spanish, which Dryden mirrors in *The Indian Emperor*.

Dryden foreshadows this sympathetic identification in the epilogue of *The Indian Queen* when Montezuma, speaking on behalf of the playwright, directly addresses English theatergoers as follows:

> *[We] hope it is below your aim to hit*
> *At untaught Nature with your practic'd Wit:*
> *Our naked* Indians *then, when Wits appear,*
> *Wou'd as soon chuse to have the* Spaniards *here*. (Dryden 1665, V.i.7–10)

This passage analogizes the audience's reception of the play and the Spanish treatment of the indigenous Mexicans. If Restoration theatergoers sink "below [their] aim" to "hit" the "untaught Nature" of the "naked Indians" with "practic'd Wit," then Montezuma and the playwright he represents will prefer the presence of the vilified Spaniards. As the word "hit" implies, mocking Dryden's play would be an act of violence that mirrors the Spanish colonization of Amerindians. In other words, "naked Indians" in these lines are defenseless against English "practic'd Wit," which Montezuma represents as a weapon. The equation of Amerindians with "untaught Nature" gives them a prelapsarian innocence from Dryden's perspective that Europeans are morally obligated to refrain from harming. Because England used violence against Amerindians in order to secure and maintain its colonies, the difference between that country and Spain is minimal or nonexistent, but Dryden encourages selective national amnesia. While the epilogue of *The Indian Queen* only hints at Dryden's invocation of the Black Legend of the Spanish, I argue that it is the dominant theme of the sequel.

Immediately upon discovering the torture that Pizarro, the Christian Priest, and the Spanish soldiers have put Montezuma through, the stage directions indicate that Cortez "Runs to take [the Mexican king] off the Rack," "Embrac[es]" him, "kneels by" Montezuma, and "weeps" over the injuries he has suffered (Dryden 1665, V.ii.114, 117, 137). Cortez's highly emotional reaction to Montezuma's pain anticipates the sentimental masculinity of eighteenth-century works such as Steele's *The Conscious Lovers* (1722) and Mackenzie's *The Man of Feeling* (1771), and Cortez's reaction, as an English surrogate, demonstrates the supposedly humane and morally superior way that the English treated West "Indians" in North American, Surinamese, and Caribbean colonies. Although the torture of English subjects by Spanish Inquisitors was isolated to a few highly publicized incidents, they loomed disproportionately large on early modern and Restoration stages. I argue that one cause of this phenomenon was Dryden's and other Englishmen's frustration at having ended up with the far less lucrative colonies in the Americas than Spain. Consequently, the English viewed themselves as victims of Spain, or at least placed in a position of powerlessness, in a manner similar to Amerindians.

Thus Dryden's identification with, and pity toward, Montezuma, an indigenous Mexican, over his fellow European Spaniards makes sense. Dryden expected his audience to side with a non-Christian "Indian" against Spaniards who technically believed in the same religion that most English men and women did, albeit from a Catholic rather than a Protestant perspective. Montezuma's royal bearing under duress gives him a moral superiority over Pizarro, a lower-class Christian. Intra-European antagonisms therefore outweigh nominal allegiances to Christianity in Dryden's *The Indian Emperor*.

Yet this sympathetic identification between England and the indigenous peoples of the Americas only extended so far since, after all, the former had already encroached on North American territory. As Cortez puts an end to the ongoing torture in act five, he says, "Ah Father, Father, what do I endure / To see these Wounds my pity cannot Cure!" (Dryden 1667, V.ii.117–18). Cortez's use of the word "Father" implies a subservient attitude and his "pity" appears to be a benevolent sentiment, but Montezuma is quick to point out the power relations associated with the latter term by saying, "Am I so low that you should pity bring, / And give an Infants Comfort to a King?" (V.ii.119–20). In this passage, Montezuma argues that an object of pity is inherently looked down upon by the one who expresses the sentiment. One must be perceived as "low" for others to feel pity, which makes the sympathetic party "high" or powerful by extension. Montezuma reiterates his title of "King" as a way to regain some of the dignity that torture and defeat by the Spaniards has robbed him of, and to some extent Dryden endorses an aristocratic ethos that transcends national boundaries. Yet, like Heylyn, Dryden cannot overlook the fact that the Spanish conquered Central and South America, and thus pity and condescension color his narrative in a way that does not occur in *Aureng-Zebe*, a play that features a country far more powerful, militarily superior, and wealthy than England. Derek Hughes contends that Dryden "tactfully admonish[es]" Charles II's "sex life" by showing the "hero-king" Montezuma "as being gravely weakened by imprudent love" (Hughes 2004, 2: 92). Although I disagree with Hughes' point that Montezuma's "imprudent love" represents Dryden's admonishment to Charles II,[25] two implicit ideas behind this statement mesh well with my argument. First, Montezuma is depicted in a "gravely weakened" state that is characteristic of Dryden's, and other seventeenth-century Englishmen's, portrayals of West "Indians." Second, the idea that Montezuma could serve, in some capacities, as a surrogate Charles II reveals a limited sympathetic identification between English playwrights and their West "Indian" characters.

DRYDEN, CATHOLICISM, AND CHARLES II

The selection of Cortez as the mouthpiece for English attitudes toward colonialism was potentially problematic for Dryden beyond the fact that Cortez was Spanish; he was also Catholic. Yet Dryden shrewdly circumvented the controversy of a positive depiction of a Catholic by refashioning the historical Cortez into an idealized nonpartisan Christian, neither explicitly Catholic nor Protestant, who represented the "proper" moral way to colonize the Americas in contrast to the lower-class brutality of Pizarro. Dryden's humane, Anglicized Cortez, who is welcomed into the Americas by the indigenous peoples, therefore served as a fantasy metaphor for European expansion in the Americas, and a justification for English conquests in North America, Surinam, and the Caribbean. Dryden therefore creates a version of Cortez, who, while technically being Catholic and Spanish, actually represents the ideal English way of colonizing the peoples of the Americas. In doing so, Dryden makes *The Indian Queen* and *The Indian Emperor* plays that invite, and create a need for a larger English presence in the Americas. At the same time, Dryden uses Pizarro's character as a scapegoat for all the alleged cruelty of Spain and the Inquisition, thereby assuring Dryden's English readers that he did not side with a country that was very unpopular or publicly with Catholicism, which was generally out of favor in England at the time.

Unlike many of his fellow English men and women, Dryden did not believe Catholicism was inherently wicked. He publicly announced his conversion in the early 1680s out of loyalty to James II, and Dryden was probably a crypto-Catholic or at least sympathetic to the faction for decades beforehand as his former Stuart patron Charles II was rumored to be. The dedication that Dryden often expressed toward Charles II and James II appears to have been genuine since Dryden refused to change his religion or political affiliation even when it would have been personally advantageous to do so under William of Orange's rule (DeMaria 2001, 173). The wording of Charles II's "Proclamation Commanding All Jesuites and Popish Priests to Depart this Kingdom" in 1663 reveals much about his public and private attitudes toward Catholicism, and Dryden likely followed suit. In the proclamation, Charles makes it clear that the "Lords and Commons in this present Parliament Assembled" were pressuring him to make a public declaration against Catholicism, "notwithstanding [his] unquestionable Affection and Zeal to the true Protestant Religion, Manifested in [his] constant Profession and Practice, against all Temptations whatsoever" (Stuart 1663). "Temptation" implies desire, and had Charles II's "Affection and Zeal to the true Protestant Religion" truly been "unquestionable," such a proclamation would not have been necessary. By outwardly "Commanding All Jesuites and Popish Priests to Depart this Kingdom," Charles placated his people, despite what he personally may have believed. Queen Elizabeth ushered in an age of a strongly Protestant preference in most English people that lasted long beyond the end of her reign in 1603, and seventeenth-century rulers who openly opposed that predilection seriously undermined public support for their reigns, as James II would later find out when he faced the Exclusion Bill in 1679.

Because Dryden followed the example of whichever male[26] Stuart monarch happened to be in power at the time, he avoided any explicit endorsements of Catholicism until after Charles II's death in 1685. As Dryden became more directly financially dependent upon Charles II in the years following the publications of *The Indian Queen* and *The Indian Emperor*, as Poet Laureate from 1668–88 and Historiographer Royal from 1670–88, depictions of the monarch became transparently flattering and idealized. However, Dryden had to adapt and reconfigure these representations of Charles II in relation to contemporary Mughal India in his 1676 play *Aureng-Zebe*, a country whose power in relation to England vastly differed from the Americas in the sixteenth century.

NOTES

1. All dates refer to the first publications of the respective plays. The initial performance dates were as follows: *The Indian Queen* (1664), *The Indian Emperor* (1665), and *Aureng-Zebe* (1675) (Zwicker, *Cambridge Companion* viii, x). The *Indian Queen* is sometimes attributed solely to Sir Robert Howard, such as in *Four New Plays as They Were Acted by His Majesties Servants at the Theatre-Royal* (1665) and *Five New Plays* (1692 and 1700). The 1735 and 1762 reprints of *The Indian Queen* credit both "the Honourable Sir Robert Howard and Mr Dryden." However, at least one text, a 1695 edition of *The Songs in the Indian Queen* lists "John Dryden" as the author of the original play without mentioning Howard, and the *Cambridge Companion to John Dryden* includes *The Indian Queen* among Dryden's works with a parenthetical reference to it being written "with Sir Robert Howard" (viii). Because the verse style and vocabulary in *The Indian Queen* and *The Indian Emperor*, which was composed solely by Dryden, are essentially indistinguishable, I believe Dryden and not Howard wrote the vast majority of *The Indian Queen*. The fact that Dryden took the time to write an entire sequel within a year of the first performance of *The Indian Queen* also suggests that he was more invested in the subject matter than Howard. In the introduction to *The Dramatic Works of John Dryden*, Sir Walter Scott affirms the central role that Dryden played in the composition of *The Indian Queen* by saying, "The versification of this piece, which is far more harmonious than that generally used by Howard, shows evidently, that our author had assiduously corrected the whole play" (1: 69).

2. Derek Hughes' book *Dryden's Heroic Plays* falls into this category as well. Specifically, Hughes argues that these three plays reveal Corneille's influence on Dryden (1981, 2–3).

3. Whereas most Restoration prologues, such as the ones for *The Indian Emperor* and *Aureng-Zebe*, contain self-reflexive pleas by the playwright for mercy from the audience, *The Indian Queen* immediately begins a contextual narrative dialogue between characters. Moreover, contemporary notes about the January 27, 1664, premiere of *The Indian Queen* specifically state that the prologue occurred "after the curtain opened," which implies that not all Restoration plays followed that format. Consequently, I treat the prologue of this particular play as especially important and intratextual (Van Lennep 1965, 1: cxxxvi).

4. The Spanish conquest of Mexico that Dryden chronicles in *The Indian Emperor* took place from 1519 to 1521, whereas the Incas were not invaded until 1532 (Moseley 1992, 11).

5. According to N. D. Shergold and Peter Ure, Dryden "owned," "read," "had a positive interest in," and "borrow[ed] sources from" "Spanish books" (1966, 370). However, out of convenience and to save time, Dryden would more likely choose translations in his native language as source material if they were available, and not all, or even most, of his English audience was fluent enough in Spanish to read accounts of the Quetzalcoatl legend in their original tongue.

6. Although Purchas faithfully provides his readers with the English-translated version of his Spanish source(s), his gloss in this section expresses dissent from the narrative that he mediates. Purchas' marginal notation reads as follows: "Cortes

admits diuine worship agreeing more with his couetous designes then Christian religion, which thriued there according to these beginnings" (1625, 3: 1,022). Thus while Purchas' Spanish sources idealized Cortez's invasion of Mexico, Purchas himself condemned the conquistadors' "couetous designes." Purchas' attitude is not surprising considering the fact that war broke out between Spain and England in the year *Purchas his Pilgrimes* was published (1625).

7. Although Behn did not publish *Oroonoko* until 1688, her account of the indigenous peoples of Surinam was inspired by her residence in that country from 1663–64 (Behn 1688, 356). Dryden would not have read her account at the time he wrote *The Indian Emperor*, then, but Behn's memory or invention of Amerindian deification of English people was contemporaneous with Dryden's play and thus illustrates the larger point about documented instances of seventeenth-century examples of this phenomenon.

8. In addition to taking land by force, Englishmen forged alliances with several tribes against the French and their own Indian allies by the late seventeenth century.

9. For a more extensive analysis of the woman-as-land metaphor in seventeenth-century literature, see Hutner (2001), especially pages 8–9, 15–16, 22, 24, 36, 63–64.

10. Because Old Testament chronology depicts the earth as much newer than modern archeological estimates, seventeenth-century writers such as Heylyn and Dryden thought that the first "Indians" in the Americas arrived thousands, or possibly even hundreds, of years before the European "discovery" rather than at least ten thousand.

11. English soldiers had already fought the First (1609–13) and Second (1644–46) Anglo-Powhatan Wars, and the Pequot War (1637) against the indigenous peoples of the Americas by 1664.

12. Quevira's description of the New World invokes the pagan tradition of the Golden Age and anticipates Lockes's *Two Treatises of Government* when he idealistically creates a fiction of the Americas as a place of inexhaustible natural resources. For a more extensive analysis of the Golden Age motif in early modern England, see Markley, "Land."

13. Just as Dryden resents the Spanish for holding more valuable New World territories than England, Behn laments that "the Dutch have the advantage" of Surinam after 1667, a region that allegedly held the fabled "mountains of gold." Behn says, "'Tis to be bemoaned what His Majesty lost by losing that part of America" (Behn 1688, 125). Behn associates "that part of America," South America, with wealth that England's Caribbean and North American colonies did not possess. Like Dryden, she attempts to differentiate England's treatment of the indigenous inhabitants of the New World from other European colonizers by claiming that the Dutch "used them [the Surinamese] not so civilly as the English" (120).

14. In addition to the seventeenth-century Anglo-Spanish wars I listed in chapter 2, these two countries also fought from 1585 to 1604.

15. In 1660, the EIC gave £3,000 of silver to Charles II and loaned him another £10,000 in 1662. Over the years of Charles II's reign, the Company loaned him at least £150,000 (Keay 1994, 131).

16. Dryden perpetuates the stereotype of Hollanders as an unmerciful people by including a torture scene of English men by Dutch merchants in act five of his play

Amboyna (1673), which was based on actual events in 1623. This historical moment was already considered an outrage to the English in the seventeenth century, so Dryden's dramatization and resurrection of the incident fanned the flames of an already long-burning fire of indignation. See Markley, *Far East* 143.

17. Purchas also included part of Las Casas' work in the 1625 edition of *Purchas his Pilgrimes*.

18. A complete armor suit for ""fighting on foot" from Madrid around 1530 weighed, for example, seventy-nine lbs. (ffoulkes 1912, 119). Even if the Spaniards" only wore part of a complete set of armor, say, fifty lbs., that would be an enormous burden during long marches and sustained combat.

19. For the three examples of the word "ignorance" in the play, see I.160, III.210, IV.i.112.

20. Similarly, Dryden depicts another great English rival, the Dutch, as a country whose inhabitants enjoy torturing innocent people in *Amboyna*.

21. Dryden had by far the most plays performed at Charles II's court, a total of ten including *Aureng-Zebe* on Monday, May 9, 1676 (Van Lennep 1965, 244). The next most popular playwrights at Charles II's court, including Aphra Behn among others, only had four of their respective plays performed at the king's private theaters at the Palace of Whitehall, St. James' Palace, and Windsor Castle (Boswell 1932, 9, 58–59, 107).

22. The first Theatre Royal between Bridges Street and Drury Lane, built in 1663, where both of Dryden's earlier "Indian" plays premiered (*The Indian Queen*: January 27, 1664; *The Indian Emperor*: April of 1665) was slightly larger than the very first theaters of Charles II's reign because it could accommodate "seven hundred souls" (Van Lennep 1965, cxxxvi, 87). Even with the larger seating capacity, however, this theater was expensive. According to Charles Beauclerk, prices "tended to be doubled on the first night of a play" there, and it was "richly appointed" with "three galleries," "chandeliers," benches with "green baize and gilt leather," "embroidered side boxes," and an orchestra pit in a "recess beneath the stage" (2005, 56, 59).

23. Indeed, the play was very successful. According to Robert Shiells, Dryden's *The Indian Emperor* was "acted with great applause" (1753, 3: 88). The play was reprinted twenty-five times between 1667 and 1759 (about once every four years for nearly a century), and it went through at least ten performances (one of which was at court) and five additional possible revivals before 1700. Sir Walter Scott says that this play "was probably the first of Dryden's performances which drew upon him, in an eminent degree, the attention of the public" (*Dramatic Works*, 71). Pepys saw *The Indian Emperor* four times and called it a "very good play indeed," and *The Gentleman's Journal* in January of 1691/2 remarked that the play "hath been revived many times" (Van Lennep 1965, 132, 402).

24. During the Restoration, playwrights received the third-night's proceeds from their plays, provided they lasted that long (Langhans 2003, 5). Thus Dryden depended on pleasing his audiences in *The Indian Emperor* at least long enough to make a profit.

25. Charles II, unlike Dryden's Montezuma, was not prone to pining for a monogamous relationship, and the phrase "imprudent love" only applies to the English king if it is a very loose euphemism for "lust." Given Dryden's lifelong deference and

arguably even obsequiousness to figures of authority, it is unlikely that he would presume to chide his sovereign, "tactfully" or otherwise.

26. Apparently Dryden's loyalty to the Stuarts did not extend to women since Mary II, William of Orange's wife, was the daughter of James II. Yet William III was seen as a direct replacement for, and rival of, James II, so Dryden could not pledge his allegiance to both Mary and her father simultaneously. Because James II still lived until 1701, Dryden may have held out hope for a second Restoration. In other words, gender could have played a less important role in his monarchical allegiances than prior pledges of loyalty.

Chapter 4

Mughal History and Dryden's *Aureng-Zebe*

Although Dryden depicts a militarily dominant European presence in the West Indies in *The Indian Queen* and *The Indian Emperor*, he does not adopt the same attitude in the East Indian play *Aureng-Zebe*. The different perspectives toward East and West "Indians" in these three theatrical works represent the vastly dissimilar positions English men and women occupied in relation to the distinctive groups of peoples in the latter half of the seventeenth century. In his plays set in Mexico, Dryden reimagines the commencement of the European colonization of the indigenous peoples. Dryden's dramatic work that takes place in India, by contrast, never directly mentions Europeans. Indeed, the presence of Europeans in the Mughal Empire in India was almost inconsequential from Aurangzeb's perspective.

While critics such as Achsah Guibbory and Derek Hughes argue that bits of advice for Charles II are embedded within Dryden's plays, there has been little study of the collaborative aspects of the relationship between these two men.[1] Dryden's *Aureng-Zebe* is especially conducive to this analysis because it depicts one of the English king's trading partners and the dedication of the play states that Charles II read it before "the last hand was added to it" and modified "the most considerable event of it" (1667, 10). Even if Dryden's patron and sovereign only directly changed a single line, the knowledge of his interest in the play must have had an effect on the Poet Laureate/ Historiographer Royal. Unlike the previous historical figures upon whom Dryden's characters were based, Aurengzeb was no long-dead leader (ruled 1658–1707). Early drafts of *Aureng-Zebe* have not survived so the full extent of Charles II's input is unknown; however, we can compare the play to its source, François Bernier's *Travels in the Mogul Empire* (first English edition 1671). Dryden's play transforms the account of Aurangzeb provided by the French surgeon Bernier, who served in the Indian succession wars, almost beyond recognition. This kind of transformation is characteristic of Dryden's writing. Most scholars agree with Steven Zwicker's description of Dryden's poetic form as comprised of a "technique of denial and misrepresentation" and Ros Ballaster's claim that "Dryden plays fast and loose with the historical facts" of Bernier's narrative (Zwicker 1984, 39–43; Ballaster 2005, 279). The critical consensus is far less overwhelming when it comes to the question of how scholars should interpret Dryden's distortions. This chapter argues that the play acts as a collaborative public relations' spectacle that presents a highly sanitized version of Aurangzeb to English theatergoers, and possibly even to the emperor himself, in order to reinforce support for England's incredibly lucrative trade arrangement with the Mughal Empire. At the same time, moments of slippage within the predominately flattering rendition of Aurengzeb in the play reflect the disparities in power and ambivalent values of Dryden and his sovereign.

In Balachandra Rajan's book *Under Western Eyes*, he devotes an entire chapter to Dryden's *Aureng-Zebe* that, I argue, does not fully take into account the historical power relations between India and England in the mid 1670s. Although Rajan concedes that Mughal India was "still being treated as a sovereign state and not as a potentially subject territory," he nonetheless reads nineteenth-century British people's condescension toward their subjugated colonies into Dryden's *Aureng-Zebe* (1999, 67). For instance, Rajan says that "Mughal history is treated by Dryden with a disrespect that no writer would have thought of bringing to bear on the Greek and Roman past. Such a disrespect points to a stubbornly resident devaluation of the Orient" (76). In the context of the relative economic and military positions of England and India in the 1670s, however, there would have been few reasons for Dryden to "disrespect" or "devalu[e]" the latter country, especially since it was an ally. As Heylyn's *Cosmographie* and other contemporary voyage collections make clear, India and its surrounding islands provided valuable spices, cloth, and precious metals and stones for the English market, and the Mughal Empire was far more powerful than England at this time. Because these voyage collections were enormously popular, almost all English men and women in the seventeenth century knew that their country was weaker than India. Under Aurangzeb's rule, the Mughal Empire achieved its largest territorial size ever, and his military forces dwarfed England's (Keay 2000, 314). Consequently, Dryden's implicit parallels between Aurangzeb and Charles II, though unrealistic, would have been flattering to the English monarch upon whom Dryden depended for his income as Poet Laureate and Historiographer Royal.

Moreover, Rajan's argument that Dryden singled out the Orient's history to "disrespect" by implicitly drawing attention to the discrepancy between *Aureng-Zebe* and India's "historical reality" does not factor in the playwright's general tendency to exercise extreme poetic license. Rajan explains his theory of Dryden's allegedly disingenuous idealization of the Mughal

Empire as follows: "The play offers itself as an endeavor to display India as exemplary, but the very comprehensiveness of its effort to do so draws attention to a historical reality that is quite the reverse of the play's apparent intentions" (Rajan 1999, 77). In fact, though, Dryden distorts the history of **every** nation, Eastern or Western, to serve his political purposes. He characteristically twists English history to reinforce Stuart interests. In *Annus Mirabilis*, for instance, Dryden describes the Great Fire of 1666 as a boon, rather than a tragedy, for London since the city was: "More great than humane, now, and more *August*, / New deifi'd she from her fires does rise" (1667, lines 1177–8). This celebration of the fire and its phoenix-like resurrection from the ashes was far from a unanimously accepted "historical reality."

After all, roughly 13,200 houses were destroyed, hundreds of millions of pounds' worth of property and goods were lost, at least four people died, and 436 acres burned, leaving only about seventy-five acres within the walls of London untouched. Mobs of Englishmen spread reports that Dutch, French, and Roman Catholics who were in London at the time had deliberately started the fire, and some were even physically assaulted or had their homes set ablaze so that, according to one blacksmith, "the conflagration might become more general" (Bell 1923, 8, 31–33, 174, 177). Quakers and Nonconformists portrayed London as a contemporary Babylon destined for divine destruction, and the fire, along with the Plague outbreak that killed at least 30,000 people the year before, appeared to confirm their prophesies. In a proclamation issued in 1666, Charles II voiced a qualified agreement with these sentiments: "it hath pleased God to lay this heavy judgment upon us all in this time, as an evidence of our sins." Unlike the Babylon analogy, however, London's devastation, from a Stuart perspective, was not a sign that God had permanently forsaken and destroyed an incorrigible city. The king hoped, after this "due humiliation," that God would enable Londoners to build a "much more beautiful city" as a "new instance of his signal blessing upon us" (Stuart 1666, 3). This passage reveals the persistence of the Job metaphor[2] in Englishmen's explanations of their country's afflictions from works such as Heylyn's *Cosmographie* in 1652 to Charles II's Proclamation in 1666. Dryden followed this train of thought in *Annus Mirabilis* and even took Charles II's explanation a step further by transforming what many people considered to be a national disaster into a means for England's cleansing and redemption. By constructing a one-sided, idealistic Carolean[3] account of a catastrophic event that occurred in his own country, Dryden showed a transparent disregard for "historical reality" that was certainly not confined to his depiction of India.

My chapter consists of five sections. In the first part, I offer a new interpretation of the reasons for Dryden's changes to Bernier's depiction of Aurangzeb. Unlike previous scholars such as Samuel Johnson, I assert that Dryden wrote with the apprehension that the Mughal ruler, who could destroy

England's vital trade network in the East at the slightest provocation, may have been watching. By flattering Charles II and possibly even Aurangzeb himself, Dryden helped maintain cordial international relations with India, which were crucial for the EIC's survival. Section two analyzes the different meanings the word "history" had in seventeenth-century England in order to evaluate the extent to which Dryden would have felt bound to retain the "truth" of the events surrounding Aurangzeb's ascension to the throne of India. In the third section, I show that, although Dryden was familiar with and occasionally even employed what Achsah Guibbory calls a "more modern" perspective of history (scientific, skeptical, and secular) in his work, he explicitly rejected this historical perspective in *Aureng-Zebe* in favor of a grossly distorted flattering portrayal of the reigning Mughal emperor (1973, 188–89). Section four explores the implicit parallels between Charles II and Aurangzeb in the play as a partial explanation of the dramatic whitewashing that Dryden performed on the merciless figure depicted in Bernier's narrative. Dryden could not malign Aurangzeb without simultaneously insulting the king of England. In the final section I summarize my argument by claiming that because Charles II depended on the EIC financially and he paid Dryden's pension as both Historiographer Royal and Poet Laureate, it was in Dryden's best interests personally and professionally to reinforce the fiscal connection among the Mughal emperor Aurangzeb, the EIC, and the English king.

THE MISSING LINK: FAZELKAN

In a discussion of Dryden's play in the *Lives of the Poets* series, Samuel Johnson says that if Aurangzeb "had known and disliked his own character, our [England's] trade was not in those times secure from his resentment." While Johnson claims that the possibility of Dryden's play coming to Aurangzeb's attention was unlikely because "His country is at such a distance," Dryden himself probably did not share this view (qtd. in Bernier 1968, x–xi). Dryden wrote and published *Aureng-Zebe* believing that there was at least some possibility that the Mughal ruler would hear of it. In the first English edition of Bernier's *Travels in the Mogul Empire*, the main source for Dryden's *Aureng-Zebe*, a letter precedes the narrative from "M. de Monceaux the younger" to "Henry Ouldinburgh," the translator, which clearly states that Fazelkan, an important counselor to Aurangzeb himself, procured and read "European Books." The letter claims that Bernier taught Fazelkan "the principal languages of Europe," and because Bernier spent time at Surat, Agra, Ahmedabad, Moka, Kásimbázár, and Masulipatam, all of which contained EIC factories at the time, it is possible that English was one of those languages (xxvi–xxvii, xvi–xvii). There were also Mughal merchants who spoke English and translators were common at court.

Dryden therefore may have anticipated news of his play eventually reaching Aurangzeb through Fazelkan or other English speakers at the Mughal court. The English playwright could not have missed Bernier's references to Fazelkan since one of the "Indian lord" or "Omrah" characters in *Aureng-Zebe* is named "Fazel Chan," and "Chan" was a variant spelling of "Khan," which meant noble (Dryden 16676, 16). In the dedication of the play, Dryden boasts that Charles II read *Aureng-Zebe* before "the last hand was added to it" and modified "the most considerable event of it" (10). Since he was the official Poet Laureate and Historiographer Royal of his country and his play was endorsed and edited by the English king, Dryden's work would be considered a flattering gesture from England if Aurangzeb ever learned of it.

Because almost half of the EIC's factories were in the reigning emperor's jurisdiction in the late seventeenth century, the maintenance of his continued goodwill was essential to England's economic prosperity.[4] India's "cloths" or "wove[n] goods" were one of the most important products in the EIC's trade network. They could be sold at Achen, Tecoo, Bantam, Jacatra, Jambi, Siam, Japan, Socodania, Macassar, and Banda. These factories in turn provided one or more of the following items for EIC merchants to trade: gold, camphor, pepper, silver, deerskins, copper, iron, diamonds, bezoar stones, rice, nutmegs, and mace (Mill 1826, 1: 33). Without factories in India and the supply of cloth that they provided, England's presence and profits in the East would have been significantly diminished.

Mughal rulers could and did renege on the firmans that they issued to EIC representatives at any time and for any reason. For instance, one learns in *Purchas his Pilgrimes* that William Hawkins used "Gifts" to obtain permission from Jahangir for "the English" to establish a "Factorie" and "freely trade [at] Surat," only to have the firman revoked and the "presents lost" after a nobleman in the Mughal court objected to the emperor. Although Hawkins states that "without gifts and bribes, nothing would either goe forward or bee accomplished," signs of respect were also important. Hawkins had to "make obeisance . . . according to the custom" in order for the Mughal emperor even to consider his request for a firman at Surat (qtd. in Purchas 1625, 1.2: 214–15). In order to thrive amongst fickle Mughal emperors who expected and demanded deferential behavior, Hawkins had to use caution. Dryden expresses a similar general wariness of royalty in the dedication of *Aureng-Zebe* when the Poet Laureate paraphrases Montaigne's "severe reflection on princes": "we ought not, in reason, have any expectations of favor from them; and . . . 'tis kindness enough if they leave us in possession of our own" (1676, 2–5). Although Dryden hastily adds that England is an exception to this rule, the fact that these words precede all others makes the qualification suspect. The fear of Stuart and possibly even Mughal surveillance therefore likely prevented Dryden from depicting the brutal and unflattering actions that India's reigning emperor committed against his own family members.

In Foucault's classic example of the Panopticon, prisoners cannot see into the guard tower to verify that sentinels are indeed watching them at any particular moment, but the *possibility* of surveillance leads inmates to act as if they are being watched at all times (1977, 201). The same principle applied to Dryden as he wrote a play about a reigning emperor who was capable of dismantling England's trade in the East at the slightest provocation. While trade in India was crucial for England in the seventeenth century, it had little effect on the Mughal Empire. The seventeenth-century Italian voyager Pietro Della Valle, who spent months in India, confirms this assertion by saying:

> the *Mogòl* is a very great and wealthy King, whose Revenews arise from his own Lands and not from the Sea; and one to whom that little which is to be had from the Sea (how great soever it may be) is nothing, and nothing he accounts it; because it accrues rather to some small Captain of his, as the Governour of *Suràt*, and the like, than to the King himself. So what is he concern'd for it? But indeed he will be concern'd for such an injury done to him in his own jurisdiction, as the English have done by making reprisal on ships, which Princes much inferior to the *Mogòl* would not have suffer'd from any admitted as Friends into their Countries. (1892, 418–19)

As this passage suggests, Mughal emperors did not profit from the EIC once the initial gifts or bribes were presented for firmans, and the leaders of India, like all "Princes," were touchy about any perceived insults. The expendability of the EIC to Aurangzeb and the natural arrogance of royalty made it unwise for Dryden to publish a play that could be interpreted by the Mughal emperor as degrading, especially since Charles II openly endorsed and "added the last hand" to it. While a lone English playwright's work probably would not have attracted the Mughal emperor's attention, a play that was coauthored by a king who was Aurangzeb's trading partner might. One historian says that "to Aurangzeb the Company was still a mere flea on the back of his imperial elephant" (Keay 1994, 146). Because of Aurangzeb's indifference toward the EIC, then, Dryden had to use caution so as not to provoke the emperor to swat the "flea" and destroy England's trading network in the East.

BERNIER'S "HISTORY" OF AURANGZEB'S ASCENSION AND DRYDEN'S ALTERATIONS

When Dryden and Bernier wrote their respective accounts of the Mughal emperor Aurengzeb in the seventeenth century, the word "history" had a variety of meanings. Dryden himself was "Historiographer Royal" to Charles II, but Edward Saslow convincingly argues that the title meant "proficiency in prose" whereas the Poet Laureateship signified "proficiency in verse." Saslow points out that when Charles wanted histories written, such as those of the Second Dutch War and the Rye House Plot, he turned, not to Dryden, the official Historiographer Royal, but rather to John Evelyn and Thomas Sprat (Saslow 1978, 263). "History" as a term became further complicated in the latter half of the seventeenth century because it could refer to the length and cost of a work rather than its style or content. Lori Newcomb maintains that, at least as early as the 1680s, booksellers used the category of "history" to denominate longer, costlier, "more or less fictional" narratives (2002, 267). Achsah Guibbory identifies three interrelated methods of history in Dryden's work: the classical, Christian, and "more modern" perspectives. In the classical model, history is a series of cycles that endlessly repeat themselves. The Christian view of history is teleological and unfolds under the direction of divine providence. The last historical perspective that Guibbory describes is the "more modern" one, and it is the vantage point with which Bernier, an eyewitness French surgeon in Mughal India and the main source for Dryden's *Aureng-Zebe*, explicitly identifies.

Guibbory's "more modern" perspective of history strives for a scientific, skeptical, and secular approach to its subject matter. Practitioners of this method actively seek out "authentic sources" and prioritize natural rather than supernatural causality (1973, 188–89, 191, 195). Bernier insists that his work follows this technique by saying, "[I] hope I shall not be suspected of a wish to supply subjects for romance. What I am writing is a matter of history, and my object is to present a faithful account of the manners of this people." Bernier's contrast between history and romance, and his stated desire to provide a "faithful account," reveal his priorities as he recounts his narrative.[5] For events that he did not personally witness during the succession crisis in Mughal India in the 1650s and 60s, Bernier tells his readers that "different" accounts or tales exist, and he will only relate what he can assert "with confidence" (1968, 12, 112, 114). Thus although the term "history" could refer to a work on the basis of style, length, cost, perspective, or content, Bernier's conception of the term anticipates the disciplinary conventions of modern historians.[6]

Bernier consistently depicts the Mughal ruler Aurangzeb as ruthlessly ambitious. The emperor imprisoned most of his family in order to punish perceived offenses: his own son, two nephews, his father, two brothers, one of his pregnant wives, and all of her female relatives. These prison sentences ended in starvation in the latter cases, execution for his two brothers, and lifelong confinement for Aurangzeb's son and father. In Bernier's narrative, Aurangzeb bribes soldiers in his brothers' armies to act as spies, violates oaths he swears on the Koran, holds his own son's wife as a hostage, and sends the decapitated head of his brother Dara to their father.[7] According to Bernier, Aurangzeb outwardly disdains the crown of India, as the following quotation from a letter to Morad-Bakche suggests: "I need not remind you, my brother, how repugnant to my real disposition are the toils of government. While *Dara* and *Sultan Sujah* are tormented with a thirst for dominion, I sigh only for the life of a *Fakire* [religious mendicant]." Yet Bernier makes it clear that statements such as these are insincere: "*Aureng-Zebe* concealed under the garb of disinterestedness and purity of intention his raging passion for sovereignty" (Bernier 1968, 26–27, 56). Throughout Bernier's narrative, Aurangzeb's Machiavellian strategies are consistently exposed.

In Dryden's play, by contrast, all of these events are either omitted entirely or, as Shawn Lisa Maurer argues, attributed to Morat (2005, 160–61). Because Charles II was a minor contributor and reader of the play, Dryden likely felt a certain degree of pressure to represent the English king's trading partner in a favorable way to theatergoers and possibly even to Aurangzeb himself. Dryden makes his role quite explicit when Morat says, "'Tis every painter's art to hide from sight, / And cast in shades, what, seen, would not delight" (Dryden 1667, V.i.147–8). The fact that Dryden identifies with the duplicitous villain perhaps reflects his resentment of Charles II's intrusive attempts to appropriate the play for his own political purposes.[8]

Dryden not only selectively elides unethical aspects of Aurangzeb's rise to power; the Poet Laureate also makes his titular hero close to the epitome of virtue. The Indian lords discuss the respective limitations of three out of the four brothers fighting for the throne: Darah is "to implacable revenge inclined," Sujah is "a bigot of the Persian sect," and Morat is "too insolent" (Dryden 1667, I.91, 95, 98). When the lords reach Aureng-Zebe, however, their criticism turns to praise. Arimant gives the following summary of Aureng-Zebe's character:

> [He is] by no strong passion swayed
> Except his love, more temp'rate is, and weighed.
> This Atlas must our sinking state uphold;
> In council cool, but in performance bold.
> He sums their virtues in himself alone,

> And adds the greatest, of a loyal son;
> His father's cause upon his sword he wears,
> And with his arms, we hope, his fortune bears. (I.102–109)

The outward expressions of the Indian lord characters, at least, support the notion that Aureng-Zebe is an exemplary hero, with the possible minor exception of him being "swayed" by the "strong passion" of "his love."

Yet there has been a considerable debate about how readers should interpret statements such as these. Derek Hughes concisely sums up the critical responses to Dryden's heroes; they are intended to be "ironic," to "invite unmixed admiration," to be "initially unruly" but "subjected to a process of education," or to elicit "simultaneous admiration and laughter" (1981, 168–69). In the specific case of Aureng-Zebe, Hughes argues that the character is "neither an exemplary hero nor even a near-paragon with just sufficient flaws to make him human. On the contrary, Dryden once again creates a hero strikingly akin in mentality and achievement to his villainous counterparts" (Hughes 1981, 149). As evidence for this claim, Hughes cites the following speech from Aureng-Zebe when he suspects Indamora of infidelity:

> Speak; answer. I would fain yet think you true:
> Lie; and I'll not believe my self, but you.
> Tell me you love; and I'll pardon the deceit,
> And, to be fool'd, my self assist the cheat. (Dryden 1667, IV.465–68)

Hughes says that, "In itself, this outburst seriously compromises Aureng-Zebe's claim to be regarded as an ideal and exemplary hero" because it reveals his jealousy, mistrust, and egocentricity (1981, 128). Compared to the French romances that Hughes cites, Aureng-Zebe indeed falls short. However, when one looks at this fairly mundane lovers' quarrel in relation to the horrifying behavior of Bernier's Aurangzeb, which Hughes does not even mention, a different picture emerges.

While both Bernier and Dryden give renditions of Aurangzeb's ascension to the Mughal throne, Dryden presents a far more sympathetic set of motives. Bernier makes clear that a "raging passion for sovereignty" is the driving force behind Aurangzeb's actions whereas Dryden's version of the figure fights against his brothers out of a sense of filial duty, romantic love, and basic survival. The Indian lords at the beginning shed light on Mughal politics through the following statement from Arimant:

> When death's cold hand has closed the father's eye,
> You know the younger sons are doomed to die.
> Less ills are chosen greater to avoid,

> And nature's laws are by the state's destroyed.
> What courage tamely could to death consent,
> And not, by striking first, the blow prevent? (Dryden 1667, I.40–45)

In Arimant's view of Mughal court culture, nature's laws against fratricide are destroyed by the state's desire to prevent civil wars by reducing the number of rival claimants for the throne. This passage reveals that inaction or meek submission on Aureng-Zebe's part will result in his own death, and Arimant equates such passivity with cowardice. Failure on Aureng-Zebe's part to participate in this conflict would be a refusal to play a divinely ordained role, as the following lines from Arimant show: "What Heav'n decrees, no prudence can prevent. / . . . [the brothers must] prove by arms whose fate it was to reign" (Dryden 1667, I.21, 36). Therefore both the warrior ethos of honor and a mixed pagan/Christian conception of fate/heaven compel Aureng-Zebe to participate in the battle with his brothers. Aureng-Zebe's ascension at the end of the play represents a transition from the chaos of civil war to the relative stability of a single ruler. At least some English theatergoers in 1675 would have lived through the British Civil Wars in the 1640s, and others doubtless heard of the bleak conditions from parents and grandparents. When Dryden presents Aureng-Zebe as a leader sent by heaven to unify a country, much as Charles II was portrayed by his supporters in 1660, English men and women most likely responded sympathetically to the Mughal representative of order and stability.

In addition to a desire for honor and survival, Dryden's Aureng-Zebe battles his brothers out of filial duty and love for Indamora. The Indian lord Solyman reveals these additional motives for Aureng-Zebe:

> Two vast rewards may well his courage move:
> A parent's blessing and a mistress' love.
> If he succeed, his recompense, we hear,
> Must be the captive queen of Cassimere. (Dryden 1667, I.110–113)

While most Carolean viewers of *Aureng-Zebe* had never personally been in the position of competing for a throne, romantic love and the desire for parental favor were common emotions. Dryden therefore changes the Mughal ruler's motives from Bernier's assessment, a "raging passion for sovereignty," to the more sympathetic and identifiable ones of love and filial duty.

Another Restoration convention that Dryden employs to sway public opinion in Aureng-Zebe's favor is that of the younger lover competing for a woman against an elderly suitor. In this case, the rival is Aureng-Zebe's own father, Shah Jahan, who has lived "seventy winters" (Dryden 1667, I.27). In the speech quoted earlier by Solyman, we learn of a contract between Shah

Jahan and his son; if Aureng-Zebe fights on his father's behalf, the "captive queen of Cassimere," Indamora, will be the reward. Aureng-Zebe honorably upholds his end of the bargain, but Shah Jahan violates the contract, as Indamora angrily points out to him in the following lines:

> Yes, in a father's hand whom he [Aureng-Zebe] has served,
> And with the hazard of his life preserved
> But piety to you, unhappy prince,
> Becomes a crime, and duty an offense. (Dryden 1667, II.187–190)

By reneging on his agreement with his son, Shah Jahan vilifies himself and makes Aureng-Zebe look heroic in contrast. Shah Jahan further increases audience sympathy for Aureng-Zebe when the aging emperor tyrannically proclaims: "My son by my command his course must steer; / I bade him love, I bid him now forbear" (II.177–78). Indamora understandably expresses her dismay when the seventy-year-old Shah Jahan announces that he will take the place of his son as her lover:

> Was't not enough you took my crown away,
> But cruelly you must my love [Aureng-Zebe] betray?
> I was well pleased to have transferred my right,
> And better changed your claim of lawless might
> By taking him whom you esteemed above
> Your other sons, and taught me first to love. (Dryden 1667, II.171–76)

As this passage suggests, Shah Jahan arbitrarily revokes an arrangement that Indamora was "well pleased" with, and she also draws attention to the unjust manner in which she became the "captive queen of Cassimere." Shah Jahan becomes one of the main hostage-takers and aggressors in the play, which is a role that Aurangzeb plays in Bernier's narrative. By assuming the elderly blocking-figure role who temporarily prevents two younger lovers from uniting, Shah Jahan would have been a recognizable stock villain to Restoration audiences. Dryden invents the character of Indamora and Aureng-Zebe's struggles as a younger lover competing against his seventy-year-old father. Consequently, Dryden's Aureng-Zebe would have been far more palatable to English theatergoers than the same figure in Bernier's version.

Like Indamora, Aureng-Zebe displays his confusion and disappointment at the sudden change that comes over Shah Jahan. Although Aureng-Zebe expects a hero's welcome for his part in defending his father's realm, the titular character instead receives a frosty reception. Because Shah Jahan courts Aureng-Zebe's promised bride while he is off fighting on his father's behalf, the aging emperor guiltily responds to his son's triumphant return:

> Turn the discourse; I have a reason why
> I would not have you speak so tenderly.
> Knew you what shame your kind expressions bring,
> You would in pity spare a wretched king. (Dryden 1667, I.302–305)

Aureng-Zebe expresses his bafflement at this treatment when he says:

> A king! You rob me, sir, of half my due;
> You have a dearer name,—a father too. . . .
> What have I said or done,
> That I no longer must be called your son?
> 'Tis in that name, Heaven knows, that I glory more,
> Than that of prince, or that of conqueror. (Dryden 1667, I.i.306–10)

Filial loyalty is indeed part of the rhetoric of Bernier's Aurangzeb, who expressed "duty and submission" to his father and "acknowledged the duty of implicit obedience to his father's commands" (Bernier 1968, 21, 166). Yet Bernier points out the irony of these statements since they were made while Aurangzeb had Shah Jahan imprisoned at Agra, and the French surgeon leaves no doubt about the future emperor's motives:

> The Prince . . . was reserved, subtle, and a complete master of the art of dissimulation. When in his father's court, he feigned a devotion which he never felt, and affected contempt for worldly grandeur while clandestinely endeavouring to pave the way to future elevation. (1968, 10)

Whereas Bernier draws attention to the discrepancy between Aurangzeb's words and true intentions, however, Dryden presents them as genuine sentiments and eliminates the part of the narrative in which Aurangzeb puts his father under house arrest. No characters, other than Shah Jahan whose motives are explicitly stated as jealousy over Indamora, contradict Aureng-Zebe's assertions of devotion to his father in the play.

CONSTRUCTING SHARED VALUES BETWEEN AURANGZEB AND CHARLES II

Because Aurangzeb was of royal blood and restored order to a country torn apart by civil wars,[9] his resemblance to Charles II would have seemed natural to English men and women in the latter half of the seventeenth century. In fact, Dryden sets his play in 1660, the year that Charles II returned to England to claim his throne, rather than 1658, the year that Aurangzeb became emperor. Maurer argues that Dryden deliberately changed the date of his play from

1658 to 1660 in order to reinforce the connection between Aurangzeb and Charles II (2005, 170). Dryden may also follow Bernier's lead since he says:

> In this manner terminated the war which the lust of domination had kindled among these four brothers. It lasted between five and six years; that is to say, from about the year 1655 to the year 1660 or 1661; and it left *Aureng-Zebe* the undisputed master of this mighty Empire. (Bernier 1968, 115)

This passage implies that Aurangzeb was not the "undisputed master" or monarch of the Mughal Empire until 1660 or 1661 so Dryden most likely reproduced Bernier's date. Nevertheless, the temporal proximity of the beginning of Aurangzeb's and Charles II's respective reigns would not have escaped the notice of Dryden, his king, or Restoration theatergoers. With these similarities in place, Dryden had to use caution when depicting the Mughal ruler since any negative characteristics would likely be projected onto Charles II by extension. By cleansing Aurangzeb of most of the ethical taint that he acquired during his rise to power, Dryden turned the Mughal emperor into an acceptable surrogate for the reigning English sovereign. In other words, Dryden enabled two vastly different rulers to appear to be equals. The number of people under the control of these two respective monarchs gives a sense of the stretch Dryden made to give them even a semblance of equality. Although 100 million of the 140 million people in the Indian subcontinent lived within Mughal territory in the 1600 population estimate I listed by Keay in this monograph's introduction, that number would have been far closer to 140 million by 1675 since Aurangzeb ruled over much more territory than his predecessors (whereas England's population did not grow much beyond the five million people it had at the beginning of the seventeenth century). With a population of close to 140 million people, Aurangzeb could and did assemble armies of astounding proportions.

Dryden's decision to add Bernier's phrase "the Great Mogul" as an alternate title to *Aureng-Zebe* reveals the English playwright's attitude toward this ruler before the play even begins (Bernier 1968, 1). The *OED* cites Dryden as one of the first writers to use the word "mogul" in the sense of "An important, influential, or dominant person; an autocrat" ("Mogul"). Dryden's "autocrat[ic]" notion of "mogul" emperors came from Bernier, who states:

> as the land throughout the whole empire is considered the property of the sovereign, there can be no earldoms, marquisates or duchies. The royal grants consist only of pensions, either in land or money, which the king gives, augments, retrenches or takes away at pleasure. (5)

With no permanent hereditary "earldoms," "marquisates," "duchies," or other confident nobles who could contest the power of a Mughal emperor, Aurangzeb had an autocratic government, which meant that the civil wars with his brothers were for absolute authority. However, John Keay argues that this notion of Mughal emperors, while widespread among seventeenth-century Europeans, was not entirely accurate: "Bernier thought the problem lay in the absence of individual property rights. Like most Europeans he mistook revenue rights for outright ownership and so considered the king, as the bestower of these rights, to be the 'sole proprietor of the land'" (Keay 2000, 322). In other words, although Aurangzeb was in fact very powerful, Dryden believed, after reading Bernier's narrative, that the Mughal emperor had even more control over India than he did. Dryden's "Great Mogul" is therefore synonymous with absolute power.

In the 1670s, the European sovereign who bore the closest resemblance to a "Great Mogul" or autocrat was Louis XIV, not Charles II. Even by European standards, Charles II was not a powerful or widely respected king. The Earl of Rochester depicted Charles II as a monarch ruled by his mistresses and nearly impotent, as the following lines from "On King Charles" reveal:

> His scepter and his Prick are of a Length;
> And she may sway the one, who plays with th' other. . . .
> This you'd believe had I but Time to tell you
> The Pains it Costs the poor laborious Nelly
> Whilst she employs, hands, fingers, mouth, and thighs
> Ere she can raise the Member she enjoys. (Wilmot lines 9–10, 26–29)

Charles II did little to dispel the notion that he was more interested in women than government since he appeared publicly with his mistresses. The king's relative impotence, or, more importantly, his poverty would have been especially noticeable to contemporaries because the monarch had the misfortune to reign at the same time as the "Sun King," Louis XIV, whose name was equated with nearly absolute power and, in England, tyranny. During the Dutch War (1672–79), Louis XIV had, according to Peter H. Wilson, "the largest army in Europe since the Roman Empire," a force of 270,000 men (144). Even with this impressive land force, Louis XIV's lack of a concomitant navy led to his inability to defeat the Netherlands. Charles II, in contrast, was "penniless" at this time and had a meager force of 30,000 men that both Louis XIV and Parliament were constantly pressuring the king of England to disband (Coote 2000, 302).

In the dedication of *Aureng-Zebe*, Dryden shrewdly conceals Charles II's weakness by emphasizing his merciful nature, respect for his subjects' rights, and desire to stay within the boundaries of English law. Dryden begins the dedication by paraphrasing Montaigne's "severe reflection" on "princes," which states "that we ought not, in reason, to have any expectations of favour from them; and that it is kindness enough, if they leave us in possession of our own" (3). Yet Dryden immediately voices his disagreement with Montaigne's assertion when it pertains to Charles II: "subjects of England may justly congratulate to themselves, that both the nature of our government, and the clemency of our king, secure us from any such complaint" (Dryden 1667, 3). Although Dryden makes Charles II's "clemency" and respect for the "nature of [England's] government" appear to be voluntary, the reality was that the king had little choice.

By beheading Charles II's father in 1649, English men and women made it clear that the divine right of kings no longer protected monarchs even in theory. Because of this action, Charles II knew he had to tread carefully with the English people in order to avoid the same fate that his father met. Consequently, he began courting their favor prior to his return to England in 1660 by issuing a proclamation assuring his supporters that he recognized the Magna Carta as a legitimate document that established boundaries on his power. In a pamphlet written in Brussels, published in Antwerp, and distributed in London in 1659, Charles II promised his potential subjects that they would not "be burdened with Taxes," forced to swear "Oaths," "debarred of their Liberties," or "questioned for their lives or Estates, for any cause or pretence whatsoever, but by the ancient and known Laws of the Land, according to the *Magna Charta*" ("By the King's Most"). When Charles II's first Parliament met in 1660, they ratified even more of the Magna Carta's principles (Turner 2003, 162). With the specter of his executed father constantly in the back of his mind, and restrictions on his power by law, Parliament, powerful hereditary nobles, and vigilant English men and women, attempts by Charles II to seize or exercise absolute power would have been suicidal.

Although Charles II was careful not to upset the delicate balance of power that allowed him to rule England, he devised a series of morbid, small-scale theatrical displays designed to deter would-be regicides. According to Stephen Coote, Charles II had "the corpses of Cromwell and two other leading Parliamentarians dug up and displayed" (2000, 183). The English king also imprisoned some of the men who conspired to oust his father from the throne and had them paraded through London annually to suffer the jeers of the crowds who gathered to watch the spectacle. Men who Charles II said were "the immediate murderers of [his] father" were hung or drawn and quartered (Coote 2000, 183). The way that the sovereign justified his punishments is worth noting since he created the public persona of a devoted son avenging the death of his father rather than a king attempting to secure his position and prevent a similar fate from happening to himself. Dryden incorporates this image of Charles II into *Aureng-Zebe* when Arimant says that Aureng-Zebe, and by extension Charles II, possesses the "greatest" virtue, being a "loyal son." Arimant continues his speech by emphasizing Aureng-Zebe's commitment to the principles of hereditary succession: "His father's cause upon his sword he wears" (Dryden 1667, I.i.108). This passage suggests that the primary motive for Aureng-Zebe's decision to risk his own life in battle was a sense of duty toward Shah Jahan, and the titular hero reinforces this idea when he asks, "Why did my arms in battle prosperous prove, / To gain the barren praise of filial love?" (I.i.348–9). By making filial loyalty the epitome of virtue and comparing Charles II to a character who personally fought battles on his father's behalf in *Aureng-Zebe*, Dryden magnifies the reigning English sovereign's dramatic gestures of devotion to Charles I to epic proportions.

Another of Aureng-Zebe's "virtues" that appears on numerous occasions in the dedication and the play itself is constancy.[10] Dryden commends the Earl of Mulgrave for

> firmness in all [his] actions. . . . A prince, who is constant to himself, and steady in his undertakings. . . . such an one cannot but place an esteem, and repose a confidence in him, whom no adversity, no change of courts, no bribery of interests, or cabals of factions, or advantages of fortune, can remove from the solid foundations of honour and fidelity. (Dryden 1667, 6)

The phrase "no change of courts," concealed within the list of temptations to waiver, is ironic considering the fact that Dryden was not "constant" to the Stuart cause throughout the interregnum. In 1659, Dryden published "Heroic Stanzas to the Glorious Memory of Cromwell," which was also printed in a short anthology of elegies with poems by Edmund Waller and Thomas Sprat. The last four lines of Dryden's contribution echo and sum up the reverent tone of the entire poem:

> His Ashes in a Peaceful Urn shall rest,
> His Name a great Example stands to show,
> How strangely high Endeavours may be bless'd,
> Where Piety and Valour jointly go. (*Works* lines 145–8)

The fact that he had, like many others, publicly backed the losing party must have been an embarrassment for Dryden, and a couplet from the play spoken by Indamora is especially important in this context. After hesitating to commit suicide when she hears false reports of Aureng-Zebe's death, Indamora says, "Not that I valued life, but feared to die: / Think that my weakness, not inconstancy" (Dryden 1667, V.i.517–18). Indamora's apologetic tone for once failing to demonstrate extreme "constancy" to a future king reflects

Dryden's professed attitude toward Charles II. By writing *Aureng-Zebe* and many other literary works promoting the Stuart cause, Dryden hoped to prove that his "constancy" to the royalist cause was now firmly cemented into place.

Dryden's desire to praise Charles II is transparent in the dedication of the play to the Earl of Mulgrave when Dryden claims he "subsist[s] wholely by his [Charles II's] Bounty" (3). This passage gives a sense of Dryden's indebtedness and dependence on the continued favor of the reigning monarch. In his offices of Poet Laureate (1668–1688) and Historiographer Royal (1670–1688), Dryden was granted a modest pension of £200 per year (Barnard 2004, 207). There are also records of occasional payments for individual works from the royal treasury, such as *Absalom and Achitophel* (1681) and *The Medal* (1682). Although Dryden attempted to gain financial support from other patrons in addition to his pensions from Charles II in the 1670s, such as the Earl of Rochester and Sir Charles Sedley, these efforts largely backfired (Barnard 207–08). With his livelihood dependent, in part, upon Charles II's good will, Dryden produced plays that were predominately designed to ingratiate himself and prolong his royal appointments. Approximately one year before the first performance of *Aureng-Zebe*, news of the Earl of Rochester's banishment from court because of his poem "On Charles II" was widespread. Although Rochester returned to Parliament in February of 1674, and was on better terms with the king by then, the incident would have had clear implications for Dryden; if an earl who was a close friend of Charles II[11] could be banished for a poetic rendition that displeased the monarch, Dryden, who was neither a member of the nobility nor a drinking buddy, was even more vulnerable (Johnson 2004, 182). Dryden would therefore have been especially careful not to incur Charles II's wrath by repeating Rochester's mistake.

There was no shortage of courtiers who would gladly snatch Dryden's titles of Poet Laureate and Historiographer Royal, and more importantly the pensions that went with them, if he fell from the king's favor, and Dryden was well aware of that fact. In the dedication to *Aureng-Zebe*, Dryden laments the abundance of non-witty courtiers "in every court," describing them as the "mud and filth" that encompass "castles," "greatness," or kings (1667, 3). Although Dryden valued wit, he makes it clear that it was not preferable to money later in the dedication:

> As I am no successor to Homer in his wit, so neither do I desire to be in his poverty. I can make no rhapsodies, nor go a-begging at the Grecian doors, while I sing the praises of their ancestors. The times of Virgil please me better, for he had an Augustus for his patron. (Dryden 1667, 9–10)

Because Charles II served as one of Dryden's main "Augustus[es]" or patrons and the Poet Laureate states explicitly that he had no "desire" for "poverty," it makes sense that Dryden would not, like the Earl of Rochester, risk a position at court for the sake of "wit" or even truth.

Attempts by Dryden to denigrate India would have been counterproductive to Charles II's interests, and therefore Dryden's own, since India supplied England with profitable spices and a number of other trade goods. In 1674, a statement issued by the EIC listed the amount of goods re-exported abroad at twice the value of the bullion sent to India (Lipson 1934, 2: 281). The EIC also leased Bombay from Charles II in 1668 for £10 per year, which he was very relieved to be rid of. It was approximately twenty square miles of mostly water, caused seven years of expense for Charles, and carried an obligation to protect Portugal's Indian settlements that he could not meet. As mentioned in the previous chapter, the directors of the EIC gave £3,000 of silver plate to Charles in 1660, loaned him £10,000 in 1662, and approved at least £150,000 in loans during his reign (Keay 1994, 131). Thus India and the EIC provided a vital source of income for Charles II, who in turn funded Dryden's court appointments. Dryden depicts India as a wealthy and now stable empire that shares the same fundamental values as England and therefore possesses the same desire for trade.

CONCLUSION

By revealing the financial and informational links between Aurangzeb, the EIC, Charles II, and Dryden, I hope to contribute to the growing body of historicizing work on the play that supplements insightful close readings by critics such as Hughes.[12] Charles II's special interest in *Aureng-Zebe* likely at least partially accounts for the dramatic whitewashing of the Mughal ruler depicted in Bernier's *Travels*. Yet the play also reflects signs of slippage; Dryden manages to insert his trademark critiques of the love and honor ideal by making the titular character jealous and excessively passionate about Indamora.

NOTES

1. See, for instance, Hughes (2004, 2: 92) and Guibbory (1973, 190). I retain Dryden's spelling, "Aureng-Zebe," when I discuss the titular character. For the actual historical figure, I use the most common typographical variant of the name, "Aurangzeb."

2. For a study of the Job analogy in the eighteenth century, see Lamb.

3. In the dedication of *Aureng-Zebe*, Dryden explicitly conveys his desire to "do honor" to his "king" and "country" by writing a heroic poem about either King Arthur or Edward, the Black Prince (1667, 9). I argue that this sentiment characterizes Dryden's aims in *Aureng-Zebe* as well.

4. In order to show the extent to which the EIC depended upon Aurangzeb's favor, I have compiled the most comprehensive list to date of the company's factories from 1600 to 1674, both within and outside of Mughal territory. For some of these factories, at least five variant spellings exist since English was not standardized yet and the names came from or passed between Hindi, Persian, Portuguese, Dutch, Italian, and French. A few of these names, such as "Petapoli" (a.k.a. "Nizampatnam"), are not even remotely similar phonetically. I have cross-referenced at least a dozen sources to ensure that none of these factory names refer to the same place. All parenthetical dates that follow refer to the foundation of the respective trading posts, and I have placed an asterisk (*) next to the names of the twenty-one factories that were within the Mughal Empire during Aurangzeb's reign. Before the initial performance of *Aureng-Zebe* in 1675, the EIC's servants had set up at least fifty factories, some far more profitable and long-lasting than others, at Bantam (1602), Masulipatam* (1611), Surat* (1612), Priaman (c. 1612), Socodania (c. 1613), Achen (1613); Cambello on Ambon Island (1615); Before 1616: Jambe, Tecoo, Ferando on the Japanese island of Hirado, Japar, the Banda Islands, Macasser, Petapoli,* Patania, Beniarmasse, Jacatra, Agra,* Azmiro,* Brampore*; Calecut (1616), Cranganore (1616), Broach* (1616); Before 1617: Shiraz, Ayuthia, Udong, Baria; Polaroon (c. 1617–18), Rosengin (c. 1617–18), Ahmadābād (by 1618), Jask (1619), Patna* (c. 1620), Hariharpur* (1634), Pippli* (1635), Tatta* (1639), Madras* (1640), Basra (1640), Balasore* (1642), Hugli* (1651), Isfahan (before 1652), Kasimbazar* (1658), Bombay (1661); Before 1661: Gombroon, Mokha, Karwar,* Kayal*; Dacca* (1666), Baliapatam* (1669), Rhajapur* (1670), and Dharangaon* (1674). I put together this list by consulting the following sources: Furber (1976) 41, 68–69, 73–74; Foster (1906) v, 191–92; Fawcett (1936) 1: xix; *Encyclopaedia* (1911) "Cranganor," "Calecut," "Surat," "Cambello," "Masulipatam," "Kasimbazar," "Pippli," "Balasore," "Madras," "Dacca"; Carré (1947) 152, 156; Manucci (1913) 23; Chaudhuri (1978) 42, 47, 49; Mill (1826) 1: 38; Chaudhuri, *English* frontispiece (1965); Keay (1994) 314.

5. Although Bernier's stated "object" was not to "supply subjects for romance," his word choices nonetheless imply, as Bridget Orr points out, that Mughal history could be represented in theatrical terms (1968, 16). In *Oroonoko*, Behn adopts this type of rhetoric for a work that is largely fictional:

> I do not pretend, in giving you the history of the royal slave, to entertain my reader with the adventures of a feigned hero, whose life and fortunes fancy may manage at the poet's pleasure; nor in relating the truth, design to adorn it with any accidents, but such as arrived in earnest to him. And it shall come simply into the world, recommended by its own proper merits, and natural intrigues; there being enough of reality to support it, and to render it diverting, without the addition of invention. (Behn 1688, 75)

In the preface to *Robinson Crusoe*, which is not paginated, Defoe, posing as the editor, makes a similar claim for his work: "The Editor believes the thing to be a just History of Fact; neither is there any Appearance of Fiction in it."

6. Dryden himself makes this distinction between history and poetic license in the dedication of *The Indian Emperor*: "In it I have neither wholly follow'd the truth of the History, nor altogether left it: but have taken all the liberty of a Poet, to adde, alter, or diminish, as I thought might best conduce to the beautifying of my work; it being not the business of a Poet to represent Historical truth, but probability" (Dryden 1667, 25).

7. This summary comes from the following pages of Bernier's work: 5, 10, 20–21, 46, 56, 66, 68–9, 72, 80, 83, 87, 92, 98, 100, 103, 105, 108, 114–15. For additional changes that Dryden makes to Bernier's narrative, see Ballaster, 2005, 279.

8. Richard Braverman describes this character as "the Machiavel" of the play (132). Dryden's identification with Morat could therefore represent political shrewdness in addition to dissatisfaction.

9. In Delhi in September of 1657, the reigning Mughal emperor Shah Jahan was gravely ill. Rumors of his impending demise instigated a series of battles between his four sons (Dara Shikoh, Aurangzeb, Shuja, and Murad Baksh) for the crown of India (Keay, *India* 339).

10. Examples of the word "constant" or allusions to the concept can be found, for instance, on pages 6 and 11 of the Dedicatory Epistle and the following lines in the play: I.i.102–3, III.i.68–9, and V.i.517–18.

11. Charles II was also one of the godfathers of Wilmot's son (Johnson 2004, 136).

12. Examples can be found in Rajan 67, 76; Bhattacharya 52–55; Brown 69; and Orr 110. For the imperfections that Dryden builds into Aureng-Zebe's character, see Hughes (*Dryden's* 127–28).

Chapter 5

British Men of Feeling on "Indians" and Wealth: Addison, Steele, and Mackenzie

> What great advantage was I of to Mr. *Dryden* in his *Indian Emperor*, "*You force me still to answer You in* That, / to furnish out a Rhime to *Morat*?" (Richard Steele, *Spectator* No. 80, 1711)

As this quotation from Steele shows, he could, like Laura Brown, group Dryden's "Indian" plays together (the lines allegedly from *The Indian Emperor* are actually from *Aureng-Zebe*). Yet Steele's *Spectator* No. 11, first published on Tuesday, March 13, 1711, and better known as the story of Inkle and Yarico,[1] reveals that the author was highly aware of the distinctive features of West "Indians" and their power relations with Europeans. Steele, like his primary source, Richard Ligon's *A True and Exact History of the Island of Barbados* (1657), depicts a scenario in which an Englishman sells an Amerindian noblewoman into slavery without the knowledge or consent of the indigenous sovereign. As I have shown in previous chapters, the English carefully cultivated the goodwill of the Mughal rulers in India so the abduction and sale of a member of the Islamic aristocracy by a merchant would have been unthinkable.

In this chapter, I analyze three authors who exemplify the Age of Sentiment to show how ideas about "Indians" and trade manifest themselves over the course of the eighteenth century. Although the protagonists of works by Addison, Steele, and Mackenzie all overtly subscribe to ideals of sentimental cosmopolitanism and identify with "Indians," each of these characters also seek to profit from the indigenes of non-European countries. I begin with Richard Steele's version of the Inkle and Yarico story in *The Spectator* (1711). Critical discussions of Inkle and Yarico simplify Steele's treatment of skin color, gender, and class. Kathryn Shevelow, for instance, argues that Yarico looks "very much like the virtuous and domestic English middle class wife" (1989, 144). Yet the animal physiognomy of the epigraph of this narrative, "He pardons the ravens and crucifies the doves," when read in context, partially refutes Shevelow. Skin color was not completely irrelevant to English authors, an important qualification of my general thesis, but it played a less prominent role in assessments of "Indians" than questions of religion and money. Aside from the originally untranslated Latin epigraph, the story of Inkle and Yarico makes few references to skin color. Inkle's moral behavior and the possibility of making money in the Americas, in contrast, factor prominently. Like Behn, Steele had a personal connection to the West Indies. In addition to owning a Barbadian plantation, Steele had access to Richard Ligon's *True and Exact History of the Island of Barbados* (1657), the first version of the Inkle and Yarico tale. Steele is typical of his age in that he pities an individual slave without attempting to undermine the institution of slavery itself. On his Barbadian plantation, Steele had slaves of color working alongside white indentured servants, which shows that class also played an important role in eighteenth-century labor distribution (Blanchard 1942, 283). In the next section, I argue that Joseph Addison, like his *Spectator* coauthor Steele, was preoccupied with trade and at least the semblance of international goodwill. I base this contention on Addison's essay on the Royal Exchange (No. 69) in *The Spectator*. The chapter concludes with a discussion of Mackenzie's *The Man of Feeling* where I make the case that Edwards' pity toward an East Indian (and simultaneous desire to profit from him) mirrors Dryden's and Steele's attitudes toward West "Indians." Mackenzie's novel therefore reflects the conflation of East and West "Indians" that became possible only after Clive's victory at the Battle of Plassey in 1757.

INKLE AND YARICO

The Inkle and Yarico tale is certainly full of ambivalent material for New Historicist, postcolonial, and feminist critics to sift through, which makes sense when one considers the author's complex background. Steele was a perpetually debt-ridden, Oxford-educated, Whiggish Irishman writing to and desperately needing to sell his work to both sexes of a predominately English audience in the midst of Whig and Tory struggles to gain power during the final years of Queen Anne's reign (Winton 1964, 34, 107, 131). By tying close readings to the historical and personal contexts in which Steele wrote, this chapter will attempt to provide a more complex picture of the ideological forces at work in *Spectator* No. 11 than scholars have offered to date. In general, critical discussions of Steele's essay tend to fit the story of Inkle and Yarico into oversimplified categories of gender, race, and class. The epigraph of this story ("He pardons the ravens and crucifies the doves"), when applied in context, refutes the idea that Steele completely homogenizes

Yarico sexually and racially; at the same time, however, the Latin phrase turns out to be a virtually impenetrable class barrier and its problematic traditional imagery undermines much of Steele's egalitarian message.

When attempting to clarify who the target audience for Steele's *Spectator* No. 11 was, and the extent to which it was a politically progressive text in terms of social class, gender, and race, one can begin by examining the type of knowledge the tale presupposes. At least some of Steele's readers did not understand the classical allusions and their relevance to the story at hand, and education traditionally served as both a marker of social status and a gateway to it. Two of the primary ways someone might have become acquainted with the classics in the late seventeenth and early eighteenth centuries would have been to have a tutor, which generally implied an aristocratic upbringing, or to attend a "public" school and then University. Women, of course, were still centuries away from admittance to Oxford. While public schools in England such as Charterhouse, the one Steele attended, were ostensibly founded, in the words of seventeenth-century author Samuel Herne, "for the relief of poor men," admittance sometimes depended on political connections more than charity (qtd. in Winton 1964, 20). Herne goes on to say that "The way to obtain a place for a young lad" in one of these schools was "to make an address to any single governor the person ha[d] most interest in, by way of friends, petition, or any other method of application" (Winton 1964, 20). It seems that Herne had good reason to suspect the political nature of admittance to such schools since Steele's own registration in the Charterhouse reads as follows: "Richard Steele admitted *for* the Duke of Ormond, in the room of Phillip Burrell—aged 13 years 12th March next" (Emphasis added, Winton 1964, 20). The fact that Steele was admitted "for the Duke of Ormond," his uncle Henry Gascoigne's employer, leaves little doubt as to who was pulling the strings behind Steele's education. In Steele's later development as an Oxford student, he explicitly asked Gascoigne to use his connections, as the following letter reveals: "the election of students is not very far off now; if you would be pleased to speak with him[2] or purchace from my Lord[3] a word or two; it would perhaps get me the most Creditable preferment for young men in the whole university" (Steele 1690, 7). As this passage demonstrates, "preferment" within the hierarchical social structure of the University depended to some extent, in Steele's and most of his readers' minds, on connections with "Lord[s]" and other powerful figures.

In 1711, the year Steele published Inkle and Yarico, the people most likely to catch Steele's allusions to Greco-Roman literature, which was predominately by, for, and about men, would therefore have been males with influential social connections. On a broad level, Norman Simms discusses this patriarchal legacy by saying that Steele's decision to allude to but not to retell the story of the Ephesian Matron presupposes a certain audience:

"To know the story is to be well-educated, to be part of the patriarchal order which underlies classical education and its institutions, and thus to be at least tacitly complicit in the hatred of women which is at the core of the tradition" (Simms 1996, 94). While Simms correctly points out that knowing this story and being "well-educated" often meant exposure to a tradition that favored men, his claim that such exposure necessarily tainted its pupils by rendering them "tacitly complicit in the hatred of women" is perhaps an overstatement. After all, Steele's decision to add the Ephesian Matron story as a parallel to Ligon's tale overtly problematizes classical gender depictions by setting up a dialogue between this story and its predecessors.

Steele implicitly criticizes the depiction of women in the Ephesian Matron narrative and offers a positive alternative through his reworking of Ligon's story. In all likelihood, Steele was aware of Roman attitudes toward funereal rites since his epigraph in *Spectator* No. 11 also comes from Juvenal's *Satires* (1965 translation, 2.63). Indeed, Steele directly incorporates this belief into his own tale but reverses it by giving Inkle the power to condemn Yarico to a secular hell, slavery, which he chooses to do for the transitory satisfaction not of sex, but money. Moreover, like Petronius, Steele prefaces his Inkle and Yarico tale with a comparison between old stories and new ones, but by 1711 the Ephesian Matron had become the "instance . . . from ancient traged[y]" that would be mentioned but not recited. Instead, Steele chooses a roughly contemporary account, with his own modifications of course, Richard Ligon's *True and Exact History of the Island of Barbados* (1657). However, the narrator Arietta in Steele's version of the story makes it clear that unlike Petronius' "inventions," her adaptation of Ligon consists of "Facts from plain People" who "have not either Ambition or Capacity to embellish their Narrations with any Beauties of Imagination" (Steele 1690, 35). Steele's emphasis on the truth of this tale as opposed to the fictional nature of Petronius' story might have been based on a genuine belief in Ligon's presentation of his own account as factual. However, with Steele's extensive knowledge of the classics, it seems unlikely that he would miss the story's uncanny resemblance to an episode in Virgil's *Aeneid*. In both cases, a traveler in a hostile land (Inkle/Aeneas) receives aid from a prestigious female native (Yarico/Dido) and then spends time with her in a cave before eventually abandoning her.[4] Regardless of whether Steele suspected the truth of this tale or not, his use of the Ephesian matron story implies that in old fictional stories written by men, women may have had unbridled sexual appetites, but not in contemporary accounts that have any semblance of truth.

In Ligon's account, in contrast, the framing device around the story is a semipornographic anthropological voyage narrative that represents West "Indian" women in Barbados as a cross between sexualized objects and exotic beasts. For instance, Ligon first introduces the Yarico figure, who remains nameless, as an example of Amerindian women who refuse to wear clothing like *civilized* peoples: "We had an Indian woman, a slave in the house, who was of excellent shape and colour, for it was a pure bright bay; small brests, with the nipls of a porphyrie colour, this woman would not be woo'd by any means to weare Cloaths" (Ligon 1657, 54). Ligon's elaborate description of this woman turns her into a sex object, a collection of body parts. In addition to this sexual objectification, Ligon emphasizes the woman's otherness by telling the story of how she went alone into a wood, gave birth to a child not from the Inkle figure but from a "Christian servant," and came back three hours later (54–55). Had Steele kept this part of the story, his readers would probably have had trouble identifying with this woman. After all, in *Moll Flanders*, published eleven years after *Spectator* No. 11, all three options or "bills" that the Midwife presents to the protagonist for her "Lying-Inn" involve "Three Months Lodging," "a Nurse for the Month," "Linnen" bedding material, and Christening fees (Defoe 1722, 223–24). For Englishwomen who were not among the lowest rungs of the laboring classes, birthing was an elaborate "Three Month" process and for West "Indian" women, in Ligon's account, it took a mere "three hours" alone in a wood.

It was in attempting to turn the Amerindian woman in Barbados from a mere spectacle or object of sexual desire, as Ligon depicts her, into a human being, then, that Steele introduced and counterbalanced the Ephesian Matron story, which represented another related problematic portrayal of women. Like Ligon's version of the Inkle and Yarico narrative, the Ephesian Matron story emphasizes the woman's sexuality. Rather than lasciviously cataloging and gawking at her body parts, though, the narrator ridicules her complete inability to curb her sexual appetite. Indeed, Eumolpus, the narrator of the tale in Petronius' version, tells the story as an example of "the inconstancy of women" and will not "bring instances from ancient tragedies, or personages notorious to antiquity." Eumolpus vows instead to relate a "story within the circle of his own memory" (Petronius 1999 reprint, 290). Interestingly enough, Eumolpus lumps "ancient tragedies," which would today be considered literature (i.e., fictional), into the same category as "personages notorious to antiquity," which sounds more like a modern conception of history (i.e., truthful accounts of real people). The main contrast, then, is not between the true and the false, but between the very old and the roughly contemporary. In other words, the preface to Petronius' tale attempts to establish the idea that the "inconstancy of women" was not merely a problem of the past (Eumolpus' allusion to feminine frailty in antiquity implies that he could give numerous instances of it from then as well) but ongoing and universal. The Ephesian Matron was reputed to be "the only true example of love and chastity" because of her elaborate and self-mortifying grieving over her husband (291). Yet, within the span of a few days, this supposed paradigm of fidelity ceased her lamentations and "receiv'd" the "embraces" of a soldier, "Not only that night they struck up the bargain, but the next and the next night after" (292). As this passage reveals, Eumolpus emphasizes that this transgression was repeated often and that it was not simply a moment of feminine weakness.

Meanwhile, someone buries the body of a crucified criminal the soldier was supposed to be guarding. Because he would face punishment if his negligence were detected, the Ephesian Matron offers the body of her dead husband to fill the place of the missing corpse. In addition to suggesting the interchangeability of male lovers, this story would have been particularly unsettling in the period that Petronius and Juvenal wrote in (c. the first and second century C.E.) because of Roman beliefs in the relationship between the rites and treatment of a corpse and its departed soul's ability to enter the underworld, as the following passage from the third of Juvenal's *Satires* reveals:

> Who'd know the people's bodies dashed to bones?
> Like souls, the poor crushed limbs would disappear. . . .
> And while they work, the deadworld's new arrivals
> shudder to see a deadly river's slick.
> Their lips lack copper for
> boatfare and hope of that all-soothing bank. (1965 translation, 259–60, 264–67)

In other words, losing the physical parts of the body is tantamount to losing the soul and the fact that the dead man has no coin in his mouth to pay Charon the ferryman for passage to the underworld means that the former is stuck. Because of her inability to control her sexual desires, then, the Ephesian Matron has perhaps doomed her dead husband's soul to eternal unrest. Crucifixion, after all, was a particularly dishonorable form of capital punishment in Rome that was often followed by mutilation of the corpse or by exposing it to the elements and wild animals. The primary rhetorical technique that Petronius employs to convince readers of female infidelity, then, is hyperbole; the Ephesian Matron, who is initially a paragon of virtue and faithfulness to her husband's memory, cannot resist having sex with another man for the mere span of a few days, even when it means condemning her husband's soul. If this especially fortuitous woman cannot curb her sexual appetite under such dire conditions, then the rest of the feminine world stands almost no chance whatsoever of maintaining female virtue.

Some women understandably found this mean-spirited attack on their sex offensive. Delarivière Manley, for instance, recorded the following reaction to the story in her 1710 *Memoirs of Europe*: "Can anything be more unnatural than a beautiful Lady . . . just expiring thro' Grief and Abstinence, tempted to dishonour herself . . . [with] a despicable common sentinel! . . . Petronius's

Designs were doubtless to expose the Frailty of the Sex" (qtd. in Felsenstein 1999, 289). A brief sampling of Manley's word choices here, "unnatural," "dishonour," "despicable," leaves little doubt of her unfavorable response to the tale as a depiction of her sex. On a purely practical level, Steele needs to tread lightly when introducing this story if he hopes to retain female subscribers, which he overtly states his desire to do in *Spectator* No. 4:

> In a Word, I shall take it for the greatest Glory of my Work, if among reasonable Women this Paper may furnish *Tea-Table Talk*. In order to it, I shall treat on Matters which relate to Females, as they are concerned to approach or fly from the other Sex, or as they are tied to them by Blood, Interest, or Affection. (Steele 1711, 16)

Part of this catering to "reasonable women" doubtless had to do with Steele's conception of himself as a gallant gentleman. From a more pecuniary standpoint, though, he could not afford to alienate potential subscribers because he was in debt throughout most of his life and was even briefly imprisoned for failure to pay his creditors in 1709 (Winton 1964, 106–7).

If Steele imagined women and men who subscribed to ideals of gallantry as his audience, he had some work to do if he was to include Ligon and Petronius in his periodical, though the former needed considerably less pruning. Steele's penchant for using and modifying extant literature makes sense both from the standpoint of reaffirming his credentials as an educated gentleman, and in terms of the production schedule under which he labored. In between his legal battles with his creditors and his duties as a husband, father of two, and Commissioner of the Stamp Office, Steele both co-wrote and co-edited *The Spectator*, which appeared six days a week with extensive advertising in the heated partisan struggles during the reign of Queen Anne. To give some idea of the pressure Steele was under, he once produced twenty-five papers in thirty-one days (Winton 1964, 118, 131, 133). In this politically volatile situation, stories from antiquity provided nonpartisan content, though it could be subtly twisted, and a ready body of text that needed only modification rather than time-consuming original work.

Under these trying conditions, Steele needed to produce a periodical that was ideologically moderate enough to sell to Whigs and Tories, men and women, and aristocrats and members of the laboring classes. I argue that Steele did not, by implicitly suggesting that this diverse audience should recollect or, in Norman Simms' words, make "the effort to track down the unspoken story," expose them to "the inherent structures of misogyny" in the "study of the classics" (1996, 94). Simms' insistence on the word "misogyny" is imprecise and extreme. Moreover, he uses the Ephesian Matron story from Petronius' *Satyricon* as a representative of all classical literature, when in fact it is one of the more radical examples. His argument holds considerably less weight if one uses, say, Penelope from *The Odyssey* as the embodiment of classical male attitudes toward women since she chastely awaits her husband's return for years. In actuality, Steele rails against precisely the type of generalizations based on scant evidence that Simms employs. For instance, Arietta, who appears to be one of Steele's mouthpieces in *Spectator* No. 11, says that one should not credit authors who "leave behind them Memorials of their Resentment against the Scorn of particular Women, in Invectives against the whole Sex" (Steele 1711, 35). In other words, one should not make hasty generalizations about women based on a few limited encounters or examples.

Steele shows that the reception of the classics need not be uncritical through Arietta's interpretation of one of Aesop's fables, "The Man and the Lion." Arietta cites this fable to illustrate the idea that the person who represents something has the power to manipulate its image as he or she pleases:

> The man walking with that noble animal, showed him, in the ostentation of human superiority, a sign of a man killing a lion. Upon which the lion said very justly, *We lions are none of us painters, else we could show a hundred men killed by lions, for one lion killed by a man.* You men are writers, and can represent us women as unbecoming as you please in your works, while we are unable to return the injury. (Steele 1711, 35)

In this brief allusion, Arietta reveals that one need not swallow the skewed portrayals of women that some classical authors employ. In fact, she shows how one can use other classical authors against the ones who represent women unfavorably. Rather than throwing up his hands at the "inherent structures of misogyny" in classical education, then, Steele attempts to counter one aspect of that tradition.

In order for his representation of women to be convincing, Steele had to tone down the sexuality of the Yarico figure in Ligon's narrative, which he indeed did. He cut out the lengthy descriptions of the Amerindian woman's breasts and her naked birth of a child in the woods. More importantly, the Inkle character becomes the father of her child rather than some "Christian servant" who *knew* her, in both the literal and biblical sense, before the central male character's ship ever arrived in the West "Indian" settlement. Because Ligon's account gives no temporal cues between the birthing anecdote and the Inkle and Yarico story, it does give the impression that the woman had the child of one man and then immediately "fell in love" with another one (Ligon 1657, 55). Yet, in critical discussions of *Spectator* No. 11, this monograph argues that some scholars tend to slightly exaggerate the extent to which Steele normalizes Yarico's sexuality. Daniel O'Quinn, for instance, says that

Steele's key innovation is to stage the erotic play between Inkle and Yarico according to the conventions of metropolitan courtship. This effectively incorporates the Inkle and Yarico story into contemporary constructions of femininity and heterosexuality, and in the process Yarico's racial otherness is subsumed in the constitution of gender normativity. (O'Quinn 2002, 391)

Kathryn Shevelow makes a similar claim by saying that Steele's Yarico "behaves very much like the virtuous and domestic English middle class wife whose husband's needs and comforts are her primary study" and exhibits an "Impulse toward domestication that is innately female" (1989, 144). Steele tones down Yarico's sexuality, and O'Quinn and Shevelow fit her into a paradigm of "English" femininity, but there are important parts of the story that do not fit their theory such as Yarico's ability to physically carry Inkle considerable distances. For the remainder of this section, my analysis of the epigraph will suggest the ways in which Steele retains Yarico's otherness and sexuality. The epigraph is also the truly class divisive and cumbersome bit of cultural baggage that Steele inherits rather than the Ephesian Matron allusion.

In an apparent attempt to minimize any interpretational ambiguity readers might encounter, Steele, in the guise of Mr. Spectator, provides them with a textual roadmap that manifests itself in the form of the following epigraph: "*Dat veniam corvis, vexat censura columbas*" (1711, 34). The inclusion of this phrase not only flaunts the narrator's erudition and mastery of languages, but it also assumes that readers shared his knowledge of Latin. While later editions of *The Spectator*, starting at least as early as 1864, often include English translations either alongside the epigraphs or in a footnote, they were notably absent in the original publication. From the outset of the essay, then, Mr. Spectator singles out and privileges a select group within the vast contemporaneous English audience who read the story. Put differently, one must first pass a test in order to share the thoughts and feelings of Mr. Spectator. As my next few paragraphs reveal, though, his Inkle and Yarico story implicitly asks this elite audience to overlook boundaries of gender, skin color, education, and propriety in a cosmopolitan gesture that will enable them to identify with a highly unusual heroine: a lascivious Amerindian woman who exhibits some conventionally masculine traits such as exceptional physical strength. Mr. Spectator articulates this seemingly universal message of commiseration, however, through an ethnocentric epigraph and an ideology that works on the principle of exclusion.

Let us, then, using Robert DeMaria's translation, enter into the elite textual conversation that the epigraph begins: "He pardons the ravens and crucifies the doves" (Steele 1711, 501). If one thinks about traditional Western iconography, it can safely be assumed that Mr. Spectator intends the doves rather than the ravens to elicit our sympathy. After all, the former represent peace, whiteness, and purity while the latter are black birds that have often been associated with death. These symbols depend upon a kind of animal physiognomy in which the exterior color of the bird represents something about its moral character. Yet this metaphor goes even further. The raven, by eating raw putrefying flesh, exhibits behavior that, in humans, would violate the laws of cleanliness established in the Old Testament; for instance, God purportedly told Moses that

> every soul that eateth that which died *of it self*, or that which was torn with beasts, (*whether it be* one of your own countrey, or a stranger) he shall wash his clothes, and bathe *himself in water, and be unclean until the even: then shall he be clean. But if he* wash *them* not, nor bathe his flesh; then he shall bear his iniquity. (*Holy Bible* 1695, Lev. 17.15–16)[5]

As this passage suggests, the physical act of consuming less-than-fresh flesh results in moral contamination or "iniquity." Whoever the pronoun "he" refers to in Mr. Spectator's opening epigraph, then, has perverted morality by indulging a black beast that exhibits unorthodox behavior and censuring an innocent white creature. When the chosen readers peruse the subsequent article, they therefore already know that Mr. Spectator wants them to sympathize with the dove and condemn the raven and the "he" who indulges it.

Readers must then determine the narrative's character embodiments of the epigraph's figures. One might begin by looking for a male whose evaluation of merit inverts the traditional notion that virtue should be rewarded and vice punished, in short, the "he." Perhaps the most obvious candidate for this position is the Common-Place Talker, who "repeat[s] and murder[s]" celebrated works of fiction, such as Petronius' *Satyricon*, to emphasize the "Perjuries of the Fair, and the general Levity of Women" (1999 reprint, 34). According to the Common-Place Talker and Petronius, then, women deserve censure while men, by implication, warrant indulgence. Arietta counters this accusation by claiming that Petronius "invented the pleasant Aggravations of the Frailty of the *Ephesian* Lady" (35). Arietta's use of the word "invented" casts doubt on the veracity of the story as an example of women's "Frailty." In other words, Arietta argues that the Common-Place Talker censures the doves (falsely accused women) and indulges the ravens (untruthful misogynistic men such as Petronius). Arietta then proceeds, like the Common-Place Talker, to illustrate her point with a story.

The Inkle and Yarico tale, however, appears to subvert the very epigraph that it ostensibly illustrates. According to the animal symbolism, creatures with dark exteriors and strange behaviors are evil whereas those with white covering and conventional conduct are good. Although Arietta attempts to present Yarico as the sympathetic heroine of this framed narrative, the latter's skin color immediately complicates the situation. While Yarico herself "delight[s] in the Opposition" of "Colour" between Inkle's hair and her own hand, it is not entirely clear a contemporaneous English audience would have wholeheartedly shared her sentiment (Steele 1711, 36). Some illustrations of Yarico represent this "Opposition" of "Colour" as not just darker than white but black. Arietta also radically inverts traditional gender roles; Yarico, the "Naked American," opens Inkle's "Bosome, then laugh[s] at him for covering it," brings "him a great many Spoils, which her other Lovers had presented to her," and "carr[ies] him in the Dusk of the Evening" (36). Unlike the dainty white virginal figures who abound in eighteenth-century sentimental fiction, Yarico acts as a sexual aggressor, mocks what appears to be a gesture of modesty in Inkle, and has premarital sex with him and perhaps some of her countrymen, depending on the exact meaning of "other Lovers."[6] In addition to usurping the casual attitude toward sexuality conventionally espoused by a male rake or perhaps a female character in a comedic Restoration play, Yarico appropriates roles traditionally held by men: she obtains food and earns commodities while Inkle stays "at home," she protects him from other men, and she physically carries this grown man over an apparently considerable distance. Readers could not have missed this reference since at least one illustration depicts Yarico with the muscular development of a man. Yarico therefore acts as both an exotic temptress and a mother-figure to a man who seems as helpless as a child. In other words, she is a complex amalgam of roles and not, as Shevelow and O'Quinn seem reductively to think, so "very much like the virtuous and domestic English middle class wife."

As for Inkle, he can only resume his quest toward "proper" English manhood and wealth when he renounces this doubly inappropriate relationship. In fact, it is only when he reenters "*English* territories" that he considers selling his Amerindian lover into slavery:

> Mr. *Thomas Inkle*, now coming into *English* territories, began seriously to reflect upon his loss of time, and to weigh with himself how many days interest of his money he had lost during his stay with Yarico. This thought made the young man very pensive, and careful what account he should be able to give his friends of his voyage. Upon which considerations, the prudent and frugal young man sold *Yarico* to a *Barbadian* merchant. (Steele 1711, 37)

In this passage, Inkle's physical proximity to "English territories" directly contributes to a change in his worldview. Steele alters this section from Ligon's version, which simply reads, "But the youth, when he came ashore in the *Barbadoes*, forgot the kindness of the poor maid, that had ventured her life for his safety, and sold her for a slave" (1657, 55). Forgotten "kindness," rather than "careful" calculations of "loss of time" and "interest" influenced by "English territories" and "friends," motivates Ligon's Inkle equivalent. Unlike Ligon's version of the story, Steele implies that being "pensive," "frugal," and "prudent" are national character traits associated with Englishness. While Arietta doubtless uses these adjectives in an unflattering way, they are not, in and of themselves, disreputable characteristics for an English merchant to cultivate. Steele himself belonged to the Whig party, which advocated these values, and he owned, as Rae Blanchard points out, a West "Indian" plantation with both "White servants" and "two hundred negro slaves" (1942, 283). He therefore supported the institution of slavery while simultaneously identifying with the plight of an individual slave. By retelling Ligon's story as a counterexample to the idea that women are inherently unfaithful, Arietta attempts to persuade her readers to disown the conventional English dove (Inkle) and identify with the unorthodox raven (Yarico).

Steele's decision to include the excerpt from Juvenal as an epigraph that summarizes his story in a nutshell rather than as a problematic relic to be wary of put his early eighteenth-century English audience in an awkward situation; in order to commiserate with Yarico, they would need to overlook her foreignness, her sexual openness, and her assumption of a traditionally masculine role. English readers would also need to disavow those bourgeois[7] traits in Inkle that were widespread in their own culture, making it difficult to separate black from white and raven from dove. Steele probably did not intend for everyone to adopt this perspective, and certainly not "Common-Place" people. Instead, he targeted a portion of society who considered themselves to be hypersensitive and well-educated individuals, like Arietta and Mr. Spectator, and who were capable of sympathizing with the poor "Naked American." Fortunately for Steele, many people thought of themselves in this flattering way. *Unfortunately, though, his ethnocentric and elitist epigraph compromises a story that otherwise includes some exciting progressive elements.*

ADDISON'S ROYAL EXCHANGE

Like Steele, Joseph Addison and Henry Mackenzie, who Sir Walter Scott dubbed the "Scottish Addison,"[8] portray men in their texts whose love of humanity brings them to tears (qtd. in Bending and Bygrave). The social effect that these tears were supposed to elicit in their eighteenth-century audience and the groups of peoples who were included under the heading of "humanity," however, were significantly different in Addison's essay about the Royal Exchange (1711) and Mackenzie's novel *The Man of Feeling* (1771). In a recent article on the latter, Maureen Harkin claims that some scholars of Mackenzie's novel, namely John Mullan, Nicholas Phillipson, and

Richard Dwyer, see it as an attempt to carve out a community on the basis of a shared sentimental ethos (317–18). Although Erin Mackie does not refer specifically to this criticism on Mackenzie, she nonetheless posits a similar reformatory and community-delineating urge behind *The Spectator*, the popular journal for which Joseph Addison wrote (Mackie 1998, 14). On the surface, the community that both Addison and Mackenzie construct looks quite similar, with sentiment as the governing principle and without bias toward any particular country. As one examines these texts with greater scrutiny, however, it becomes clear that the community Addison envisions marginalizes all who are not English whereas Mackenzie's hypothetical community genuinely coheres on the basis of sentimentality rather than nationality.

Part of Addison's failure, whether intentional or not, to produce a model for a truly inclusive international community is that he tries to build it on a tenuous foundation; more specifically, his ethical code depends upon a reconciliation of two bourgeois virtues that possess an uneasy relationship with one another: self-interest and self-sacrifice. Addison attempts to elicit this reconciliation by positing a general theory in which these two traits are directly rather than inversely proportional to one another. Perhaps his most concise articulation of this theory occurs in the following description of his own reaction to the Royal Exchange:

> I am wonderfully delighted to see such a Body of Men thriving in their own private Fortunes, and at the same time promoting the Public Stock; or in other Words, raising estates for their own Families, by bringing into their Country whatever is wanting, and carrying out of it whatever is superfluous. (Addison 1711, 213)

According to Mr. Spectator, then, the pursuit of "private Fortunes" and the promotion of "Publick Stock" correspond to one another in a one-to-one ratio; as private fortunes go up, the general living conditions of all nations connected to this economic network also improve. Behavior that appears to be mere self-interest therefore turns out to be in the best interests of everyone in Mr. Spectator's opinion. To support this claim, Addison's narrator follows in the footsteps of contemporary philosophers by wedding his ideas to a supposedly "natural" order:

> Nature seems to have taken particular Care to disseminate her Blessings among the different Regions of the World, with an Eye to this mutual Intercourse and Traffick among Mankind, that the Natives of the several Parts of the Globe might have a kind of Dependance upon one another, and be united together by their common Interest. (Addison and Steele 1711, 213)

In other words, because different commodities are spread out over diverse countries, it is only "natural" that humans should trade with one another so that everyone may benefit from the fruits of the earth. Yet this paradigm presupposes a highly benevolent view of human nature. In a more Hobbesian framework, of course, people would merely steal from one another in the state of nature and could only be forced to accept this system if some punitive apparatus were constructed in order to ensure fair play. Even Adam Smith, whose "invisible hand" theory of economics closely resembles this one, acknowledges the potential abuses of this system; excessive self-interest might lead to large monopolies that would severely disrupt the otherwise harmonious flow of unbridled capitalism (1761, 273–74). In Mr. Spectator's description, though, there is no indication that people might steal rather than trade or form monopolies to gratify their own self-interest at the direct expense of others. In fact, there is no explicit acknowledgment in Addison's essay that such a thing as *excessive* self-interest even exists.

While Mr. Spectator's theory does not deal directly with the possibility of excessive self-interest, the details of his argument implicitly address the question. Aside from a few second-hand quotations of Sir Andrew and an Egyptian merchant who bows and grimaces, Mr. Spectator is the only character in this essay who exemplifies Addison's view of human nature. If the rest of humanity feels even half the pleasure that Mr. Spectator claims to have when witnessing his fellow creatures prosper, then we must be a fine species indeed. Mr. Spectator describes his feelings about the Royal Exchange as follows: "As I am a great Lover of Mankind, my Heart naturally overflows with Pleasure at the sight of a prosperous and happy Multitude, insomuch that at many publick Solemnities I cannot forbear expressing my Joy with Tears that have stolen down my Cheeks" (Addison and Steele 1711, 213). According to this passage, Mr. Spectator sympathizes so strongly with the joy of others that he feels it himself to the point of tears. If he, as our sole representative of humankind, experiences this degree of empathy, it follows that humans would not experience joy from their commodities if these items were produced through the suffering of others. Within Addison's idealistic view of human nature, the possibility of excessive self-interest is therefore in some sense unthinkable. Because of this extreme sympathetic identification that humans feel for one another, then, any proper or "natural" system of economics must have universal benefits.

THE MAN OF FEELING

However, in Mackenzie's *The Man of Feeling*, excessive self-interest not only exists, but it also leads to an ambitious pursuit of wealth that appears to be inextricably tied to corruption. At first glance, one might attribute this sentiment chiefly to Harley. Indeed, much of the novel focuses on his lack of ambition, unfitness for the commercial world, and outright denunciation of actions that result in profit at the expense of morality. For instance, Harley responds to Edwards' reminiscences about the British presence in India by saying, "You describe the victories they have gained; they are sullied by the cause in which they fought: you enumerate the spoils of those victories; they are covered with the blood of the vanquished!" (Mackenzie 1771, 77). Yet the fact that Harley utters this idea that wealth taints its possessor complicates our task as readers, especially since the chapter is entitled "The Man of Feeling Talks of What He Does Not Understand." This phrase, like so many of the implicit and explicit commentaries on Harley in the narrative, is highly ambiguous. It could mean that he does not understand how human beings could treat each other this way (how is it ethically possible?) or it could refer to the fact that Harley lacks sufficient experience in the world to comment authoritatively on this issue (what does a sheltered, naïve rural aristocrat know about real suffering and international politics?). Aside from the comparatively trifling and brief uneasiness that Harley experiences over whether or not he is the true recipient of Miss Walton's affections, his suffering is always second-hand, once-removed from actual hardship. Mackenzie's narrator, however, reduces the ambiguity of this passage when Edwards, who has directly experienced the brutality of imperialism, affirms that Harley's "maxims" are "certainly right" (77).[9] For Edwards, these ideas are more than just "maxims"; he uses his own body as a type of currency that can be exchanged for the alleviation of others' suffering. Whereas Harley makes gestures of sympathy toward the disenfranchised by offering them coins and a few kind words, thus perpetuating the capitalist idea that money and rhetoric can cure a host of social ills, Edwards disrupts this economy by substituting his own body for the punishment intended for others, namely his son and the Indian man; implicit in these self-sacrificial actions is the idea that money and words are not sufficient in and of themselves to bring about real change.

    This section shares the assumption of John Mullan and others that *The Man of Feeling* attempts to provide an ethical code that will forge and govern a community. These critics view it as a failed attempt because of Harley's ineffectuality and ambiguous depiction. Maureen Harkin counters this argument by claiming that Harley's powerlessness, in conjunction with the fragmentary form of the work, is Mackenzie's deliberate exposure of the transient and ultimately limited power of the sentimental novel to elicit real political change (Harkin 1994, 319). If one takes the family as the basic unit of bourgeois politics in the eighteenth century, though, Mackenzie's novel contributes to social stability through the framed narrative of Emily Atkins and her father. Emily succumbs to Mr. Winbrooke's seduction partially because "His figure, his address, and conversation, were not unlike those warm ideas of an accomplished man which [her] favourite novels had taught [her] to form" (Mackenzie 1771, 43). While seduction novels contribute to Emily's unhappy descent into prostitution, Mackenzie envisions her cautionary story as a socially beneficial document. Emily's father says:

> Could such tales as mine, Mr. Harley, be sometimes suggested to the daughters of levity, did they but know with what anxiety the heart of a parent flutters round the child he loves, they would be less apt to construe into harshness that delicate concern for their conduct, which they often complain of as laying restraint upon things. (Mackenzie 1771, 55)

In order to combat the deleterious effects of seduction novels, Mackenzie proposes "such tales" as the one Mr. Atkins relates. By focusing on parental grief rather than romantic desire, Mackenzie counterbalances one form of fiction with another.

Critics rightly point out that the novel appears to be a failure *if* we view Harley as the sole embodiment of the ethical code that will form Mackenzie's hypothetical community. Because Edwards embodies self-sacrificial action when he risks his own safety and comfort for his son, grandson, daughter-in-law, and the Indian man, he fulfills this role rather than Harley. Harkin's suggestion that Mackenzie writes a sentimental novel about the uselessness of sentimental novels outside of a purely aesthetic realm does not take into account the fragmentary form of the narrative, which forces readers to sift actively through the rubbish in order to find the gems (such as the story of Edwards). In a 1770 letter, Mackenzie claimed that the story of Edwards was his "favorite passage" of all in *The Man of Feeling*, and four magazines published it separately between 1778 and 1810 (Bending and Bygrave 2001, 117). These facts suggest that the author and his contemporaries viewed Edwards' portion of the narrative as especially important. The active work of interpretation that the reader must perform therefore mirrors Edwards' active approach to self-sacrifice and opposes the gullible passive reception of stories that Harley often engages in.

The Man of Feeling seems to disagree with Addison's essay about who exactly benefits from English foreign policy. Both concede that the English profit by the arrangement, but the "gains" of the other nations appear to be a point of contention. Mr. Spectator argues that England's self-interested economic policies benefit other nations in addition to their own whereas Edwards, the authoritative figure in *The Man of Feeling*, believes that the English profit at the direct expense of the countries that they interact with. Upon closer examination, however, Mr. Spectator unwittingly acknowledges that the British not only took unfair advantage of other countries, but also that they *ought to* in his opinion. Though he claims to be a "Citizen of the World," Addison's narrator appears curiously partial to England's economic growth (Addison and Steele 1711, 212). In the second sentence of this work, for instance, Mr. Spectator says, "It gives me a secret Satisfaction, and, in some measure, gratifies my Vanity, as I am an *Englishman*, to see so rich an Assembly of Country-men and Foreigners consulting together upon the private Business of Mankind, and making this Metropolis a kind of *Emporium* for the whole Earth" (212). Despite Mr. Spectator's supposed willingness to identify himself as a Dane, Swede, or Frenchman, then, he takes a special joy in observing that an *English* "Metropolis" is the Mecca of this commercial activity. In fact, the way he positions himself in this passage results in the construction of binary categories in which he and his fellow "Country-men" are on one side and a diverse mixture of ethnic groups lumped together under the broad category of "Foreigners" are on the other.

This bias in favor of his native country becomes increasingly apparent as the story progresses. For example, Mr. Spectator claims that the distribution of "superfluities" between nations benefits everyone and yet England trades "Tin" and "Wooll" for "Gold" and "Rubies" (Addison and Steele 1711, 214). The latter two items seem quite a bit less "superfluous" than the former two. Although all countries may indeed benefit from this arrangement, it is clear that England gets a far better deal. More disturbing still is the propriety language that Addison's narrator and his English friend Sir Andrew begin to employ toward the end of the essay. One such instance occurs when Mr. Spectator says, "Trade, without enlarging the *British* Territories, has given us a kind of additional Empire" (Addison and Steele 1711, 206). In this passage, one catches another glimpse of Mr. Spectator without his mask of cosmopolitan rhetoric. Words such as "us" and "Empire" make this universally beneficial trade system seem far more unilateral. Unlike Mr. Spectator, Edwards truly seems to want global happiness and prosperity; by risking his own safety to help the Indian man escape, Edwards displays a type of self-sacrifice and universal compassion that transcends boundaries of skin color and nationality.

Although both Addison and Mackenzie adopt the discourse of sentimentality as the cornerstone for their envisioned international communities, then, only the latter provides a workable model of that principle in action, and only in a small section of his novel. Edwards, unlike Mr. Spectator or Harley, consistently stands in for others to prevent their suffering rather than merely weeping for them as they prosper or weeping with them after they recount their misfortunes. Moreover, the actively interventionist sentimental ethical code that Edwards embodies is not limited to British people, nor is it content to toss a few coins at the victims of systemic oppression. Maureen Harkin therefore rightly points out that Mackenzie was skeptical about the sentimental novel's ability to elicit change, but he did not go through the trouble of writing one just to articulate that idea. Instead, he isolates and ridicules the problematic elements of sensibility, embodied chiefly by Harley and his sentimental predecessors such as Mr. Spectator, and proposes a modified ethical code based on self-sacrificial actions rather than mere sympathetic rhetoric.

EPILOGUE: EAST INDIAN OBJECTS OF PITY

Like Heylyn, Dryden, and Addison, Mackenzie's Harley feels the ties of nationhood. Harley emphasizes his devotion to England when he says, "I have a proper regard for the prosperity of my country: every native of it appropriates to himself some share of the power, or the fame, which, as a nation, it acquires" (Mackenzie 1771, 76). Yet Harley's "regard" for the "prosperity," "power," and "fame" of "every native" of his "country" has its limits since he finishes the previous sentence with a qualification: "but I cannot throw off the man so much as to rejoice at our conquests in India" (76). As the pronouns "*my* country" and "*our* conquests" suggest, Harley identifies with his fellow Englishmen and even feels a share of the responsibility for British actions abroad. The British presence in India puts him in a difficult bind in which he simultaneously desires the "prosperity" of "every native" of his country yet cannot "throw off the man" or the ethical consequences of this prosperity. Harley's notion that, from a financial standpoint at least, "every native" of England benefits from the British conquest of India ignores the EIC's stock losses. As Stephen Bending and Stephen Bygrave point out, "massive speculation in the East India Company . . . led to the 1766 collapse in stock and huge financial losses for many individuals" (Bending and Bygrave 118). In keeping with the ethos of sentimental novels, Mackenzie likely simplified the financial element of England's presence in India so that the moral consequences would take center stage. Harley's ambivalence about England's imperial role in India was widespread since the government rewarded Clive with a knighthood and an Irish peerage, but then impeached him in 1767, the year that Mackenzie began *The Man of Feeling* (Bending and Bygrave 2001, 118).

The idea of "conquests" in India was fairly new to the British in 1771. Edwards' description of what he witnesses as a British soldier in India leads Harley to question the consequences of the new relations between that country and England:

> You tell me of immense territories subject to the English: I cannot think of *their* possessions without being led to inquire by what right *they* possess them. *They*

came there as traders, bartering the commodities *they* brought for others which *their* purchasers could spare; and however great *their* profits were, *they* were then equitable. But what title have the subjects of another kingdom to establish an empire in India? to give laws to a country where the inhabitants received them on the terms of friendly commerce? (emphasis added, Mackenzie 1771, 76)

Whereas Harley associates himself with Englishness via the personal pronouns "our" and "my" in the previous sentences, this passage represents his dissociation from his country's actions in India by consistently switching to "they" and "their." The notion of the British going from "traders" to possessing an "empire in India" with "immense territories" and a legal system that governs the indigenous inhabitants presupposes the absence of Mughal resistance. Roe's 1615 warning to his fellow Englishmen to avoid conflicts with India, Heylyn's awe of Mughal military power in 1652, and Dryden's reverence for Aurangzeb in 1675 all reflect a different set of power relations than what Harley describes in this passage. India's newer position in relation to England, from trading partner to subjugated colony, represents an ethical turn for the worse in Harley's opinion. Harley considers "friendly commerce" between "traders" that results in "profits" that are "equitable" to be just because of the give-and-take nature of the arrangement. By "bartering the commodities they brought for others which their purchasers could spare," British merchants use the surplus value of their own country to enhance the number of goods that the people of India use. Because the people of India "received" the British "on the terms of friendly commerce," Harley compares the imposition of laws by visitors to a violation of the time-honored tradition of hospitality.

Whereas the trading arrangement depends on England contributing commodities to India's economy, the imperial relation is one-sided from Harley's perspective. Harley continues this discussion with Edwards: "You say they are happier under our regulations than the tyranny of their own petty princes. I must doubt it, from the conduct of those by whom these regulations have been made. They have drained the treasuries of Nabobs, who must fill them by oppressing the industry of their subjects" (Mackenzie 1771, 76). In this passage, Harley weighs a possible benefit of British rule, fairer "regulations," but he rejects this putative contribution as empty rhetoric. He envisions a two-fold scenario in which the British steal from the Nabobs, and to recompense their losses they in turn exploit the natives. Unlike the previous give-and-take trade arrangement, commodities now flow only in one direction: toward the British. The reciprocity of trade implies ongoing renewal, but Harley's word "drain" to describe England's new role suggests a situation in which India's wealth will eventually dry up. By pointing out the moral problems with England's parasitical relation to India and longing for a simpler time, Harley expresses his desire for national reform.

In fact, Mackenzie's inclusion of a torture scene raises some troubling comparisons, most importantly to Spain's conquest of the Americas. Like the Spanish in Mexico and Peru in the sixteenth century, the British were uniquely positioned to loot the treasure of the inhabitants of India after the Battle of Plassey in 1757. As I argued in chapter 3, the British took great pains to distance themselves from the torturous practices of the Spanish and the Dutch. Yet the story Edwards recounts of British soldiers torturing an Indian man to find the location of his treasure bears a striking resemblance to Dryden's scene in *The Indian Emperor* when Spaniards perform the same act on Montezuma for exactly the same reason. When Spaniards torture Montezuma in Dryden's play, the Aztec emperor defiantly exclaims: "Know I have Gold, which you shall never find, / No Pains, no Tortures shall unlock my Mind" (Dryden 1667, V.ii.19–20). The British soldiers in Mackenzie's novel are even worse in some ways since the Indian man "declared he had none" (Mackenzie 1771, 70). Unlike the Spanish, the British torture an "Indian" without even knowing with certainty that he possesses the treasure they seek. Later in the story, the Indian man gives Edward "two hundred pieces of gold," which means that he lies to his torturers (70). Mackenzie's representation of an Indian character therefore relies on the paradoxical stereotype of non-European peoples as both deceitful and innocent. In Mackenzie's view, the greed and cruelty associated with Spain for centuries now contaminate his own country. England occupies the position that Spain did centuries earlier in the Americas in the minds of contemporary Europeans, and Harley fears for the national character of which he is a part.

As Harley speaks, he continues to return to the question of "what title" or right the British have to rule in India, or more generally for any country to conquer another. Unlike previous British writers, Mackenzie's character states that "the fame of conquest" is a "barbarous" motive (Mackenzie 1771, 77). Yet Harley follows these anti-imperial and pacifist sentiments with a paragraph of rhetorical questions that provide examples of acceptable reasons for conquest:

> Could you tell me of some conqueror giving peace and happiness to the conquered? did he accept the gifts of their princes to use them for the comfort of those whose fathers, sons, or husbands, fell in battle? did he use his power to gain security and freedom to the regions of oppression and slavery? did he endear the British name by examples of generosity, which the most barbarous or most depraved are rarely able to resist? did he return with the consciousness of duty discharged to his country, and humanity to his fellow-creatures? did he return with no lace on his coat, no slaves in his retinue, no chariot at his door,

and no burgundy at his table?—these were laurels which princes might envy—which an honest man would not condemn! (Mackenzie 1771, 77)

Although the allegedly positive aspects of imperialism are ethical (promoting peace, happiness, generosity, humanity), Harley does not specifically mention Christianity or sati as later British writers would. His description of the most "barbarous" and "depraved" peoples of India who cannot resist "generosity," however, subtly reinforces notions of non-European peoples who can be reclaimed through Christian values. Harley therefore targets not imperialism in and of itself, but rather a certain form of the practice. In its putatively benevolent form, Harley envisions several ways in which imperialism could "endear the British name" in other countries.

Mackenzie balances Harley's indictment of British soldiers looting India with Edwards' more realistic response. After Harley's paragraph of impassioned rhetorical questions about England's role in India, Edwards replies:

Your maxims, Mr. Harley, are certainly right . . . I am not capable of arguing with you; but I imagine there are great temptations in a great degree of riches, which it is no easy matter to resist: those a poor man like me cannot describe, because he never knew them; and perhaps I have reason to bless God that I never did; for then, it is likely, I should have withstood them no better than my neighbours. (Mackenzie 1771, 77)

Although he "is not capable of arguing" with Harley's critique of British plundering in India, Edwards also sympathizes and identifies with the situation that his countrymen found themselves in. Clive's statement before Parliament that he "walked through vaults which were thrown open to [him] alone, piled on either side with gold and jewels" makes a similar appeal to the overwhelming "temptation" that such an opportunity presented (qtd. in Keay 2000, 386).

His trial made Clive something of a celebrity and a symbol of the returning nabob in England, and Mackenzie may have had him specifically in mind since Edwards says:

For you know, sir, that it is not the fashion now, as it was in former times, that I have read of in books, when your great generals died so poor, that they did not leave wherewithal to buy them a coffin; and people thought the better of their memories for it: if they did so now-a-days, I question if any body, except yourself, and some few like you, would thank them. (Mackenzie 1771, 77)

Edwards mentions "great generals" in the discussion of India, and Clive, whose rank was Major-General, was the leading British figure in that country. Although Edwards claims that "few" people wanted generals to refrain from amassing great wealth in India, the objections were not merely on moral grounds. The nobility feared the redistribution of power that returning nabobs represented, even though, as Philip Lawson and Jim Phillips show, most EIC servants either died prematurely or made insignificant profits (1984, 226). Mackenzie himself acknowledges the aristocracy's fears of nouveaux riches when Harley's aunt complains about the "pert hussy" in the chandler's shop who comes from the "mushroom-gentry who wear their coats of arms in their purses" (1771, 81). While financial considerations made stockholders disgruntled with the EIC after 1757 and class conflicts led nobles to fear returning nabobs, Mackenzie focuses on the moral dimensions of the exploitation of India's peoples.

Until the death of Aurangzeb in 1707, there was no need for Europeans to show compassion for Mughal Indians since the latter were wealthier, better armed, and more globally respected than the former. After Aurangzeb's forty-nine years in power ended in 1707, the average reigns of Mughal emperors decreased dramatically, one of many indications that their power was in decline. Even though there was unrest from Maratha rebels under Aurangzeb's leadership, the next four Mughal emperors after him reigned a mere five years or less. His predecessors, in contrast, had far longer tenures as rulers: Shah Jehan (thirty-one), Jahangir (twenty-two), Akbar (forty-nine), Humayun (twenty-six) (Keay 2000, 329, 365). The inability of Mughal rulers immediately after Aurangzeb to hold power for even a fraction of the time of earlier emperors signaled to the English that the empire was losing momentum.

By 1757, the weakening of the Mughal Empire had proven to be a lasting phenomenon. As John Keay puts it, "The next seven months, or 'the Famous Two Hundred Days,' would witness the British conquest of the richest and possibly the largest of the Mughal provinces. Bengal duly became the 'bridgehead,' 'springboard' and 'foundation' of British rule in India" (Keay 2000, 381). Clive's conquest of Bengal brought with it a plundering of Mughal coffers that greatly expedited the collapse of what little power the empire had left. In 1765, the crown prince of what remained of the Mughal Empire, Shah Alam II, "formally inducted the Company, in the person of Clive, into the Mughal hierarchy. As *diwan*, or chancellor, for Bengal, the Company received a title which was now tantamount to sovereignty over a province that enjoyed virtual autonomy" (Keay 2000, 382). Eventually, Clive was called to account for his actions before a parliamentary committee, one of the first expressions of British concern for the ethical ramifications of their newly acquired power. In his own defense, Clive said:

> A great prince was dependent on my pleasure; an opulent city lay at my mercy; its richest bankers bid against one another for my smiles; I walked through

vaults which were thrown open to me alone, piled on either side with gold and jewels. Mr Chairman, at this moment I stand astonished at my own moderation! (qtd. in Keay 2000, 386).

Mughal India therefore moved from the "almost infinite" armies described by Heylyn in 1652 to being "at [Clive's] mercy" after 1765.

Henry Mackenzie's *The Man of Feeling* (1771) reflects this change in British attitudes toward Mughal India. Harley, the protagonist, listens as Edwards tells about a time when he was "ordered to the East Indies" as a sergeant in the British military. Edwards witnesses "an old Indian . . . suffer fifty lashes every morning" until he revealed the location of a treasure he was believed to possess by some British officers. "Oh! Mr. Harley," Edwards continues:

> had you seen him, as I did, with his hands bound behind him, suffering in silence, while the big drops trickled down his shrivelled cheeks and wet his grey beard, which some of the inhuman soldiers plucked in scorn! I could not bear it, I could not for my soul, and one morning, when the rest of the guard were out of the way, I found means to let him escape. (Mackenzie 1771, 70)

In return for this favor, the elderly Indian man gives Edwards "a purse with two hundred pieces of gold in it" and says "You are an Englishman . . . but the Great Spirit has given you an Indian heart" (70). The Indian equates an "Indian heart" with compassion, and his association of this characteristic with Edwards marks the latter as an exception to the cruelty now associated with being an "Englishman" in India. Through an act of sympathy, Edwards extracts the very treasure from the Indian that other English officers could not obtain through torture.

This situation mirrors Dryden's concerns a century earlier with morally acceptable methods of plundering the wealth of the Americas. Similarly, Steele continues a tradition of pity for West "Indians" that Dryden evokes in *The Indian Emperor* when Cortez weeps for Montezuma (see chapter 3). Mr. Spectator is "so touch'd" by Yarico's enslavement that he leaves "the Room with Tears in [his] eyes," and Ligon refers to Yarico as "the poor maid" and "poor Yarico" after the same scenario takes place in his narrative (Ligon 1657, 55; Addison and Steele 1711, 37). These expressions of sympathy for West "Indians" by Europeans were therefore typical of the seventeenth and eighteenth centuries. British pity, whether real or feigned, for "Indians" of the Western hemisphere since the "discovery" of the Americas, however, became possible for East Indians only after the British had taken control of the Mughal Empire in the latter half of the eighteenth century.

In this monograph, I have argued that before the foundation of the East India Company in 1600 and after the death of the last great Mughal emperor in 1707, British writers viewed South Asians with condescension and pity. During this period, however, Europeans were in awe of the wealth, military sophistication, civility, and power of Mughal Indians, especially because of a common misconception about emperors' land revenue rights that made them appear to be even more potent than they actually were. In the Americas, misunderstandings about the limitations of European weapons and constant retellings of the Spanish conquest of Mexico such as Dryden's *The Indian Emperor* led to an inflated sense of superiority over Amerindians. These skewed perceptions of the indigenous peoples of the Eastern and Western hemispheres therefore caused British writers to employ religious rhetoric paradoxically to explain away their secular weakness in comparison to Mughal Indians, and simultaneously to attempt to justify morally the colonization of Amerindians.

NOTES

1. The Inkle and Yarico story occurs within the framed narrative of a discussion between Arietta, Mr. Spectator, and the common-place talker. In addition to these stories, *Spectator* No. 11 either alludes to or retells portions of Juvenal's *Satires* (epigraph), Petronius' version of the Ephesian matron tale, Aesop's "Fable of the Lion and the Man," and Richard Ligon's *A True and Exact History of the Island of Barbadoes*.

2. Henry Aldrich, former tutor of the 2nd Duke of Ormond and Dean of Christ Church, Oxford from 1689–1710 (*Correspondence* 5–6).

3. The 2nd Duke of Ormond, Chancellor of the University (5).

4. Cf. book 4, especially the opening summary or "argument" (296). As the epigraph of this chapter reveals, Steele read Dryden. It is therefore possible that Steele consulted Dryden's 1697 translation of Virgil's *Aeneid*.

5. Although this chapter cites a 1695 version of the Bible that Steele may actually have come across, the point is not that he had this specific passage in mind when he chose to include Juvenal's quotation in his article, but rather that the Judeo-Christian taboos against certain eating practices were well-documented during the period in which he lived.

6. None of the three definitions of *lover* in Samuel Johnson's *Dictionary of the English Language* explicitly mean that people are having sex (1. "One who is in love" 2. "A friend; one who regards with kindness" 3. "One who likes any thing") ("Lover"). However, the *Oxford English Dictionary* states that the sexual form of the word ("one who loves illicitly; a gallant, a paramour") dates back at least as early as 1611 ("Lover"). In fact, Steele himself uses *lover* in this sense when he says that Yarico shows Inkle "where to lie down in Safety" and "hold[s] him in her Arms. . . . In this manner did the *Lovers* pass away their Time" (Emphasis added, Steele 1711,

36). Since Yarico ends up "with Child" after these encounters, one can assume they consisted of more than mere cuddling (37).

7. When Inkle sells his lover into slavery, he reveals an ungentlemanly obsession with money rather than upper-class and supposedly disinterested virtues.

8. In appendix one of the Oxford edition of *The Man of Feeling* (2001), Stephen Bending and Stephen Bygrave mention this epithetical phrase in Scott's dedication of *Waverley* to Mackenzie.

9. Edwards articulates the mutual exclusivity of morality and the pursuit of wealth more explicitly earlier in the text when he says, "I . . . might have picked up some money, if my heart had been as hard as some others were; but my nature was never of that kind, that could think of getting rich at the expence of my conscience" (Edwards 1994, 69). Yet Edwards ends up taking the Indian man's money after he "insisted" (70). In other words, the acquisition of non-European peoples' wealth becomes acceptable so long as it is not "at the expence" of "conscience."

References

Addison, Joseph, and Richard Steele. 1711, reprinted 1967. *The Spectator*. Edited by Gregory Smith. London: Dent.
Anderson, Philip. 1856. *The English in Western India* [. . .]. 2nd ed. London: Smith and Elder.
Anderson, Robert Charles. 1995. *The Great Migration Begins: Immigrants to New England, 1620–1633*. Vol. 1. Boston: New England Historic Genealogical Society.
Andrea, Bernadette. 2007. *Women and Islam in Early Modern English Literature*. Cambridge: Cambridge UP.
Aravamudan, Srinivas. 2011. *Enlightenment Orientalism*. U of Chicago P.
Armstrong, Virginia, ed. 1971. *I Have Spoken: American History Through the Voices of the Indians*. Chicago: Swallow P.
"Arquebus." 1989. In *The Oxford English Dictionary*. 2nd ed. Oxford UP.
"Balasore." 1911. In *Encyclopædia Britannica*. 11th ed.
Ballaster, Ros. 2005. *Fabulous Orients: Fictions of the East in England, 1662–1785*. New York: Oxford UP.
———. 1992. *Seductive Forms: Women's Amatory Fiction from 1684 to 1740*. Oxford: Clarendon P.
Barnard, John. 2004. "Dryden and Patronage." *The Cambridge Companion to John Dryden*. Edited by Steven N. Zwicker, 199–221. New York: Cambridge UP.
Barnard, John. 1683. *Theologo-Historicus, or, The True Life of the Most Reverend Divine and Excellent Historian Peter Heylyn*. London.
Beauclerk, Charles. 2005. *Nell Gwyn: A Biography*. London: Macmillan.
Behn, Aphra. 1688, reprinted 1922. *Oroonoko, The Rover and Other Works*. 1688. Edited by Janet Todd. New York: Penguin.
Bell, Walter George. 1923. *The Great Fire of London in 1666*. 3rd ed. London: John Lane.
Bending, Stephen, and Stephen Bygrave. 2001. Appendix to *The Man of Feeling*, by Henry Mackenzie, 99–103. Edited by Brian Vickers. Oxford: Oxford UP.

Bennett, H. S. 1970. *English Books and Readers 1603–1640: Being a Study in the History of the Book Trade in the Reigns of James I and Charles I.* Cambridge: Cambridge UP.

Bernier, François. 1968. *Travels in the Mogul Empire: A.D. 1656–1668.* 2nd ed. Translated by Irving Brock. New Delhi: S. Chand.

Blanchard, Rae. 1942. "Richard Steele's West Indian Plantation." *Modern Philology* 39, no. 9, 281–85.

Boswell, Eleanore. 1932. *The Restoration Court Stage, 1660–1702.* Cambridge: Harvard UP.

Botero, Giovanni. 1601. *The Travellers Breviat* [. . .]. London.

Brecht, Bertolt. 1964, "Short Description of a New Technique of Acting Which Produces an Alienation Effect." *Brecht on Theatre: The Development of an Aesthetic.* Edited and Translation. John Willet. London: Methuen.

Brewer, John. 1989. *The Sinews of Power: War, Money, and the English State, 1688–1783.* New York: Alfred A. Knopf.

Brown, Laura. 2004. "Dryden and the Imperial Imagination." *The Cambridge Companion to John Dryden.* Edited by Steven N. Zwicker, 59–74. New York: Cambridge UP.

Burton, Jonathan. 2005. *Traffic and Turning: Islam and English Drama, 1579–1624.* Newark: U of Delaware P.

Canny, Nicholas, ed. 1998. *The Oxford History of the British Empire.* Vol. 1. New York: Oxford UP.

Carré, Barthélemy. 1947. *The Travels of the Abbé Carré in India and the Near East, 1672–1674.* Translated by M. Fawcett. London: Hakluyt Society.

Chapman, Walter. 1967. *The Golden Dream: Seekers of El Dorado.* Indianapolis: Bobbs-Merill.

Chatterji, S. K. 2001. *Vintage Guns of India.* New Delhi: Macmillan.

Chaudhuri, K. N. 1965. *The English East India Company: The Study of an Early Joint-Stock Company, 1600–1640. New York: Frank Cass.*

———. 1978. *The Trading World of Asia and the East India Company: 1660–1760.* New York: Cambridge UP.

Childs, John. 2001. *Warfare in the Seventeenth Century.* London: Cassell.

Clarke, Samuel. 1640. *A Generall Martyrologie* [. . .]. 2nd ed. London: Thomas Ratcliffe.

"Colony." 1755. In *A Dictionary of the English Language* [. . .]. 2 vols. London.

"Colony." 1989. In *The Oxford English Dictionary.* 2nd ed.

"Condescend." 1989. In *The Oxford English Dictionary.* 2nd ed.

Coote, Stephen. 2000. *Royal Survivor: A Life of Charles II.* New York: St. Martin's.

Cressy, David. 1987. *Coming Over: Migration and Communication Between England and New England in the Seventeenth Century.* New York: Cambridge UP.

Davenant, Sir William. 1673. *The Works of William Davenant.* London: T.N.

d'Avity, Pierre. 1615. *The Estates, Empires, and Principallities of the World.* London.

Defoe, Daniel. 1711, reprinted 1989. *The Fortunes and Misfortunes of the Famous Moll Flanders.* Edited by David Blewett. New York: Putnam-Penguin.

———. 1725. *A New Voyage Round the World* [. . .]. London.

———. 1719, reprinted 2007. *Robinson Crusoe*. Edited by Thomas Keymer and James Kelly. New York: Oxford UP.
de León, Fernando González. 2004. "Spanish Military Power and the Military Revolution." *Early Modern Military History, 1450–1815*. Edited by Geoff Mortimer, 27–52. New York: Macmillan.
Della Valle, Pietro.1892. *The Travels of Pietro Della Valle in India: From the Old English Translation of 1664*. Vol. 1. Translated by G. Havers. London: Hakluyt Society.
de Madariaga, Salvador. 1942. *Hernán Cortés: Conqueror of Mexico*. Coral Gables: U of Miami P.
Demaria, Robert, ed. 2001. *British Literature, 1640–1789: An Anthology*. 2nd ed. Malden: Blackwell.
Denevan, William M. 1992. "Native American Populations in 1492: Recent Research and a Revised Hemispheric Estimate." *The Native Population of the Americas in 1492*. Edited by William M. Denevan. 2nd ed. Madison: U of Wisconsin P.
Derrida, Jacques. 1988. "Structure, Sign and Play in the Discourse of the Human Sciences." *Modern Theory and Criticism: A Reader*. Edited by David Lodge. London and New York: Longman.
Diaz del Castillo, Bernal. 1928. *The Broadway Travellers. The Discovery and Conquest of Mexico: 1517–1521*. Translated by A. P. Maudslay. Edited by Genaro Garcia. New York and London: Harper.
Dryden, John. 1883. *Amboyna. The Works of John Dryden: Illustrated with Notes, Historical, Critical, and Explanatory, and a Life of the Author*. Vol. 5. Edited by George Saintsbury. Edinburgh: William Paterson.
———. 1956. *Annus Mirabilis. The Works of John Dryden*. Vol. 1. Edited by Edward Niles Hooker and H. T. Swedenberg. Berkeley and Los Angeles: U of California P.
———. 1971. *Aureng-Zebe*. Edited by Frederick M. Link. Lincoln: U of Nebraska P.
———. 1956. "Heroique Stanzas to the Glorious Memory of Cromwell." *The Works of John Dryden*. Vol. 1. Edited by Edward Niles Hooker and H. T. Swedenberg. Berkeley and Los Angeles: U of California P.
———. 1667, reprinted 1966. *The Indian Emperor, or, The Conquest of Mexico by the Spaniards: Being the Sequel of* The Indian Queen. *The Works of John Dryden*. Vol. 9. Edited John Loftis. Berkeley and Los Angeles: U of California P.
———, and Sir Robert Howard. 1665, reprinted 1966. *The Indian Queen, A Tragedy. The Works of John Dryden*. Vol. 8. Edited by Edward Niles Hooker and H. T. Swedenberg. Berkeley and Los Angeles: U of California P.
Edwards, Philip. 1994. *The Story of the Voyage: Sea-Narratives in Eighteenth-Century England*. Cambridge: Cambridge UP.
"Factory." 1755. *A Dictionary of the English Language* [. . .]. 2 vols. London.
Fawcett, Charles. 1936. *The English Factories in India*. Vol. 1. Oxford: Clarendon P.
Felsenstein, Frank. 1999. Afterword to *English Trader, Indian Maid: Representing Gender, Race, and Slavery in the New World; An Inkle and Yarico Reader*. 289–90. Baltimore and London: Johns Hopkins UP.
ffoulkes, Charles. 1989. *The Armourer and His Craft from the XIth to the XVIth Century*. 1912. Salem: Ayer.

"Firman." 1989. In *The Oxford English Dictionary*. 2nd ed. 1989.
Foster, William, ed. 1906. *The English Factories in India, 1618–1621: A Calendar of Documents in the India Office, British Museum and Public Record Office*. Oxford: Clarendon P.
Foucault, Michel. 1977. *Discipline and Punish: The Birth of the Prison*. Translated by Alan Sheridan. New York: Pantheon.
Foxe, John. 1958. *Actes and Monuments* [. . .]. 2nd ed. Vol. 2. London: John Day, 1583.
Freud, Sigmund. *The Interpretation of Dreams*. Translated and edited James Strachey. New York: Basic.
Furber, Holden. 1976. *Rival Empires of Trade in the Orient, 1600–1800*. Minneapolis: U of Minnesota P.
Gentles, Ian. 1998. "The Civil Wars in England." *The Civil Wars: A Military History of England, Scotland, and Ireland, 1638–1660*. Edited by John Kenyon, 103–55. Oxford: Oxford UP.
Gillespie, Susan D. 1989. *The Aztec Kings: The Construction of Rulership in Mexica History*. Tucson: U of Arizona P.
Goldsmith, Oliver. 1846. *Pinnock's Improved Edition of Dr. Goldsmith's History of England: From the Invasion of Julius Caesar to the Death of George II* [. . .]. 1771. Philadelphia: Thomas.
Greenblatt, Stephen. 1978. "Marlowe, Marx, and Anti-Semitism." *Critical Inquiry* 5, no. 2, 291–307.
———. 1986. "Psychoanalysis and Renaissance Culture." *Literary Theory/ Renaissance Texts*. Edited by Patricia Parker and David Quint, 210–24. Baltimore: Johns Hopkins UP.
———. 1988. *Shakespearean Negotiations: The Circulation of Social Energy in Renaissance England*. Berkeley: U of California P.
Guibbory, Achsah. 1973. "Dryden's Views of History." *Philological Quarterly* 52, no. 2, 187–204.
———. 1986. *The Map of Time: Seventeenth-Century English Literature and Ideas of Pattern in History*. Urbana: U of Illinois P, 1986.
Hakluyt, Richard. 1599–1600. *The Principal Nauigations, Voyages, Traffiques and Discoueries of the English Nation*. 2nd ed. Vol. 3. London: George Bishop.
Hammond, Paul. 1991. *John Dryden: A Literary Life*. New York: St. Martin's P.
Harkin, Maureen. 1994. "Mackenzie's *Man of Feeling*: Embalming Sensibility." *ELH* 61, no. 1, 317–40.
Head, Richard. 1996. *The English Rogue: Being a Complete History of the Most Eminent Cheats of Both Sexes*. London: New English Library.
Heath, James. 1982. *Torture and English Law: An Administrative and Legal History from the Plantagenets to the Stuarts*. In *Contributions in Legal Studies* 18. Westport and London: Greenwood P.
Heylyn, Peter. 1652. *Cosmographie in Four Books* [. . .]. 4 vols. London: Henry Seile.
———. 1612. *Microcosmus*. Oxford.
———. 1625. *Mikrokosmos*. Oxford: John Linchfield.

"Heylyn, Peter." 2004. *The Oxford Dictionary of National Biography*. Oxford: Macmillan.
Historical Atlas of the World. 1995. Map. Maplewood: Hammond.
"History of the Monarchy." 2010. On *The Official Website of the British Monarchy*.
Hobbes, Thomas. 1651. *Leviathan* [. . .]. London.
Holy Bible: King James Version. 1611. London.
Holy Bible: King James Version. 1695. Oxford.
Hughes, Derek. 1981. *Dryden's Heroic Plays*. London and Basingstoke: Macmillan P.
———. 2004. "Theatre, Politics and Morality." Vol. 2. Edited by Joseph Donohue. *The Cambridge History of British Theatre*. New York: Cambridge UP.
———. 2007. *Versions of Blackness: Key Texts on Slavery from the Seventeenth Century*. New York: Cambridge UP.
Hutchinson, J. R. 1914. *The Press Gang Afloat and Ashore*. New York: E. P. Dutton.
Hutchinson, Richard. 1677. *The Warr in New-England Visibly Ended* [. . .]. London.
Hutner, Heidi. 2001. *Colonial Women: Race and Culture in Stuart Drama*. New York: Oxford UP.
"India."1989. In *The Oxford English Dictionary*. 2nd ed.
Jameson, Fredric. 1981. *The Political Unconscious: Narrative as a Socially Symbolic Act*. Ithaca: Cornell UP.
Jardine, Lisa. 1995. "Strains of Renaissance Reading." *English Literary Renaissance* 25, no. 3, 289–306.
Jenkins, Eugenia Zuroski. 2013. *A Taste for China: English Subjectivity and the Prehistory of Orientalism*. Oxford UP.
Johnson, James William. 2004. *A Profane Wit: The Life of John Wilmot, Earl of Rochester*. Rochester: U of Rochester P..
Jokić, Olivera. 2011. "Commanding Correspondence: Letters and the 'Evidence of Experience' in the Letterbook of John Bruce, the East India Company Historiographer," *Eighteenth-Century Studies* 52, no. 2, 109–36.
Juvenal. 1965. *Satires*. Translated by Jerome Mazzaro. Ann Arbor: U of Michigan P.
Kadian, Rajesh. 1990. *India and its Army*. New Delhi: Vision.
Kamen, Henry. 1991. *Spain, 1469–1714: A Society of Conflict*. 2nd ed. London and New York: Longman.
Kaul, Suvir. 2009 *Eighteenth-Century British Literature and Postcolonial Studies*. Edinburgh UP.
Keay, John. 1994. *The Honourable Company: A History of the English East India Company*. New York: Macmillan.
———. 2000 *India: A History*. New York: Grove.
Khan, Iqtidar. 2004. *Gunpowder and Firearms: Warfare in Medieval India*. Oxford: Oxford UP.
Kincaid, Dennis. 1938. *British Social Life in India, 1608–1937*. London: G. Routledge.
King, Gregory. 1771. "A Scheme of the Income and Expence of the Several Families of England Calculated for the Year 1688." Vol. 2. *The Political and Commercial Works of That Celebrated Writer Charles D'avenant*, 184. London.

Koch, Peter O. 2006. *The Aztecs, the Conquistadors, and the Making of Mexican Culture*. Jefferson and London: McFarland.

Lach, Donald and Edwin Van Kley. 1993. *Asia in the Making of Europe, Volume II: Trade, Missions, Literature*. Chicago/London: U of Chicago P.

Lamb, Jonathan. 1995. *The Rhetoric of Suffering: Reading the Book of Job in the Eighteenth Century*. New York: Oxford UP.

Langhans, Edward A. 2003. "The Theatre." *The Cambridge Companion to English Restoration Theatre*. Edited by Deborah Payne Fisk, 1–18. New York: Cambridge UP.

Lawson, Philip, and Jim Phillips. 1984. "'Out Execrable Banditti': Perceptions of Nabobs in Mid-Eighteenth-Century Britain." *Albion: A Quarterly Journal Concerned with British Studies* 16, no. 3, 225–41.

León-Portilla, Miguel, ed. 2006. *The Broken Spears: The Aztec Account of the Conquest of Mexico*. Boston: Beacon.

Ligon, Richard. 1657. *A True and Exact History of the Island of Barbados* [. . .] London: Humphrey Mosley.

Lipson, E. 1934. *The Economic History of England*. 2nd ed. Vol. 2. London: Macmillan.

Lloyd, T. O. 1984. *The British Empire, 1558–1983*. New York: Oxford UP.

Loomba, Ania. 2002. "'Break Her Will, and Bruise No Bone Sir': Colonial and Sexual Mastery in Fletcher's *The Island Princess*." *Journal for Early Modern Cultural Studies* 2, 68–108.

———. 1989. *Gender, Race, Renaissance Drama*. Manchester and New York: Manchester UP.

"Lover." 1967. In *A Dictionary of the English Language* [. . .]. 1755. New York: AMS P.

"Lover." 1989. In *The Oxford English Dictionary*. 2nd ed.

Mackenzie, Henry. 1771, reprinted 2001. *The Man of Feeling*. Ed. Brian Vickers. Oxford: Oxford UP.

Mackie, Erin. 1998. "Introduction: Cultural and Historical Background." *The Commerce of Everyday Life: Selections from* The Tatler *and* The Spectator. Ed. Erin Mackie, 1–32. Boston: Bedford/St. Martin's.

MacLean, Gerald M. 2004. *The Rise of Oriental Travel: English Visitors to the Ottoman Empire, 1580–1720*. New York: Palgrave Macmillan.

Maltby, William S. 1971. *The Black Legend in England: The Development of Anti-Spanish Sentiment, 1558–1660*. Durham: Duke UP.

Mancall, Peter. 2007. *Hakluyt's Promise: An Elizabethan's Obsession for an English America*. New Haven: Yale UP.

Manucci, Niccolao. 1913. *Storia do Mogor or A Pepys of Mogul India, 1653–1708* [. . .]. Translated by William Irvine. New York: J. Murray.

Markley, Robert. 2006. *The Far East and the English Imagination, 1660–1730*. New York: Cambridge UP.

———. 1999. "'Land Enough in the World': Locke's Golden Age and the Infinite Extension of 'Use.'" *The South Atlantic Quarterly* 98, no. 4, 817–37.

———. 2003. "Riches, Power, Trade, and Religion: The Far East and the English Imagination, 1600–1720." *Renaissance Studies* 17, no. 3, 494–516.
Marvell, Andrew. 1984. *The Complete Poems*. Edited by George de Forest Lord. New York: A. A. Knopf.
Matar, Nabil I. 1998. *Islam in Britain, 1558–1685*. New York: Cambridge UP.
Mather, Increase. 1676. *A Brief History of the War with the Indians in New-England* [. . .]. London.
Maurer, Shawn Lisa. 2005. "Fathers, Sons, and Lovers: the Transformation of Masculine Authority in Dryden's *Aureng-Zebe*." *The Eighteenth Century: Theory and Interpretation* 46, no. 2, 151–73.
Mayhew, Robert J. 2000. "'Geography is Twinned with Divinity': The Laudian Geography of Peter Heylyn." *Geographical Review* 90, no.1, 18–35.
McKeon, Michael. 1987. *The Origins of the English Novel*. Baltimore and London: Johns Hopkins UP.
Mill, James. 1826. *The History of the British in India*. 3rd ed. Vol. 1. London: Baldwin, Cradock, and Joy.
Mitsein, Rebekah. 2018. "Trans-Saharan Worlds and World Views in Aphra Behn's *Oroonoko*," *Eighteenth-Century Fiction* 30, no. 3, 339–68.
"Mogul." 1989. In *The Oxford English Dictionary*. 2nd ed.
Mooney, James. 1907. "The Powhatan Confederacy, Past and Present." *American Anthropologist 9*, no.1, 129–52.
Moseley, Michael E. 1992. *The Incas and their Ancestors: The Archaeology of Peru*. London: Thames and Hudson.
———. 2002. *Peru's Golden Treasures*. Chicago: Field Museum of Natural History, 1978.
Newcomb, Lori Humphrey. 2002. *Reading Popular Romance in Early Modern England*. New York: Columbia UP.
"New England." 1911. In *The Encyclopædia Britannica*. 11th ed.
Nichols, Philip. 1967. *Sir Francis Drake Revived* [. . .]. London: Edward Allde, 1626.
Nietzsche, Friedrich. 1967. *On the Genealogy of Morals: Ecce Homo*. Translated by Walter Kaufmann. New York: Vintage.
O'Quinn, Daniel. 2002. "Mercantile Deformities: George Coman's *Inkle and Yarico* and the Racialization of Class Relations." *Theatre Journal* 54, 389–409.
Orr, Bridget. 2001. *Empire on the English Stage, 1660–1714*. New York: Cambridge UP.
Pan American Union. 1954. *Francisco Pizarro*. Washington, D.C.: Pan American Union.
Petronius. 1999. "The Ephesian Matron." *English Trader, Indian Maid: Representing Gender, Race, and Slavery in the New World; An Inkle and Yarico Reader*. Edited by Frank Felsenstein. Baltimore and London: Johns Hopkins UP.
Prescott, William H. 1892. *History of the Conquest of Peru, with a Preliminary View of the Civilization of the Incas*. Vol. 1. Philadelphia: David McKay.
"Press-gang." 1989. In *The Oxford English Dictionary*. 2nd ed.
Price, David A. 2005. *Love and Hate in Jamestown: John Smith, Pocahontas, and the Heart of a New Nation*. New York: Alfred A. Knopf.

Pritzker, Barry M. Introduction. 2000. *A Native American Encyclopedia: History, Culture, and Peoples*. New York: Oxford UP.
Purchas, Samuel. 1613. *Purchas his Pilgrimage* [. . .]. London.
———. 1625. *Purchas his Pilgrimes* [. . .]. 4 vols. London: William Stansby.
Rajan, Balachandra. 1999. *Under Western Eyes: India from Milton to Macaulay*. Durham: Duke UP.
Raleigh, Sir Walter. 1596. *The* Discouerie of the Large, Rich, and Bevvtiful Empire of Guiana. London: Robert Robinson.
Raman, Shankar. 2001. *Framing "India": The Colonial Imaginary in Early Modern Culture*. Stanford: Stanford UP.
Rediker, Marcus. 1987. *Between the Devil and the Deep Blue Sea: Merchant Seamen, Pirates, and the Anglo-American Maritime World, 1700–1750*. Cambridge: Cambridge UP.
Ricketts, Howard. 1962. *Firearms: Pleasures and Treasures*. New York: Putnam.
Robson, Mark. 2008. *Stephen Greenblatt*. Routledge Critical Thinkers. London and New York: Routledge.
Russell, Carl P. 1957. *Guns on the Early Frontiers: From Colonial Times to the Years of the Western Fur Trade*. Berkeley and Los Angeles: U of California P.
Said, Edward. 1979. *Orientalism*. New York: Vintage.
———. 1998. Interview. *Edward Said on Orientalism*. Directed by Sut Jhally. Media Education Foundation.
Salomon, Frank, and Stuart B. Schwartz. 1996. Introduction. *The Cambridge History of the Native Peoples of the Americas*. Vol. 3. Edited by Salomon and Schwartz. 1–18.
Saslow, Edward. 1978. "Dryden as Historiographer Royal, and the Authorship of 'His Majesties Declaration Defended.'" *Modern Philology* 75, no. 3, 261–72.
Schwoerer, Lois G. 1974. *"No Standing Armies!": The Antiarmy Ideology in Seventeenth-Century England*. Baltimore: Johns Hopkins UP.
Scott, Sir Walter. 1882. Introduction to *The Dramatic Works of John Dryden with a Life of the Author*, by John Dryden. Edited by George Saintsbury. Vol. 1. Edinburgh: William Patterson.
Shergold, N. D., and Peter Ure. 1966. "Dryden and Calderón: A New Spanish Source for *The Indian Emperor*." *Modern Language Review* 61, no. 3, 369–83.
Shevelow, Kathryn. 1989. *Women and Print Culture: The Construction of Femininity in the Early Modern Periodical*. London and New York: Routledge.
Shiells, Robert. 1753. *The Lives of the Poets of Great Britain and Ireland*. Vol. 3. London: R. Griffiths.
Simms, Norman. 1996. "A Silent Love Affair: Frances Seymour's *Inkle and Yarico*." *Journal of the Australasian Universities Modern Language Association* 85, 93–101.
Smith, Adam. 1761. *The Theory of Moral Sentiments*. 2nd ed. London.
Stearn, E. Wagner, and Allen E. Stearn. 1945. *The Effect of Smallpox on the Destiny of the Amerindian*. Boston: Bruce Humphries.
Steele, Richard. 1690. Letter to Henry Gascoigne. 31 Mar. Reprinted 1968. *The Correspondence of Richard Steele*. Edited by Rae Blanchard. Oxford: Clarendon P.

———. 1711. *Spectator No. 80.*
Stuart, Charles II. 1663. *By the King: A Proclamation Commanding All Jesuites and Popish Priests to Depart this Kingdom.* London: John Bill and Christopher Barker.
———. 1659. *By the King's Most Excellent Majesty, A Proclamation.* Antwerp.
———. 1666. *His Majesties Declaration to His City of London, upon the Occasion of the Late Calamity by the Lamentable Fire.* London.
———. 1660. *His Majesties Gracious Speech to Both Houses of Parliament, on the 29th Day of August 1660.* Edinburgh: Christopher Higgins.
———. 1661. *A Proclamation Concerning His Majesties Gracious Pardon, in Pursuance of His Former Declaration.* London: John Bill.
Swift, Jonathan. 2001. *Gulliver's Travels.* Edited by Robert DeMaria, Jr. London: Penguin.
"Swine." 1989. In *The Oxford English Dictionary.* 2nd ed.
Thomas, Edward. 1967. *Chronicles of the Pathan Kings of Delhi* [. . .]. Delhi: Munshiram Manoharlal.
Tompson, Benjamin. 1676. *Sad and Deplorable Newes from New England* [. . .]. London.
Torrey, Clarence Almon. 1985. *New England Marriages Prior to 1700.* Baltimore: Genealogical.
Trigger, Bruce G., and William E. Washburn. 1996. Introduction. *The Cambridge History of the Native Peoples of the Americas.* Vol. 1. New York: Cambridge UP.
Truschke, Audrey. 2017. *Aurangzeb: The Life and Legacy of India's Most Controversial King.* Stanford: Stanford UP.
Tsouras, Peter G. 2005. *Montezuma: Warlord of the Aztecs.* Washington, D.C.: Potomac.
Turner, Ralph V. 2003. *Magna Carta Through the Ages.* New York: Pearson/Longman.
Van Lennep, William, ed. 1965. *The London Stage, 1660–1800.* Vol. 1. Carbondale: Southern Illinois UP.
Vernon, George. 1682. *The Life of the Learned and Reverend Dr. Peter Heylyn* [. . .]. London.
Virgil. 1697 translation. *The Aenied. The Works of Virgil.* Translated by John Dryden. London.
Vitkus, Daniel. 2003. *Turning Turk: English Theater and the Multicultural Mediterranean, 1570–1630.* New York: Palgrave Macmillan.
Waith, Eugene. 1971. *Ideas of Greatness: Heroic Drama in England.* New York: Barnes & Noble.
Watt, Ian. 1964. *The Rise of the Novel: Studies in Defoe, Richardson, and Fielding.* Berkeley and Los Angeles: U of California P.
Weber, Max. 1958. *The Protestant Ethic and the Spirit of Capitalism.* Translated by Talcott Parsons. New York: Scribner's.
Wheeler, Roxann. 2000. *The Complexion of Race: Categories of Difference in Eighteenth-Century British Culture.* Philadelphia: U of Pennsylvania P.
Williams, Glyndwr. 1973. "'The Inexhaustible Fountain of Gold': English Projects and Ventures in the South Seas, 1670–1750." *Perspectives of Empire: Essays*

Presented to Gerald S. Graham. Edited by John E. Flint and Glyndwr Williams. London: Longman.

Williams, Noel T. St. John. 1994. *Redcoats and Courtesans: The Birth of the British Army*. New York: Macmillan.

Wilmot, John. 1964. "On King Charles." *Poems by John Wilmot, Earl of Rochester*. 2nd ed. Edited by Vivian de Sola Pinto. Cambridge: Harvard UP.

———. 1675. "A Satyr Against Mankind." London.

Wilson, Peter H. 2004. "New Approaches Under the Old Regime." *Early Modern Military History, 1450–1815*. Edited by Geoff Mortimer, 135–55. New York: Palgrave Macmillan.

Winton, Calhoun. 1964. *Captain Steele: The Early Career of Richard Steele*. Baltimore: Johns Hopkins UP.

Wood, Michael. 2000. *Conquistadors*. Berkley and Los Angeles: U of California P.

Wright, James. 1699. *Historia Histrionica*: *An Historical Account of the English Stage* [. . .]. London: G. Croom.

Zwicker, Steven N. 1984. *Politics and Language in Dryden's Poetry: The Arts of Disguise*. Princeton: Princeton UP.

Index

Addison, Joseph, 26, 115–16, 126–28, 130–32. *See also The Spectator*; Steele, Richard
Africa, 4, 14, 40
Akbar, Mughal emperor, 6, 136
America, colonial; demographics of, 3–7; New England 3–4, 70–7; relationship to England, 3–4; voyage to and from, 4
Americas: gold, 24–25, 35, 60, 63–64, 72–74; population 6, 38–39, 76–77. *See also* Aztecs; Incas; Indigenous Americans
Anderson, Philip, 6–7
Anderson, Robert Charles, 4–5, 71
Aravamudan, Srinivas, 21, 23
Arimant, 102–4, 110. *See also* Dryden, John: *Aureng-zebe*
arquebus, 76. *See also* guns
Atahualpa, 72–73. *See also* Pizarro Francisco
Aurangzeb: Bernier's depiction of, 51–52, 102–7; Dryden's depiction of, 9, 18, 25–26, 95–98, 102–8; historical person, 3–5, 9, 18, 50–51, 95–100
Aztecs, 59, 72–73. *See also* Americas; Inca-Aztec conflation; Indigenous Americans

Ballaster, Ros, 96
Barnard, John, 34, 111
Behn, Aphra, 11, 61–63
Bernier, François, 8–10, 24–25, 31–57, 95–108, 112
Bible, King James: Job, 35, 97; Leviticus, 124; Tower of Babel, 44, 97. *See also* Christianity
Botero, Giovanni, 37–38
Brown, Laura, 9, 57–58, 115

cannibalism, 43
cannons, 9, 39–40, 51, 76
capitalism, 16, 21–22, 128
Charles I, 36, 47–48, 110; Parliament under, 34–35
Charles II, 25, 58, 61, 68, 74, 81–92, 95–112; Parliament under, 47–48, 82–83, 89, 108–11
China, 8, 17, 29, 31, 53
Christianity: Catholicism, 7, 10, 25, 58, 87–89; conversion to, 71, 60; divine right of kings, 48, 67, 109; Protestantism, 7, 10, 19–22, 48, 87–89; providentialism in colonial expansion, 35, 41, 58, 62, 71, 101. *See also* worship of Europeans by native people
Clarke, Samuel, 86

Index

colony, 3, 10, 133
Columbus, Christopher, 1
Commonwealth, British, 35–39; army of, 34, 41–44; finances of, 45–46, 49. *See also* Cromwell, Oliver
Cortez: Dryden's portrayal of, 24–25, 58–61, 84–85, 88; Heylyn's portrayal of, 40; historical person, 75–76, 79–80, 84, 86, 88; Purchas's portrayal of, 61. *See also* Spain: Black Legend of
Cromwell, Oliver, 34, 36, 38, 41, 48, 74, 83, 109–10

Davenant, Sir William, 83, 86
Defoe, Daniel: *Moll Flanders*, 119; *A New Voyage*, 38, 63; *Robinson Crusoe*, 5, 11, 40–41, 48, 55, 113
Della Valle, Pietro, 7, 100
Derrida, Jacques, 15–16
Dido and Aeneas, 118
dreams, 13, 40, 63
Dryden, John: *Annus Mirabilis* 97; *Aureng-Zebe* (play), 7–10, 23–27, 57–58, 78, 88–112; Catholicism, 58, 88–90; "Heroic Stanzas," 110; *The Indian Emperor*, 8–9, 24–27, 57–92, 134, 137–38; *The Indian Queen*, 2, 24–27, 57–92

East India Company, 5–7, 10, 25, 36, 50, 54, 74, 98–100, 112, 132, 136
EIC. *See* East India Company
elephants, war, 37–40, 51, 52, 53
England: armies of, 9, 78–79; British Civil Wars in, 46–48; finances of, 70, 111–12; masculinity in, 26, 87, 126–27; mercy, ideal of, 83, 71, 74, 82–84; national identity, 26. *See also* Commonwealth, British; Europeans, skin color of
Ephesian Matron, 117–24
Europeans, skin color of, 7–9, 125–26

Fazelkan, 98–99

femininity, portrayals of, 119–20, 23
firmans, 4, 28, 99–100
Foucault, Michel, 20, 100
Foxe, John, 74–76, 86
Freud, Sigmund, 13, 16

gifts between Indians or "Indians" and Europeans, 50–51, 66, 99–100
Greenblatt, Stephen, 12–18
Guibbory, Achsah, 95, 98
gunpowder, 36, 39–40, 76. *See also* guns
guns, 9, 40–41, 51, 76. *See also* arquebus; cannons; gunpowder

Hakluyt, Richard, 2, 12, 24, 31–33. *See also* voyage narratives
Hamilton, Alexander, 7
Harkin, Maureen, 127–30, 132
harquebus. *See* arquebus
Harris, 2, 12
Hawkins, William, 52, 99
Heath, James, 81
Heylyn, Peter: *Cosmographie*, 12–18, 31–55; *Microcosmus*, 33–46, 53–54. *See also* voyage narratives
Hinduism, 8, 29, 42
historiographer royal, 25, 95–101, 111
history, conception of, 101
Hobbes, Thomas, 46–49, 128
horses, 9, 39, 76, 78–79
Hughes, Derek, 29, 88
Hutchinson, Richard, 48, 50

Inca-Aztec conflation, 59, 67. *See also* Aztecs; Incas
Incas, 59, 73. *See also* Americas; Inca-Aztec conflation; Indigenous Americans
Indamora, 103–6, 110. *See also* Dryden, John: *Aureng-zebe*
India, colonial, 10
India, imperial: armies of, 6, 36–41, 44–45, 78–79; collapse of, 9–10; English trade, control over, 97–100;

factories of, 3–7, 9–10, 98–99;
Mughal civil wars in, 12; population
of, 3–7. *See also* East India
Company; Indians, Mughal
"Indian" usage, 8, 27
Indian, American. *See*
Indigenous American
Indians, Mughal: skin color of, 8,
18, 40, 43. *See also* gifts between
Indians or "Indians" and Europeans
Indigenous Americans: armies of,
40, 39–43, 79–80; clothing of, 40,
43, 86–87, 122, 125; diseases that
infected, 18, 39, 75–78; gender
portrayals of, 122–23, 126; religion
of, 25, 70–71; skin color of, 8,
18–19, 115–16, 123–25. *See also*
gifts between Indians or "Indians"
and Europeans
Ireland, 38, 41
Islam, 8, 17, 29, 42, 115

Jahangir, 3, 28, 99, 136
James II, 28, 48, 89, 93
Jameson, Fredric, 15
Jesuit missionaries, 89
Johnson, Samuel, 4, 97–98
Jokić, Olivera, 14–15
Juvenal, 118, 120, 126

Kaul, Suvir, 21–23
Keay, John, 107–8

Lach, Donald and Edwin Van
Kley, 10–11
Las Casas, 74–77
Ligon, Richard: *A True and Exact
History of Barbados*, 115–16,
118. *See also The Spectator*: Inkle
and Yarico
London, Great Fire of, 97
Loomba, Ania, 18, 29
Louis XIV, 51–52, 108

Mackenzie, Henry: *Man of Feeling*,
127, 129–32, 137
Mackie, Erin, 127
MacLean, Gerald, 29
Magna Carta, 109
Maltby, William, 60, 74–75
Markley, Robert, 23, 31
marriage, 6–7, 69
Maurer, Shawn Lisa, 102, 106
Maximilian of Transylvania, 1
Mayans, 72
Mayhew, Robert, 31
Mexico. *See* Americas
Mitsein, Rebekah, 14
Mogols. *See* Mongols
Mongols, 8
Montezuma: Dryden's portrayal of, 59,
63–70, 72, 77, 79–88, 134; historical,
72, 77. *See also* Dryden: *The Indian
Emperor*; Dryden: *The Indian Queen*
Moseley, Michael, 72–73
Mughal. *See* India, imperial
musket. *See* guns

navigation, 4, 12, 46
Netherlands, 11, 91–92, 97; Second
Dutch War, 101, 108
New Historicism, 12–15, 18, 23, 116
Nietzsche, Friedrich, 19–23

O'Quinn, Daniel, 123, 125
orientalism. *See* Said, Edward

Peru. *See* Americas;
Indigenous Americans
Petronius, 118–22, 124. *See also*
Ephesian Matron
Pizarro, Francisco; Dryden's
portrayal of, 72, 80–82, 84–89;
historical, 72–73, 76–77, 86. *See
also* Atahualpa
poet laureate, 25, 95–102, 111
Portugal, colonies, 112
Portuguese women in India, 5–7, 10

postcolonialism, nineteenth-century, 15–18, 21–23
press-gang, 48–49
Purchas, Samuel, 31–32, 60; *Purchas His Pilgrimage*, 37, 60–61, 99. *See also* voyage narratives

Rajan, Balachandra, 1, 9–10, 96–97
Raleigh, Sir Walter, 72–74
Raman, Shankar, 18
Restoration, 80–93, 104–7, 125. *See also* Charles II
Rochester, Earl of, 49, 108, 111–12
Roe, Thomas, 5–6

Said, Edward, 21, 30, 57
Saslow, Edward, 101
savages, 40
Scotland, 38, 41
Scott, Sir Walter, 126
sentimentality, 26, 87, 125, 127, 130–32. *See also* England: masculinity in
Shah Jahan, 3, 26, 36, 50, 104–6, 110
Shergold, N. D., and Peter Ure, 72, 86
Shevelow, Kathryn, 115–16, 123, 125
Simms, Norman, 117–18, 121–22
slavery, 20, 115, 116, 118, 125–26, 134
slaves, 64, 116, 126, 135
Smith, Adam, 128
Smith, John, 6, 63
Spain: army of, 76–77; Black Legend of, 58, 71, 74–75, 77, 87; finances of, 73–74. *See also* Cortez
The Spectator: Arietta, 118, 122–26; Inkle and Yarico, 115–19, 122–24; Mr. Spectator, 123–24, 126–28, 130–32, 137

Sprat, Thomas, 101, 110
Steele, Richard, 6–7, 115–19. *See also The Spectator*
swords, 78–80

taxes, 45, 109
theater, London, 80, 83–84,
theater, theoretical conception of, 12–16
Tompson, Benjamin, 50
Truschke, Audrey, 26

Virgil, 111, 118
virtue, 10, 82, 102, 110, 120, 124
voyage narratives, 1–2, 11–13, 23–27, 43, 49, 118. *See also* Hakluyt, Richard; Heylyn, Peter; Purchas, Samuel

Waith, Eugene, 84
war, state of, 46–51. *See also* Hobbes, Thomas
weapons. *See* cannons; cavalry; elephants, war; guns; gunpowder; swords
Weber, Max, 19, 21–23
William III, 48, 89, 93
Williams, Glyndwr, 71–74
Wilmot, John. *See* Rochester, Earl of
Wilson, Peter, 108
worship of Europeans by native people 11, 59–61. *See also* Christianity: conversion to
Wright, James, 83

Zempoalla, 25, 59, 65, 68. *See also* Dryden: *The Indian Queen*

About the Author

Peter Craft received his Ph.D. from the University of Illinois, and he is currently a professor of English at Felician University. His research focuses on British literature of the early modern period, with special interests in Shakespeare and drama. He has had a total of six articles accepted for publication in peer-reviewed journals. His work has been most accepted for publication in *Studies in Medieval and Renaissance History* and the *Journal of Commonwealth and Postcolonial Studies*. He received a grant from the National Endowment for the Humanities (NEH) to study at the Folger Shakespeare Library, an experience that enhanced his book project by helping to contextualize ideas about authenticity in literary representations of the East and West Indies. A Dolores Zohrab Liebman Fellowship provided three years of research support for this project.

www.ingramcontent.com/pod-product-compliance
Lightning Source LLC
Chambersburg PA
CBHW020124010526
44115CB00008B/968